BEST *of the* BEST *from* West Virginia COOKBOOK

Selected Recipes from
WEST VIRGINIA'S FAVORITE COOKBOOKS

Fully operable, the Glade Creek Grist Mill is a re-creation of a mill which once ground grain on Glade Creek. The mill was created by combining parts and pieces from three mills. The basic structure dates back to 1890.

BEST *of the* BEST *from* West Virginia COOKBOOK

Selected Recipes from
WEST VIRGINIA'S FAVORITE COOKBOOKS

EDITED BY
GWEN McKEE
AND
BARBARA MOSELEY

Illustrated by Tupper England

QUAIL RIDGE PRESS
Preserving America's Food Heritage

Library of Congress Cataloging-in-Publication Data

Best of the best from West Virginia cookbook : selected recipes from West Virginia's favorite cookbooks / edited by Gwen McKee and Barbara Moseley ; illustrated by Tupper England.
p. cm.
Includes index.
ISBN 1-893062-36-8
1. Cookery, American 2. Cookery—West Virginia. I. McKee, Gwen. II. Moseley, Barbara.

TX715.B485652 2002
641.59754—dc21 2002069996

ISBN 1-893062-36-8

First printing, September 2002 • Second, February 2003

Front cover photo of Glade Creek Grist Mill by Roger Spencer Photography.
Back cover photo by Shawn McKee. Design by Cynthia Clark. Printed in Canada.

QUAIL RIDGE PRESS

P. O. Box 123 • Brandon, MS 39043 • 1-800-343-1583

email: info@quailridge.com • www.quailridge.com

CONTENTS

PHOTO © ROGER SPENCER PHOTOGRAPHY.

The amber-colored waters of Blackwater Falls plunge five stories (about fifty feet), then flow through an eight-mile-long gorge. The "black" water is a result of tannic acid from fallen hemlock and red spruce needles.

PREFACE

Prepare yourself for a taste of wild and wonderful West Virginia! Also known as the Mountain State, West Virginia's "wild" includes terrific fishing, canoeing, caving, hiking, skiing, and the best white water rafting in the world. As a matter of fact, more than 200,000 acres of the state have been set aside as state parks, forests and wildlife management areas. The pristine beauty and natural wonders of West Virginia are for all to enjoy.

On a trek through the state, you'll discover the site of the last battle of the American Revolution in the Northern Panhandle, the rushing rivers of the New River/Greenbriar Valley, and all the towering mountains, glistening lakes, rolling farmlands and coal mines in-between. West Virginia is the epitome of diversity with equal doses of rich history and pure Southern charm—perfect ingredients for the state's wild and wonderful reputation.

What better way to get a first-hand taste of West Virginia cooking than to welcome into your home the state's true down-home country cookin'. At any given time in a West Virginia kitchen, you are likely to find everything from Poke Pickles (page 85) to Pawpaw Pudding (page 254), from Ramp Casserole (page 109) to Molasses Stack Cake (page 199)! When you put on Cabbage Patch Supper (page 98), you can almost envision a mountaineer coming home to his log cabin on the waft of this heavenly aroma. Not all country-type food, there's the elegance of Breast of Chicken Veronique (page 147) and the audacious-delicious Mountain Momma Mudslide (page 250)! Now you can bring them all to your kitchen.

In the pages of *Best of the Best from West Virginia,* you'll also encounter photographs and facts about West Virginia that offer a more vivid view of the state. Did you know that the famous Hatfields and McCoys feuded here? Or that West Virginia has the most irregular boundary of any state? Or that it was originally named Kanawha in 1861 before it was changed to West Virginia? Interesting tidbits!

Besides delicious recipes that depict the flavor of West Virginia, this book introduces you to a wonderful variety of cookbooks from all across the state. Below each recipe is the name of its contributing cookbook. A special Catalog of Contributing Cookbooks Section (see pages 261-276) shows each book's cover, along with a description and ordering information. This section is particularly popular with cookbook collectors.

We wish to extend a heartfelt thank you to everyone who contributed to this cookbook, especially those of you who so generously offered your recipes. We appreciate the food editors and the bookstore and gift shop managers who helped guide us to the state's most popular cookbooks. Thanks also to West Virginia's tourism department and many Chambers of Commerce for providing historic and informative data. To Tupper England, we thank you for bringing the state to life with your delightful illustrations.

Enjoy cooking your way through *Best of the Best from West Virginia* as each delectable recipe delivers down-home cookin' to your neck of the woods.

Gwen McKee and Barbara Moseley

CONTRIBUTING COOKBOOKS

The All or Nothing Cookbook
Almost Heaven
The Best of Wheeling
Best Taste of Fairmont
Bootstraps and Biscuits
Cakes...Cakes...and more Cakes
Carnegie Hall Cookbook
Casseroles, Meats and Fish...Cookies
Christ Reformed Church Historical Cookbook
Cookin' in a Coal Camp
Cookin' with the Colts
Cookin' with the Stars
Cooking for the New Era
A Dooryard Herb Cookbook
Down Memory Lane
Dutch Pantry Cookin'
Dutch Pantry Cookin' Volume II
Dutch Pantry Simply Sweets
Elkins Manor Cookbook
Enjoy at Your Own Risk! Cookbook
Everything but the Entrée
Feeding the Flock—HCCLA
Feeding the Flock—MOPs of Westminister
For the Love of Kids
Generations
Good Morning West Virginia!
A Gracious Plenty
Gypsy, West Virginia 100th Anniversary Cookbook
Heavenly Helpings
Home Cookin'

CONTRIBUTING COOKBOOKS

Homemade with Love
Just Plain Country
Keaton Mills Family Cookbook
Mom-Mom's Cookbook
More...Home Town Recipes
More than Beans and Cornbread
Our Best Home Cooking
Our Daily Bread
Our Favorite Recipes
Pocahontas County Hunter's Cookbook
Recipes for You & Your Best Friends
Serving Our Best
Somebody's Cookbook
Stout Memorial Culinary Treasures
Take Two & Butter 'Em While They're Hot
A Taste of Fayette County
Third Wednesday Homemakers
Third Wednesday Homemakers Volume II
Treasured Recipes
Treasures from Heaven
Treat Yourself to the Best Cookbook
Tyrand Cooperative Ministries Cookbook
United Methodist Ministers' Wives Cook Book
The Way Pocahontas County Cooks
West Virginia Country Cooking
West Virginia Librarians (bon) Appétit
White Grass Cafe Cross Country Cooking

PHOTO BY DAVID FATTALEH, COURTESY OF WEST VIRGINIA DIVISION OF TOURISM.

Appropriately known today as West Virginia Independence Hall, the Wheeling Custom House, headquarters for federal offices for the Western District of Virginia, provided a facility for the heated political discussions and constitutional conventions that led to eventual statehood for West Virginia in 1863.

Orange Blossom Mimosa

1 (6-ounce) can orange juice concentrate, thawed
1 (12-ounce) can frozen strawberry daiquiri mix concentrate, thawed
4 cups cold water
1 (750-ml.) bottle Asti Spumante, chilled*

In pitcher, combine concentrates and cold water; stir to combine. To make 1 drink, mix equal parts juice mixture and spumante. Serve immediately. Repeat for additional drinks. Makes about 6 cups juice mixture.

*Asti Spumante is a well-known sparkling wine produced in Asti, Italy. A plain mimosa is equal parts orange juice with champagne or spumante.

Nutrition Information: 1 cup with spumante, 280 cal; 0 cal from fat; 0g fat; 0g sat fat; 0mg chol; 200mg sod; 52g carbo; less than 1g fiber.

The All or Nothing Cookbook

Dandelion Wine

3 quarts dandelion blossoms
4 pounds sugar
1 gallon water
2 lemons
2 tablespoons yeast

First, you go out and pick a lot of yellow dandelion blossoms. You pick all of your own lawn, all the neighbors lawns, and then go out into the fields and pick some more. You will need 3 quarts of flowers. Place the clean flowers in a large clean crock. Use flowers only, no stems. Dissolve the sugar in 1 gallon boiling water and add to flowers with 2 whole lemons. Let stand 3 days and nights in a cool place.

Slice the lemons and boil mixture about 15 minutes. Cool. Strain out the lemons and add yeast. Put in cool place to ferment. Strain wine slowly through several layers of clean cloth. Bottle and keep for special occasions.

Keaton Mills Family Cookbook

Punch

4 cups water
2 cups sugar
1 (20-ounce) can pineapple juice
1 (12-ounce) can frozen orange juice
1 (12-ounce) can frozen lemonade
3 bananas, mashed
2 (2-liter) bottles ginger ale, divided
2 (2-liter) bottles Sprite® or 7UP®, divided

Combine water and sugar in large container, stirring until sugar is dissolved. Add pineapple juice, orange juice, and lemonade, stirring until juices are thawed and mixed well. Add mashed bananas; stir well. Divide mixture in 1/2 and pour into 2 freezer bags. Place in freezer until ready to use.

Remove frozen punch from freezer 1 1/2 hours before serving time. Just before serving, place in punch bowl and break into pieces with wooden spoon. Add 1 bottle of ginger ale and 1 bottle of Sprite or 7-UP to each package of frozen mixture.

Each bag of frozen punch makes enough for 1 punch bowl.

Treasures from Heaven

Perfectly Pink Punch

1 quart raspberry sherbet
2 quarts ginger ale
1 quart cranberry juice
1 (32-ounce) can pineapple juice

Soften sherbet in punch bowl. Add ginger ale, cranberry juice, and pineapple juice; mix gently. Ladle into punch cups. Yields 24 servings.

The Best of Wheeling

The first court in the United States to admit videotaped evidence was Charleston Municipal Court in 1967. The judge examined a tape of an inebriated man and found him guilty of drunk driving.

Fruit Buttermilk

3 cups thick buttermilk
3 tablespoons sugar or to taste
1½ cups canned fruit juice or juice drained from canned fruit

Combine all ingredients and stir until sugar is dissolved. Serve well chilled. Will not curdle on standing. Red cherry, apricot, pineapple, peach, and grape juice all combine well with buttermilk; or mixed juices may be used.

Elkins Manor Cookbook

Strawberry-Kiwi-Banana Smoothie

8 ounces papaya juice, soy milk or other fruit juice
5–6 strawberries, fresh or frozen
1 kiwi fruit, peeled
1 banana
3 ice cubes

Put juice in blender jar. Cut fruit into chunks; add to blender with ice cubes. Blend until smooth. Makes 1 (20-ounce) smoothie.

Note: This basic recipe is easily adapted to suit available fruit and individual tastes. Bananas provide a nice texture, as does at least 1 frozen fruit. I like to add supplements such as soy protein, spirulina and bee pollen.

A Taste of Fayette County

Olive Roquefort Cheese Ball

12 ounces cream cheese
1/4 pound butter
1 (1 1/4-ounce) triangle Roquefort cheese
1/2 cup chopped green olives
1–1 1/2 tablespoons finely minced onion
Salt
Pepper
Chopped pecans or parsley flakes

In a mixing bowl, soften cream cheese, butter, and Roquefort cheese. Mix well with an electric mixer. Add olives, onion, salt, and pepper to taste. Chill. Form 1 large or 2 small cheese balls and roll in chopped pecans or parsley flakes. Refrigerate.

Almost Heaven

Dried Beef Cheese Ball

1 (4.5-ounce) package dried beef
3 (8-ounce) packages cream cheese, softened
2 tablespoons Worcestershire sauce
2 teaspoons Accent®
1 medium onion, chopped fine
2 tablespoons horseradish sauce

Rinse dried beef. Pat dry with paper towel. Mix cheese, Worcestershire sauce, Accent, onion, and horseradish. Chop beef in blender or food processor. Add 1/2 beef to cheese mixture. Form into ball and roll in remaining beef. Refrigerate.

Our Daily Bread

The crowning of the Festival Queen highlights the West Virginia Strawberry Festival in Buckhannon. The Coronation is held in the Chapel of West Virginia Wesleyan College and is followed by a reception and entertainment.

Philly Beef Ball

1 (8-ounce) package cream cheese, softened
1 (3-ounce) jar dried beef, chopped (set aside 1/3 for later)
3 long green onions, chopped
1 1/2 teaspoons Accent®
1/2–3/4 teaspoon steak sauce

Mix all ingredients together except reserved beef. Form ball and roll in reserved beef. Wrap in plastic wrap and refrigerate. Serve with crackers.

Treasures from Heaven

Pesto Cheese Ball

1 (8-ounce) package light cream cheese (not fat-free), softened
1 clove garlic, crushed
1/3 cup coarsely grated Parmesan cheese
A handful of fresh basil leaves
Chopped walnuts, pecans, or whole pine nuts

Blend cream cheese, garlic, and Parmesan cheese in food processor until well mixed. Add fresh basil leaves and process until mixed. Don't over-process or your cheese ball will be green! Form into a ball. Roll in nuts. Chill, then serve with crackers.

Take Two & Butter 'Em While They're Hot!

Approximately 250,000 whitewater rafting enthusiasts raft West Virginia waters each year.

Bacon Onion Cheesecake

2/3 cup stone-ground wheat cracker crumbs
1/3 cup finely chopped walnuts
2 tablespoons butter, softened
8 slices bacon
1/2 cup chopped onion
1 tablespoon bacon drippings
3 (8-ounce) packages cream cheese, softened
3 eggs, beaten
1/4 teaspoon garlic powder
1/2 teaspoon cayenne pepper

Combine cracker crumbs, walnuts, and butter until well blended. Press crumbs evenly in bottom of springform pan. Bake in preheated 350° oven for 10 minutes. Cool on rack. Fry bacon until crisp, reserving drippings, then crumble. Sauté onion in drippings until tender and set aside. Beat cream cheese. Gradually add eggs, garlic powder, and cayenne. Beat until smooth. Stir in bacon and onion. Spoon mixture into pan. Spread level. Bake 45–60 minutes or until cheesecake is almost set and cracks on top. Cool completely. Store in refrigerator covered with plastic wrap. Just before serving at room temperature, remove sides of pan. Serve with crackers or carrot slices. Serves 10–12.

Best Taste of Fairmont

Fresh Tomato Salsa

4 cups chopped fresh tomatoes
1/4 cup chopped onion
1 hot pepper, chopped
1 tablespoon oil
1 tablespoon vinegar
1 teaspoon ground cumin
1 teaspoon salt
1 garlic clove, minced
Fresh basil

Mix and let stand 1 hour. Good stored in refrigerator up to 2 weeks.

United Methodist Ministers' Wives Cook Book

Homemade Summer Tomato Salsa

5 1/2 pounds medium tomatoes, peeled, diced
2 onions, diced
1 (7-ounce) can diced green chiles
1/2 cup vinegar
2 tablespoons lemon juice
2 tablespoons chopped fresh cilantro
2 teaspoons salt
1 1/2 teaspoons cayenne pepper
1 teaspoon black pepper

Combine tomatoes, onions, undrained chiles, vinegar, lemon juice, cilantro, salt, cayenne, and black pepper in a saucepan. Cook until heated through. Cool slightly. Refrigerate, covered, until chilled. Yields 4 quarts.

Note: For best results, use vine-ripened summer tomatoes.

Everything but the Entrée

The Golden Delicious Apple originated in Clay County. The original Grimes Golden Apple Tree was discovered in 1775 near Wellsburg.

Mango Chutney Torta

1 cup cottage cheese
2 (8-ounce) packages cream cheese, softened
1 teaspoon ground curry
1 cup dry roasted peanuts
1 cup sliced green onions
1 cup golden raisins
1 (9-ounce) jar Major Grey's Mango Chutney

Process cottage cheese until smooth. Add cream cheese and curry. Process until smooth. Add peanuts, onions, and raisins, reserving a small amount of each for garnish. Pulse until coarsely chopped. Spoon 1/2 of the mixture into a 4x8-inch pan lined with plastic wrap. Spread with 1/4 cup chutney. Cover with remaining 1/2 of cheese mixture. Press down and cover with plastic wrap. Chill overnight. Un-mold, cover with thin layer of chutney and decorate with chopped peanuts, onions, and raisins. Serve with crackers.

A Gracious Plenty

Apple Dip

2 (8-ounce) packages cream cheese, softened
1 cup packed brown sugar
1 cup caramel ice cream topping
1/2 cup coarsely chopped walnuts
1 pound Granny Smith apples, sliced
1 pound Red Delicious apples, sliced

Blend cream cheese and brown sugar in bowl. Spread on 12-inch pizza pan. Chill for 30 minutes. Spread caramel topping over cream cheese layer; sprinkle with walnuts. Arrange apples in decorative pattern over top, alternating red and green slices. Yields 12 servings.

The Best of Wheeling

Artichoke Dip

1 (8-ounce) package cream cheese, cubed
1/2 teaspoon lemon juice
1/3 cup mayonnaise
3/4 cup milk
1 1/4 cups chopped artichoke hearts
1/2 cup Parmesan cheese
1/3 teaspoon black pepper

Put all ingredients in a saucepan. Cook over low heat, whisking often. Dip is done when the cream cheese is melted. If it is too thick, add a little more milk. Serve with warm toasted pita or bread.

A Taste of Fayette County

Curried Onion Dip

1 cup reduced-fat sour cream
1/2 cup reduced-fat mayonnaise
2 tablespoons low-fat milk
2 large green onions, with tops, finely chopped
1/4 cup finely chopped green, red or yellow pepper
1/2 teaspoon curry powder
1/8 teaspoon garlic powder

In small bowl, stir together sour cream, mayonnaise, milk, green onions, chopped pepper, curry powder, and garlic powder. Cover and refrigerate for at least 1 hour (will keep for 2 days). Serve with any fresh vegetables or chips. Makes 1 1/2 cups.

Generations

Spinach Dip

1 (10-ounce) package frozen chopped spinach, thawed and well drained
1½ cups sour cream
1 cup mayonnaise (not salad dressing)
1 (8-ounce) can water chestnuts, chopped
3 green onions, chopped
1 package Knorr® Vegetable Soup Mix

Mix all ingredients together and blend well. Cover; refrigerate at least 2 hours before serving. Stir to blend flavors and serve with pumpernickel bread.

Treasures from Heaven

Crock Pot Fondue

2 (8-ounce) packages cream cheese
1 (2¼-ounce) package dried beef, cut up
1¾ cups milk
¼ cup chopped onion
2 teaspoons dry mustard
1 loaf French or Italian bread, cut up

Combine all ingredients, except bread, in a small crock pot. Can cook on LOW all day. Serve with bread cubes.

Stout Memorial Culinary Treasures

Raw Vegetable Dip

1 cup mayonnaise
1 tablespoon minced dried onion
1 teaspoon horseradish
1 teaspoon curry powder
1 teaspoon garlic salt
1 teaspoon vinegar

Mix all ingredients well. Cover and refrigerate several hours before serving. Serve with assorted fresh vegetables.

Serving Our Best

BLT Bites

16–20 cherry tomatoes
1 pound bacon, cooked and crumbled
1/2 cup mayonnaise or salad dressing
1/3 cup chopped green onions
3 tablespoons grated Parmesan cheese
2 tablespoons snipped fresh parsley

Cut a thin slice off each tomato top. Scoop out and discard pulp. Invert tomatoes on a paper towel to drain.

In a small bowl, combine all remaining ingredients; mix well. Spoon into tomatoes. Refrigerate for several hours. Yields 16–20 appetizers.

Dutch Pantry Cookin' Volume II

Bacon Roll-Ups

1 loaf white bread
1 (8-ounce) package cream cheese, softened
1 pound bacon

Remove crust from bread and spread cream cheese on each slice, then cut in half. Cut bacon pieces in half. Roll up bread jellyroll-style and wrap halved bacon piece around bread. Secure with wooden toothpick and place on cookie sheet. Bake at 350° for 30–40 minutes until brown.

Feeding the Flock—MOPs of Westminister

Crab-Stuffed Cherry Tomatoes

36 cherry tomatoes
Salt
1/4 cup low-fat cottage cheese
1 1/2 teaspoons minced onion
1 1/2 teaspoons lemon juice
1/2 teaspoon horseradish sauce
Dash garlic salt
1/2 pound fresh crab meat, drained and flaked
1/4 cup minced celery
1 tablespoon finely chopped green pepper

Cut off top of each tomato; scoop out pulp. Sprinkle with salt and invert on paper towels to drain. Mix remaining ingredients and spoon into tomatoes. Chill until serving. Yields 36 appetizers.

Best Taste of Fairmont

Crab Meat Balls

2 (6- to 7-ounce) cans crab meat
1 cup fresh bread crumbs
1 tablespoon lemon juice
1 tablespoon grated onion
1 teaspoon dry mustard
1/2 teaspoon salt
Pepper to taste
12 bacon slices, cut in half

Drain and flake crab meat. Combine with remaining ingredients, except bacon. Mix well. Shape into walnut-size balls. Wrap with bacon, secure with toothpick, and broil until bacon is crisp (10 minutes), turning to brown. Makes about 24.

Best Taste of Fairmont

Moundsville is the site of Grave Creek Mound, the continent's largest cone-shaped prehistoric burial mound measuring 69 feet high and 900 feet in circumference at the base. In 1838, excavations began, and among the relics recovered from two burial chambers is the famous Grave Creek Stone, on which are markings that scientists and students of ancient languages have never been able to explain. No other writing like it has ever been found, and it has been suggested the stone may be a hoax.

Crab Quiche Squares

Great for a crowd.

Double pie crust pastry
10–12 ounces shredded Swiss cheese
2 tablespoons grated Romano cheese
3–4 tablespoons flour
5 eggs
1 pint half-and-half
1 (10-ounce) package frozen spinach
1 large onion, chopped
1 tablespoon minced garlic
½ cup butter
1 (12-ounce) can crab meat

Press double pie crust pastry into a 15x10x1-inch jellyroll pan and come up the sides. Pre-bake pie shell at 350° for 10 minutes. Remember to puncture crust with a fork. Cool crust.

Toss shredded Swiss and Romano cheeses with flour. Beat eggs; add half-and-half. Add spinach that has been well squeezed. Sauté onion and garlic in butter. Add sautéed mixture to egg mixture. Add crab meat. Then add to Swiss and Romano cheese mixture. Bake at 400° for 40–45 minutes until brown. Yields 60 (1½-inch) squares.

Note: This can also be placed into 2 pre-baked pie shells. Freezes well.

Treat Yourself to the Best Cookbook

Fresh Vegetable Pizza

2 (8-ounce) packages crescent rolls
1 (8-ounce) carton sour cream
1–2 tablespoons prepared horseradish
¼ teaspoon salt
⅛ teaspoon pepper
1 cup chopped tomatoes
1 cup broccoli florets
1 cup cauliflower florets
½ cup chopped green bell pepper
½ cup chopped green onions

Heat oven to 375°. Separate dough into 4 long rectangles. Place rectangles crosswise in ungreased 10x15x1-inch baking pan. Press over bottom and 1 inch up sides to form crust. Bake for 15–19 minutes or until golden brown. Cool completely.

In small bowl, combine sour cream, horseradish, salt, and pepper. Blend until smooth. Spread evenly over cooled crust. Top with remaining ingredients. Cut into appetizer-size pieces. Store in refrigerator. Makes 60 appetizers.

Heavenly Helpings

Quick and Easy Pepperoni Rolls

1 (8-ounce) stick pepperoni
2 (10-count) cans buttermilk biscuits
8 ounces mozzarella cheese, shredded
Pizza sauce (optional)

Cut pepperoni into 2-inch strips. Flatten each biscuit with hand on work surface. Place 2 strips pepperoni on each biscuit; sprinkle with cheese. Roll biscuits to enclose filling; press ends to seal. Place on baking sheet. Bake at 425° for 10–13 minutes or until golden brown. Serve with warm pizza sauce for dipping, if desired. Yields 20 servings.

Variation: May add your favorite vegetable, such as strips of green pepper or broccoli flowerets.

The Best of Wheeling

Chicken Rolls

4 skinless, boneless chicken breasts
2 thin slices Swiss cheese
2 thin slices lean ham
1 teaspoon paprika
6 tablespoons bread crumbs
1/4 teaspoon garlic salt
1/2 teaspoon dried oregano
1/2 teaspoon dried basil
2 tablespoons grated Parmesan cheese
3 tablespoons margarine, melted

Preheat oven to 350°. Pound each chicken breast to 1/4-inch thickness. Cut cheese and ham slices in half. Layer on chicken; roll to enclose cheese and ham. Secure with toothpicks. Mix paprika, bread crumbs, Parmesan cheese, garlic salt, oregano, and basil in a shallow dish. Dip chicken rolls in margarine; roll in crumb mixture to coat. Place rolls seam-side-down in a baking dish. Bake for 25 minutes or until chicken is cooked through and golden brown.

Feeding the Flock—HCCLA

Hidden Valley Ranch Burrito

2 (3-ounce) packages cream cheese, softened
1 package Hidden Valley® Original Ranch® Dressing
2 green onions, chopped
Red pepper to taste
4 large flour tortillas
2–3 stalks celery, chopped

Mix cream cheese, ranch dressing, green onions, and red pepper. Spread on tortillas. Sprinkle with chopped celery. Roll up; chill and cut into 1/2-inch slices.

Cookin' with the Stars

Organ Cave, near Ronceverte, is the third longest cave in the United States and the largest in the state.

Hidden Valley Ranch Oyster Crackers

1 package Hidden Valley® Original Buttermilk Ranch Salad Dressing Mix
¾ cup salad oil
½ teaspoon dill weed
¼ teaspoon lemon pepper
½ teaspoon garlic powder
1 (12- to 16-ounce) package plain oyster crackers

Combine dressing mix and oil; add dill weed, lemon pepper, and garlic powder. Pour over crackers. Stir to coat. Place in warm oven for 15–20 minutes.

Christ Reformed Church Historical Cookbook

Hot Pepper Mustard

36 hot peppers
1½ cups vinegar
¼ cup salt
1½ cups water
5 cups sugar
1 cup flour
1 tablespoon turmeric
1 tablespoon dry mustard
1 (16-ounce) jar mustard

Wash peppers, remove and discard seeds and grind. In a saucepan, combine peppers, vinegar, salt, and water. Cook until peppers are tender. In a mixing bowl, combine sugar, flour, turmeric, dry mustard, and mustard. Stir well, making a paste. Add to pepper mixture and cook over low-medium heat until thickened. Pour hot mixture into jars and seal.

Recipes for You & Your Best Friends

Cheese Straws

½ pound sharp Cheddar cheese, grated, room temperature
½ cup (1 stick) butter, softened
Pinch cayenne pepper
1 cup self-rising flour
3 cups cornflakes

Whip cheese and butter until fluffy. Add cayenne and flour. (If you don't have self-rising flour, substitute 1 cup all-purpose flour mixed with ½ teaspoon salt and 1 teaspoon baking powder.) Process until smooth. Measure 3 cups cornflakes, crush, then stir into cheese mixture. Form into small balls and flatten onto a greased cookie sheet. Bake at 350° for 10 minutes or until lightly browned.

Take Two & Butter 'Em While They're Hot!

Spiced Pecans

1 egg white
1 teaspoon water
1 pound large pecan halves
1 cup sugar
1 teaspoon ground cinnamon
½ teaspoon salt

In large bowl, beat egg white and water. Add pecans and stir until moistened. Mix sugar, cinnamon, and salt and pour over pecans and stir until completely coated. Put on a 10x15-inch cookie sheet and bake at 275° for 45 minutes. Stir every 15 minutes. Cool and store in a tight container.

Treasured Recipes

BREAD *and* BREAKFAST

PHOTO © MICHAEL RIBAS PHOTOGRAPHY.

The Seneca Rocks stand in stark contrast to the hay fields below. This magnificent formation rises nearly 900 feet above the North Fork River. Due to the hardness of the sandstone formation, Seneca Rocks offers rock climbers a unique opportunity found nowhere else in the eastern United States.

Beaten Biscuits

2 cups all-purpose flour
1 teaspoon sugar
½ teaspoon salt
¼ teaspoon baking powder
⅛ teaspoon cream of tartar
¼ cup lard (or shortening)
¾–1 cup ice water
Butter

In a mixing bowl, combine flour, sugar, salt, baking powder, and cream of tartar. Cut in shortening till mixture is like coarse crumbs. Hollow out center and add ¾ cup ice water. Mix well. Add additional ice water to make a stiff dough. Put dough on a lightly floured surface. Beat vigorously with a wooden mallet for 15 minutes. Turn, folding dough constantly. Roll out dough to ¼-inch thickness. Cut biscuits out with a floured 2-inch biscuit cutter. Place on ungreased baking sheet. Prick tops with a fork. Bake at 400° about 20 minutes, till light brown. Serve warm with butter. Makes about 24.

Mom-Mom's Cookbook

Yeast Rolls

4 or 5 cups flour, divided
¼ cup sugar
1 teaspoon salt
1 package dry yeast
¼ cup Crisco®
1½ cups warm water
1 egg, well beaten

Sift 2 cups flour with sugar, salt, and yeast in bowl. Soften shortening in warm water and add to flour mixture. Beat 2 minutes. Add egg; beat 1 minute. Add remaining flour until not sticky. Knead until smooth. Grease. Put in bowl. Let rise until double. Punch down and make into rolls. Put in pan and let rise until double. Bake in 350° oven for 16–20 minutes. Makes 24 rolls.

Tyrand Cooperative Ministries Cookbook

Butter-Rich Crescent Rolls

$^{3}/_{4}$ cup milk
1 package dry yeast
$^{1}/_{4}$ cup warm water
$^{1}/_{4}$ cup butter-flavored shortening
$^{1}/_{4}$ cup sugar
1 egg, beaten
1 teaspoon salt
3 cups all-purpose flour

Scald milk and let cool to lukewarm. Dissolve yeast in warm water in a large bowl. Stir in shortening, sugar, egg, and salt. Add milk, stirring well. Add flour and beat until smooth. Place dough in a greased bowl, turning to grease top. Cover and let rise in warm place, free from drafts, until doubled in size. Punch dough down (it will be slightly sticky) and divide in half. Roll each half into a circle about 10 inches in diameter and $^{1}/_{4}$ inch thick; cut in 8 wedges (like a pizza). Roll each wedge tightly, beginning with wide end. Place rolls on greased baking sheet, point-side-down. Curve into crescent shape. Cover and let rise until doubled in size. Bake at 400° for 8–10 minutes or until lightly browned. Yields 16 rolls.

Our Daily Bread

English Muffin Loaves

5$^{1}/_{2}$–6 cups flour (measure by spooning flour lightly into cup), divided
2 packages active dry yeast
1 tablespoon sugar
2 teaspoons salt
$^{1}/_{4}$ teaspoon baking soda
2 cups milk
$^{1}/_{2}$ cup water
Cornmeal

Combine 3 cups flour, yeast, sugar, salt, and baking soda. Heat liquids until very warm (120°–130°). Add to dry mixture; beat well. Stir in enough remaining flour to make a stiff batter. Spoon into 2 8$^{1}/_{2}$ x 4$^{1}/_{2}$-inch pans that have been greased and sprinkled with cornmeal. Cover; let rise in warm place for 45 minutes. Bake at 400° for 25 minutes. Remove from pans immediately and cool.

Serving Our Best

Sourdough Bread

STARTER:

2 cups flour
1 teaspoon salt
3 tablespoons sugar
1 tablespoon dry yeast
2 cups lukewarm water

Sift dry ingredients. Add water and mix. Cover with a towel and place in a warm spot to ferment for 2–3 days.

TO FEED STARTER:

1 cup flour
1 cup milk
½ cup sugar

Feed starter the first time after 3 days, then every 5–6 days after that. Starter is ready to use 3 days after first feeding.

THINGS YOU MUST KNOW:

1. Always keep at least 1 cup of starter in reserve to continue your supply.
2. Do not use starter the same day you feed it; wait 3–4 days after each feeding.
3. Always use a wooden spoon to stir, as metal will mutate the fermentation process.
4. Always keep starter in glass bowl or crock with towel covering it.
5. Do not refrigerate starter; this will stop the fermentation.

BREAD:

1 package dry yeast
½ cup warm water
1 cup sourdough starter
4 tablespoons shortening
2 cups self-rising flour
¼ teaspoon salt

Dissolve yeast in warm water. Add all other ingredients and mix well. Knead a few strokes on floured board. Let rise in greased bowl until doubled in size. Knead again and form into loaves or rolls. Let rise in greased pans until doubled in bulk. Bake at 350° for 35 minutes or until lightly browned.

West Virginia Country Cooking

Cornbread

1 cup yellow cornmeal (home-ground is best)
1 teaspoon sugar
1½ teaspoons baking powder
¼ teaspoon baking soda
½ teaspoon salt
¼ cup applesauce
1 egg
1¼ cups buttermilk
2 teaspoons shortening

Mix all ingredients, except shortening. Grease 8-inch iron skillet with shortening. Bake in 350° oven 20–25 minutes or until done.

The Way Pocahontas County Cooks

Dora Mae's Southern Corn Pone

This is an old-time recipe. You can eat it warm or cold, and it is delicious sliced thin and buttered for oven toast.

4 cups cornmeal
½ cup sugar
1 tablespoon salt
4 cups boiling water
1 cup flour
1 cup buttermilk
2 eggs
2 teaspoons baking powder
1 teaspoon baking soda, dissolved in a little water
2 tablespoons butter

Place cornmeal, sugar, and salt in large bowl. Add boiling water and stir until smooth. Cover with cloth and let stand overnight.

In the morning add flour, buttermilk, eggs, baking powder, and baking soda solution. Preheat oven to 460°. Melt butter in large iron skillet, then pour into cornmeal batter and mix well. Pour batter into hot iron skillet; place in oven for 15 minutes, then reduce heat to 350° and bake 45 minutes. Remove from oven and turn out on wire rack to cool.

Note: Try baking in a Bundt cake pan. Can be sliced thin. Looks like a cake.

Keaton Mills Family Cookbook

Jalapeño Cornbread

1 cup milk
2 eggs, beaten
$^{1}/_{2}$ cup oil
$^{1}/_{2}$ teaspoon baking soda
$^{1}/_{2}$ teaspoon salt
1 cup cornmeal
1 (16-ounce) can cream-style corn
1 medium onion, chopped
8 ounces grated sharp cheese
4 jalapeño peppers, seeded and chopped

Mix all ingredients except onion, cheese, and peppers. Pour half of mixture in 9x9-inch pan. Add onion, cheese, and peppers. Pour in remaining mixture. Bake approximately 1 hour at 325°. Serves 12.

Note: You may substitute packaged pepper cheese for cheese and jalapeños.

Somebody's Cookbook

Mexican Cornbread

$^{1}/_{2}$ pound hot sausage, cooked
$^{1}/_{2}$ cup flour
3 teaspoons baking powder
2 teaspoons sugar
$^{3}/_{4}$ teaspoon salt
$1^{1}/_{2}$ cups cornmeal
3 tablespoons butter, melted
$^{3}/_{4}$ cup buttermilk
$^{1}/_{2}$ cup cream-style corn
$^{1}/_{2}$ cup chopped green chiles
$1^{1}/_{2}$ cups grated cheese
1 egg, beaten

Combine sausage, flour, baking powder, sugar, salt, cornmeal, butter, buttermilk, corn, green chiles, cheese, and egg. Mix well. Pour into a greased 9x13-inch pan. Bake at 350° for 30–40 minutes.

Our Daily Bread

Mom-Mom's Corn Fritters

1½ cups flour
2 tablespoons sugar
2 teaspoons baking powder
½ teaspoon salt
¼ cup milk
2 eggs
1 can whole-kernel corn
1 tablespoon butter, softened
Vegetable oil for frying

Place all ingredients, except oil, in medium bowl. With mixer, beat for 30 seconds. Stop and scrape bowl, then beat for 30 more seconds. Heat about 1½–2 inches of oil in a deep skillet to about 375°. Drop batter in hot oil 1 tablespoon at a time. Turn fritters once after they start to bubble and they are golden brown; continue frying on the other side. Drain on brown paper bag. Serve immediately with maple syrup. Yields 24 fritters.

Mom-Mom's Cookbook

Squash Puppies

5 medium yellow squash
1 egg, beaten
½ cup buttermilk
1 onion, chopped
¾ cup self-rising cornmeal
¼ cup all-purpose flour

Slice squash and cook until tender. Drain squash and mash. Combine squash and remaining ingredients. Drop mixture by tablespoon into hot oil. Fry 5 minutes or until golden brown. Makes about 2½ dozen puppies.

Third Wednesday Homemakers Volume II

Settled by wealthy coal mine owners at the end of the nineteenth century, Bramwell was once dubbed "the richest small town in America." It was home to as many as nineteen millionaires who made their fortunes in the Pocahontas County coalfields.

Zucchini Bread

Zucchini is the one vegetable everyone can rely on to really grow well in the garden, and everyone always has more produce than they know what to do with. This bread freezes well and while you are sick of zucchini at harvest time, it is a delight to serve in the middle of winter.

3 eggs, beaten until foamy
2 cups sugar
3 cups flour
1 teaspoon baking soda
1 tablespoon cinnamon
1/4 teaspoon (generous) baking powder
1 teaspoon salt (optional)
1/2–1 cup raisins (optional)
1 cup vegetable oil
2 cups peeled, grated zucchini
1 tablespoon vanilla
1/2–1 cup chopped nuts (optional)

Mix together eggs and dry ingredients. Add remaining ingredients, mixing well, but do not beat. Divide batter into 2 large, greased loaf pans. Bake at 350° approximately 1 hour, or until cake tester comes out clean. Makes 2 loaves.

More than Beans and Cornbread

Poppy Seed Bread

3 cups flour
1 1/2 teaspoons baking powder
2 1/4 cups sugar
1 tablespoon poppy seeds
1 1/2 cups oil
3 eggs, slightly beaten
1 1/2 cups milk
1 1/2 teaspoons almond extract
1 1/2 teaspoons vanilla
1 1/2 teaspoons melted butter

Mix all ingredients well. Grease and flour 2 loaf pans. Pour batter evenly into prepared pans. Bake at 350° for 1 1/4 hours. Cool slightly and remove from pans to cool completely.

Feeding the Flock—MOPs of Westminister

Harvest Bread

Such a delicious fall treat!

½ cup butter, softened
1 cup sugar
2 eggs
1¾ cups flour
1 teaspoon baking soda
1 teaspoon cinnamon
½ teaspoon nutmeg
¼ teaspoon ginger
¼ teaspoon ground cloves
½ teaspoon salt
¾ cup canned pumpkin
¾ cup chocolate chips
¾ cup chopped walnuts

Cream butter and sugar in mixer bowl until light and fluffy. Beat in eggs. Mix next 7 ingredients together. Add to batter alternately with pumpkin, mixing constantly at slow speed. Stir in chocolate chips and walnuts. Spoon into greased 5x9-inch loaf pan.

Bake at 350° for 1 hour and 10 minutes. Cool in pan for 10 minutes; remove to wire rack to cool completely. Yields 12 servings.

The Best of Wheeling

Mabel's Banana Bread

3 ripe bananas, mashed
¾ cup sugar
2 eggs, lightly beaten
2 cups flour
1 teaspoon salt
1 teaspoon baking soda
Chopped nuts (optional)

Mix bananas, sugar, and eggs. Sift flour, salt, and baking soda. Add to banana mixture. Add nuts. Bake for 1 hour at 325°.

Somebody's Cookbook

West Virginia has the most irregular boundary of any state.

Raspberry Quick Bread

Winner of Quick Breads at the 1996 West Virginia State Fair.

1½ cups self-rising flour
1 cup sugar
2 eggs
Sour cream
1 teaspoon lemon flavoring
1–1½ cups raspberry pie filling

Grease and flour a loaf baking pan. Preheat oven to 350°. In a medium mixing bowl, combine flour and sugar. Break the eggs into a 1-cup measuring cup and finish filling with sour cream. Add this mixture to flour and sugar and mix for about 30 seconds. Add lemon flavoring and mix for another minute. Don't over mix. Batter will be thick. Pour batter into loaf pan. Drop raspberry filling down each side, creating 2 "tunnels" of filling. Bake until golden brown, about 30 minutes. Let set in pan for about 5 minutes after removing from oven. Turn out onto a plate. Glaze, if desired.

GLAZE:
1 cup powdered sugar
½ teaspoon lemon or vanilla flavoring
2 tablespoons water

Mix all together until smooth and creamy. Drizzle over bread.

Our Favorite Recipes

Strawberry Bread

3 cups flour
1 teaspoon cinnamon
1 teaspoon baking soda
1 teaspoon salt
1¼ cups oil
2 cups sugar
3 eggs, beaten well
2½ cups chopped strawberries
1 cup chopped nuts

Sift together in large bowl the flour, cinnamon, baking soda, and salt. Mix oil, sugar, and eggs; beat well. Gradually add dry ingredients. Add strawberries and nuts. Pour into 2 greased and floured loaf pans and bake at 350° for 1 hour. Makes 2 loaves.

Third Wednesday Homemakers

Streusel-Topped Strawberry Bread

3 cups flour
2 cups sugar
1 teaspoon baking soda
½ teaspoon salt
1 teaspoon cinnamon
4 eggs
1¼ cups vegetable oil
2 (10-ounce) packages frozen strawberries, sliced, thawed, and drained
1 cup chopped pecans (optional)

Preheat oven to 375°. Grease 2 loaf pans. Stir together flour, sugar, baking soda, salt, and cinnamon in a large mixing bowl. Make a well in center of mixture. Combine eggs, oil, strawberries, and pecans in a small bowl. Add to dry ingredients; stir well. Divide batter between loaf pans.

STREUSEL TOPPING:
½ cup light brown sugar
⅓ cup flour
4 tablespoons butter

For Streusel Topping, combine brown sugar and flour in small bowl. Cut butter in with a pastry blender or 2 knives until mixture is crumbly. Sprinkle streusel over each loaf. Bake until a toothpick inserted in center comes out clean, about 45 minutes. Cool loaves in pans for about 10 minutes. Remove from pans. Cool completely.

Dutch Pantry Simply Sweets

Apricot Nibble Bread

2 (3-ounce) packages cream cheese, softened
1/3 cup sugar
1 tablespoon all-purpose flour
1 egg
1 egg, slightly beaten
1/2 cup orange juice
1/2 cup water
1 (17-ounce) package apricot-nut quick bread mix

Combine cream cheese, sugar, and flour; beat in 1 whole egg. Set mixture aside. Combine the beaten egg, orange juice, and water. Add quick bread mix, stirring until moistened. Turn 2/3 of apricot batter into greased and floured 9x5x3-inch loaf pan. Pour cream cheese mixture over top; spoon on remaining apricot batter. Bake in a 350° oven for 1 hour and 10 minutes. Cool 10 minutes; remove from pan. Cool. Wrap in foil; refrigerate. Yields 1 loaf.

Treat Yourself to the Best Cookbook

Hobo Bread

2 cups raisins
2 1/2 cups boiling water
4 teaspoons baking soda
3/4 cup brown sugar
1 cup sugar
4 tablespoons cooking oil
1/2 teaspoon salt
3 cups sifted flour

Soak raisins in boiling water with baking soda; covered. Let stand 3 hours. Mix sugars, oil, salt, and flour with raisins and water. Grease and flour 3 (1-pound) coffee cans. Fill cans 1/2 full of dough, and bake for 1 hour at 350°. Let cool 1/2 hour before removing from cans.

Homemade with Love

Hot Cheddar Bread

¼ cup mayonnaise
4 tablespoons butter
1 cup shredded Cheddar cheese
½ teaspoon garlic powder
1 loaf French bread, cut in half

Mix mayonnaise, butter, cheese and garlic powder. Cut each half of loaf of bread in half, lengthwise. Spread cut sides of bread with mixture. Wrap each quarter in heavy foil. Bake in 350° oven or on hot grill for 10–15 minutes.

Somebody's Cookbook

Hot Cheese Toast

This can be made the day before serving.

8 slices bacon, fried crisp, drained, then set aside
⅓ cup mayonnaise
1 cup grated Cheddar cheese
1 small onion, chopped
1 egg, slightly beaten
⅛ teaspoon dry mustard
½ teaspoon Worcestershire sauce
Several dashes Tabasco® sauce
Freshly ground pepper
8 or 9 slices of bread
Paprika

Crumble bacon, then add to remaining ingredients, except bread and paprika. Cut crust from bread and toast on both sides. Spread each slice generously with cheese mixture. Cut each slice into 3 strips and sprinkle with paprika. Place on a baking sheet and cover with plastic wrap and place in refrigerator. Remove 30 minutes before baking. Bake in 350° oven for 20 minutes; serve hot.

Cookin' in a Coal Camp

The first rural free mail delivery was started in Charles Town on October 6, 1896.

Pepperoni and Cheese Loaf

1 loaf frozen bread dough, thawed
1 egg, beaten
½ cup grated Parmesan cheese
8 ounces sliced pepperoni
2 cups shredded mozzarella cheese
½ teaspoon oregano

Let the bread dough rise according to package directions. Punch down the dough. Turn onto a lightly floured surface. Roll into a large circle. Combine egg and Parmesan cheese in a bowl, mixing well. Spread egg mixture over dough to within ½ inch of the edge. Top with pepperoni and mozzarella cheese. Sprinkle with oregano.

Roll up dough jellyroll-style. Pinch seam to seal and fold ends under. Place seam-side-down on a baking sheet. Bake at 375° for 30 minutes. Cut into slices to serve. Yields 6–8 servings.

Everything but the Entrée

Pepperoni Rolls

Great for a crowd or for lunch boxes.

1 package dry yeast
1½ cups lukewarm water
½ cup dry milk
¼ cup sugar
¼ cup corn oil
1 egg
1 teaspoon salt
5 cups unbleached flour, divided
1½ pounds stick pepperoni

In a large bowl, combine first 7 ingredients plus 2 cups flour. Beat with electric mixer until smooth. Stir in additional flour until dough pulls away from sides of bowl. Turn onto floured surface and knead, adding just enough flour to make a soft dough. Place in a buttered bowl and cover; let rise 1 hour.

Slice pepperoni stick lengthwise and then cut into thin slices. Use about 3 pieces for each roll. When dough has risen, separate into 4 pieces. Roll each into a long rope and cut off 2-inch sections and wrap around 3 slices of pepperoni, punching to seal. Place on greased cookie sheet to rise 20 minutes. Bake in preheated 450° oven for 5–6 minutes. Serve warm or cold. Yields 2 dozen.

Treat Yourself to the Best Cookbook

Broccoli Calzones

1 package frozen chopped broccoli
1 cup pizza sauce, divided
1 package sliced pepperoni
¼ cup plus 1 tablespoon Parmesan cheese, divided
2 eggs
1 teaspoon basil
1 teaspoon garlic powder
1 package pizza dough
1 cup mozzarella cheese

Cook and drain broccoli. Combine broccoli, ¼ cup pizza sauce, pepperoni, ¼ cup Parmesan cheese, eggs, basil, and garlic powder. Unroll dough; press into rectangle. Sprinkle on mozzarella cheese; top with broccoli mixture. Fold and seal edges. Place on greased baking sheet. Brush with oil and sprinkle with 1 tablespoon Parmesan cheese; cut slits in top. Bake at 450° for 10–15 minutes. Serve with remaining pizza sauce. Serves 4.

Third Wednesday Homemakers Volume II

Stromboli

2 loaves frozen bread dough
1 egg, beaten, divided
¼ pound pepperoni, sliced
¼ pound ham, chopped
¼ pound hard salami, chopped
¼ pound provolone cheese
2 tablespoons Parmesan cheese
Melted butter

Thaw bread; roll 1 loaf out and brush with ½ of the egg. Put pepperoni, ham, salami, and provolone cheese on bread. Roll out other loaf of bread. Mix Parmesan cheese with other ½ of egg and brush on ingredients. Put second loaf of bread on top and pinch edges together. Brush with butter. Poke holes in top. Place loaf on cookie sheet and bake at 350° for 25–30 minutes.

Cookin' with the Colts

Chicken in a Blanket

FILLING:

1 (3-ounce) package cream cheese, softened
2 tablespoons margarine, softened
2 cups chopped cooked chicken
¼ teaspoon salt
⅛ teaspoon pepper
2 tablespoons milk
2 tablespoons chopped chives
2 tablespoons minced onion
2 tablespoons minced pimento
1 package crescent rolls

Blend cream cheese and margarine. Add remaining Filling ingredients, except rolls. Place 2 rolls together to form rectangle. Place 2 tablespoons Filling on each rectangle; bring ends together to form square and pinch to hold together. Bake at 350° for 20 minutes.

SAUCE:

1 can cream of mushroom soup
1 (8-ounce) carton sour cream
¼ cup milk
1 (4-ounce) can sliced mushrooms, sautéed
Salt and pepper to taste

Combine all Sauce ingredients and heat thoroughly. To serve, pour over hot Chicken in a Blanket.

Cookin' in a Coal Camp

With the recommendation of the Governor and a vote by public school pupils, the Legislature adopted the Rhododendron the official state flower on January 29, 1903. The Monarch Butterfly was designated the official state butterfly on March 1, 1995.

The Sustainer

2½ cups ketchup
½ cup hickory-smoked barbecue sauce
½ cup barbecue sauce
½ cup tightly packed brown sugar
2 tablespoons Worcestershire sauce
½ teaspoon salt
Dash of pepper
½ cup beef broth
3 pounds flank steak, cooked and thinly sliced
Buns or pita bread

Mix ketchup, barbecue sauces, brown sugar, Worcestershire sauce, salt, and pepper in a large saucepan. Let simmer for 20–30 minutes. Add broth and meat; simmer for 20 minutes more. Remove from heat for 15 minutes to let flavor develop. Reheat and serve on buns or in pita bread. Yields 10–12 servings.

Note: Three pounds of pork, cooked and shredded, may be substituted for the flank steak.

Almost Heaven

Herb Egg Salad Sandwiches

WATERCRESS BUTTER:
3 tablespoons chopped watercress
4 tablespoons softened butter
1 tablespoon fresh parsley

Mix all ingredients until well blended.

6 hard-boiled eggs, shelled
3 tablespoons mayonnaise
2 tablespoons chopped fresh chives
2 tablespoons chopped fresh dill
Salt and ground black pepper
Watercress Butter
8 slices white sandwich bread

Finely chop eggs in a bowl. Add mayonnaise, chives, and dill. Season with salt and pepper. Fold the mixture until well combined. If prepared ahead of time, refrigerate. Spread Watercress Butter on 1 side of each of the 8 slices of bread. Top 4 of the slices of bread with the egg mixture. Cover with remaining bread. Cut sandwiches into triangles and serve. Serves 4.

For the Love of Kids

Cinnamon Rolls

1 package yellow cake mix
2 packages dry yeast
5 cups flour
2½ cups hot water
Butter, softened
1 cup sugar
2 tablespoons cinnamon
2 sticks butter
8 tablespoons light Karo® syrup
8 tablespoons brown sugar
1 cup chopped nuts

Mix cake mix, yeast, and flour in bowl. Add hot tap water and mix. Cover; let rise 1–2 hours. The more it rises, the more it makes. Roll out ½ of dough on floured surface. Spread with softened butter. Sprinkle with ½ of sugar/cinnamon mixture. Roll; cut into 1-inch slices. Place into a greased 8-inch cake pan. Do the same with other ½ of dough. Cover rolls and let rise 1 hour. In saucepan, melt 2 sticks butter with Karo and brown sugar. Drizzle over rolls, sprinkle with nuts. Bake at 350° for 20 minutes.

For the Love of Kids

Christmas Morning Rolls

1 cup chopped pecans
1 (18-count) package frozen rolls
½ cup brown sugar
1 stick margarine
Cinnamon to taste
1 small package butterscotch pudding (not instant)

The night before serving, grease the bottom of a Bundt or solid-bottom tube pan. Cover bottom of pan with nuts. Place frozen rolls in pan. Combine sugar, margarine, and cinnamon in saucepan. Bring to a boil, then pour over rolls in pan. Sprinkle dry pudding mix over top. Leave on counter overnight to rise; don't cover. In the morning, bake at 350° for 30 minutes. Remove from oven and invert onto serving platter.

Feeding the Flock—MOPs of Westminister

Small Nut Rolls

FILLING:
1 pound ground nuts
2 cups powdered sugar
3 egg whites, beaten stiff

Mix nuts and sugar; fold in egg whites. Fill pastries.

PASTRY DOUGH:
4 cups flour
1/4 cup sugar
3/4 teaspoon salt
1/2 pound margarine
3 egg yolks
1 package yeast
8 ounces sour cream
1 whole egg

Mix dry ingredients; cut in margarine as for pie crust. In another bowl, mix egg yolks, yeast, and sour cream. Combine the 2 mixtures together. Divide Dough into 12 portions; put in refrigerator overnight. In the morning, roll thin and cut into 12 triangles and spread with Filling. Roll from wide part to thin part. Beat 1 egg and brush over Pastries before baking at 350° for 20 minutes.

Cookin' with the Colts

Cheese Danish

2 packages refrigerated crescent rolls
2 (8-ounce) packages cream cheese, room temperature
1 egg, separated
1 teaspoon vanilla
3/4 cup sugar

Grease 9x13-inch pan. Spread 1 package rolls on bottom, stretching to cover. Mix cream cheese, egg yolk, vanilla, and 3/4 cup sugar. Spread on top of rolls. Spread out other package of rolls on top of cream cheese; brush with egg white and sprinkle with additional sugar. Bake at 350° for 25 minutes or until golden brown. Cool before cutting.

Our Daily Bread

Russian Coffee Cake

¼ pound (1 stick) butter, softened
1 cup sugar
2 eggs
1 teaspoon baking powder
1 teaspoon baking soda
2 cups flour
½ pint sour cream
1 teaspoon vanilla

Cream butter and sugar; add eggs 1 at a time. Sift dry ingredients and add to creamed mixture. Add sour cream and vanilla (batter will be thick).

NUT MIXTURE:
1 cup chopped nuts
½ cup sugar
2 teaspoons cinnamon

Put ½ of cake mixture in greased tube pan, sprinkle ½ of Nut Mixture over batter, add remaining batter, then top with Nut Mixture. Bake about 45 minutes at 350°.

Cakes...Cakes...and more Cakes

Nutmeg Coffee Cake

1 cup sugar
¾ cup packed brown sugar
2 cups flour
¼ teaspoon salt
1 teaspoon nutmeg
¾ cup oil
½ cup chopped nuts
1 cup buttermilk
1 teaspoon baking soda
1 teaspoon baking powder
1 egg

Blend first 6 ingredients. Reserve 1 cup of this mixture for topping, adding chopped nuts to it. To the remaining mixture, add buttermilk, baking soda, baking powder, and egg; blend well. Pour into a greased 9x13-inch pan; sprinkle topping evenly but gently by spoon on top. Bake at 350° for 30 minutes. Cool; cut into squares. Freezes well.

Down Memory Lane

Streusel Coffee Cake

Everyone always wants this recipe—easy, delicious, and freezes well!

2 cups graham cracker crumbs (approximately 15 graham crackers)
3/4 cup chopped nuts
3/4 cup firmly packed brown sugar
1 1/4 teaspoons cinnamon
3/4 cup butter
1 (18-ounce) package yellow cake mix
1 cup water
1/4 cup vegetable oil
3 eggs

Preheat oven to 350°. Grease and flour a 9x13x2-inch pan. Combine crumbs, nuts, brown sugar, cinnamon, and butter. Mix and set aside. Mix the cake mix, water, oil, and eggs in a large mixer bowl on low speed until moistened. Beat 3 minutes on medium speed, scraping sides occasionally. Put 1/2 batter into pan; sprinkle with 1/2 crumbs. Top with remaining batter in an even layer. Top with remaining crumbs. Bake 45 minutes in a 350° oven or until toothpick inserted in center comes out clean. Cool. Yields 24–30 servings.

GLAZE:

1 cup powdered sugar
1 1/2 tablespoons water

Combine ingredients, adding more water to reach consistency for drizzling over cake.

Treat Yourself to the Best Cookbook

Apple-Filled Oven French Toast

1 (12-ounce) loaf French bread
1 (21-ounce) can apple pie filling
8 eggs
2 cups milk
2 cups half-and-half
2 teaspoons vanilla extract
½ teaspoon nutmeg
½ teaspoon cinnamon
1 cup packed brown sugar
1 cup coarsely chopped pecans
½ cup butter, softened
2 tablespoons dark corn syrup

Slice bread into 1-inch slices. Arrange a single layer of bread slices in bottom of buttered 9x13-inch baking pan. Spread pie filling over bread. Top with another layer of bread slices.

Combine eggs, milk, half-and-half, vanilla, nutmeg, and cinnamon in a blender container and process until well mixed. Pour over top of bread. Refrigerate, covered, 8–10 hours or overnight.

Combine brown sugar, pecans, butter, and corn syrup in a bowl; mix well. Spread over top of bread mixture. Bake at 350° for 60 minutes or until puffed and golden brown. Yields 8–10 servings.

Everything but the Entrée

French Toast Casserole

8 slices white bread
2 cups milk
3 eggs
1 cup sugar
1 tablespoon vanilla
½ cup raisins (optional)
3 tablespoons butter

Soak bread in milk. Squeeze with hands until well mixed. Add eggs, sugar, vanilla, and raisins. Melt butter in bottom of 2-quart casserole dish. Pour in batter and bake at 350° for 45 minutes to 1 hour. Serve with maple syrup.

Feeding the Flock—MOPs of Westminister

Cinnamon Pecan Pancakes

½ cup regular oats
1½ cups milk
2 eggs, beaten
¼ cup melted shortening or oil
1¼ cups flour
2 tablespoons sugar
1 tablespoon baking powder
1 teaspoon salt
¾–1 teaspoon cinnamon
½ cup raisins
½ cup chopped pecans

Combine oats and milk; let stand 5 minutes. Add eggs and shortening and mix well. Combine dry ingredients, add to liquid mixture, and stir only until blended. Stir in raisins and pecans. Cook on nonstick or lightly greased griddle. Cook until tops are slightly dry around edges and bubbly in middle. Turn and cook other side. Only turn once. Makes 8–10 pancakes, 4 or 5 inches in diameter.

Recipe from The Cedar House, Milton
Good Morning West Virginia!

The Best Hot Cakes I Ever Ate

1 cup oats
1½ cups buttermilk (or milk with 1½ teaspoons vinegar added)
¼ cup brown sugar
2 eggs
¼ cup margarine, melted
1 cup flour
1 teaspoon baking soda
1 teaspoon salt

Place oats in buttermilk; let stand 5–6 minutes. Stir in sugar. Beat eggs; add margarine and stir into oat mixture. Combine flour, baking soda, and salt; add to oat mixture all at once. Stir lightly until combined (will be lumpy like mashed potatoes). Fry on hot griddle.

Our Best Home Cooking

Club Soda Waffles

2 cups Bisquick® mix
½ cup oil
1 egg
1⅓ cups club soda

Mix all ingredients well and bake according to the instructions with your waffle iron. Serve hot with your favorite toppings. This is a good and easy recipe!

Recipe from Rocky Gap Bed & Breakfast, White Sulphur Springs
Good Morning West Virginia!

Poppy Seed Muffins

2 cups flour
⅓ cup poppy seeds
⅓ cup sugar
1 tablespoon baking powder
½ teaspoon salt
1 cup milk
1 egg
¼ cup unsalted butter, melted

Preheat oven to 400°. Butter standard muffin tins. In large bowl, stir and toss together flour, poppy seeds, sugar, baking powder, and salt. Set aside.

In small bowl, whisk together milk, egg, and melted butter until smooth. Add to dry ingredients and stir until blended. Fill prepared muffin tins ⅔ full. Bake until toothpick inserted in center comes out clean, 15–18 minutes. Cool in tins for 3 minutes, then remove. Makes 12 muffins.

Recipe from Aaron's Acre Bed & Breakfast, Berkeley Springs
Good Morning West Virginia!

The world's largest shipment of matches (20 carloads or 210,000,000 matches) was shipped from a match company in Wheeling to Memphis, Tennessee, on August 26, 1933.

Overnight Casserole

Delicious for breakfast or brunch.

12 slices bread, buttered on one side
6 slices American cheese
6 slices chicken or ham
1 tablespoon chopped onion
4 eggs
1 teaspoon salt
½ teaspoon pepper
2 cups milk

Trim crust from bread slices, if desired. Put 6 slices, buttered-side-down, in a 9x13-inch pan. Top with cheese, then slices of meat. Sprinkle with onion. Next, put other 6 slices of bread, buttered-side-up, on top. Beat eggs, salt, and pepper. Add milk. Pour this mixture over bread slices in pan, making sure all are wet. Refrigerate, covered, overnight. Bake at 350° for 30–35 minutes, uncovered, until golden brown.

Our Best Home Cooking

Donna's Egg Casserole

1–1½ pounds hot sausage
9 eggs, slightly beaten
3 cups milk
1½ teaspoons dry mustard
1 teaspoon salt
3 slices white bread, trimmed and cubed
1½ cups grated sharp Cheddar cheese

Brown sausage and drain on paper towels. Mix eggs, milk, mustard, and salt. Stir in bread crumbs and cheese. Pour into greased 9x13-inch pan and refrigerate, covered, overnight. Bake next morning, uncovered, at 350° for 1 hour.

Feeding the Flock—MOPs of Westminister

Breakfast Daniel

6 slices Canadian bacon or thinly sliced ham
1 cup grated Swiss or Cheddar cheese
6 eggs, divided
Salt and pepper to taste
6 tablespoons heavy cream
4 tablespoons Parmesan cheese
Parsley for garnish

Preheat oven to 450°. For each serving, place a slice of bacon or ham in greased individual ramekin, or arrange all 6 in a greased 9x13-inch glass baking dish. Scatter about 2 tablespoons grated cheese around meat. Break 1 egg on top of each slice of meat. Sprinkle with salt and pepper. Drizzle about 1 tablespoon of cream over each egg. Bake for 10 minutes. Remove from oven and sprinkle with Parmesan cheese. Return and bake until eggs are of desired consistency. Garnish with parsley. Serve immediately! Makes 6 servings.

Recipe from The James Wylie House Bed & Breakfast, White Sulphur Springs

Good Morning West Virginia!

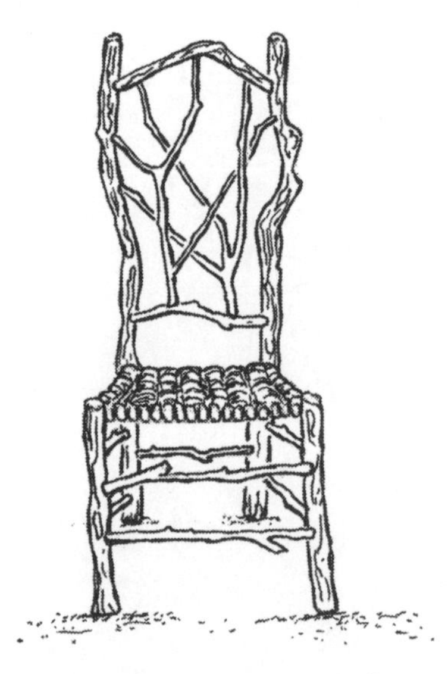

Breakfast Pizza

2 cans crescent rolls
1 pound pork sausage
6 eggs
¼ cup milk
½ cup chopped green pepper
½ cup chopped onion
2 cups Potatoes O'Brien
1½ cups grated Cheddar cheese, divided

Unroll and divide crescent rolls and arrange in a large pizza pan. Crumble sausage and brown in skillet; drain. Spread sausage over dough. Combine eggs and milk as you would for scrambled eggs. Spread green peppers, onions, potatoes, and half of the cheese over the sausage. Pour egg/milk mixture over top and cover with remaining cheese. Bake for 20 minutes at 425°. Serves 4.

A Gracious Plenty

Hilltop Manor House Specialty

6 slices bread
Butter or margarine
1 pound pork sausage
1 onion, chopped
1½ cups shredded low-fat cheese
2 cups half-and-half or non-dairy cream substitute
6 eggs
Pinch of salt or salt substitute

Remove crust from bread; butter bread, and place buttered-side-up into greased 9x13-inch casserole. Cook sausage and onion together until browned, drain well, and break up. Spoon sausage over top of bread. Sprinkle with cheese. Combine half-and-half with eggs; add a pinch of salt. Pour over bread. Cover and refrigerate overnight. Remove from refrigerator 15 minutes before baking. Bake uncovered at 350° for 45 minutes. Let stand 5 minutes.

Recipe from Hilltop Manor Bed & Breakfast, Cairo
Good Morning West Virginia!

Wild Mint Jelly

5 pounds wild yellow or green apples
2 cups mint leaves
1 package powdered pectin
9 cups sugar
Green food coloring

Gather about 5 pounds of wild yellow or green apples. Wash, seed, and cut apples. Place in a kettle and cover with water. Simmer till tender. Remove apples with a slotted spoon and set aside. Return juice to boil, and reduce until it measures 5 cups of concentrated juice. To this, add 2 cups concentrated mint juice made with 2 cups (any kind) mint leaves and 1 cup boiling water that you have let set to steep for 30 minutes. Strain. Measure liquids to equal 7 cups.

Place liquid in large jelly kettle and stir in 1 package of powdered pectin. Bring to a full rolling boil. Have ready 9 cups sugar and pour all in, slowly stirring. Bring back to a full boil, stirring for 1 minute. Remove from heat. Add a few drops of green food coloring and stir well. Remove foam. Pour into hot sterilized jars. A washed and dried mint leaf can be added to the jar, if you like. Seal. Place in a hot water bath and boil 10 minutes.

Bootstraps and Biscuits

SOUPS, CHILIES, *and* STEWS

PHOTO © ROGER SPENCER PHOTOGRAPHY.

Deep snow and sunshine brighten a country churchyard near Bearsville in Tyler County.

Chicken Vegetable Soup

1 (2½-pound) chicken, cut up
1 medium onion, chopped
5 large carrots, sliced
2 whole cloves
1 bay leaf
6 tablespoons parsley flakes
4 celery stalks, chopped (including leaves)
1½ teaspoons salt
¼ teaspoon black pepper
1 (8-ounce) can tomato sauce
2 cups or 1 (16-ounce) can chopped tomatoes
2 cups or 1 (16-ounce) can green or wax beans
⅓ cup uncooked rice (white or brown)
3 drops lemon extract or 12 drops lemon juice

Wash chicken in cold water, remove skin and fat, and place in 5-quart Dutch oven on top of stove. Add onion, carrots, cloves, bay leaf, parsley, celery, salt, and pepper, and cover with water. Bring to a boil; cover and simmer for 1 hour.

Remove from heat, uncover, and skim fat from edge of pan with spoon; remove cloves and bay leaf. Remove chicken from pot. Remove chicken from bones and return chicken to pot. Add tomato sauce, tomatoes, beans, rice, and lemon juice. Bring to a boil and reduce heat. Cover and simmer for 30 minutes.

Variation: Two cups diced raw potatoes can be substituted for rice.

Treasures from Heaven

Italian Wedding Soup

2 pounds chicken pieces
Salt and pepper to taste, divided
4–6 chicken bouillon cubes
Water
1–1½ pounds ground meat
3 eggs, divided
1 cup Parmesan cheese, divided
Bread crumbs
2 bay leaves
1 can or box spinach, drained and squeezed
½–¾ box small pasta beads
1–2 cans of chicken broth, if needed

Place chicken pieces in large Dutch oven or stockpot. Season with salt, pepper, and bouillon cubes. Cover with water. Stew until chicken is cooked. Mix well ground meat, 1 egg, and ½ cup Parmesan cheese. Add enough bread crumbs so meatballs will hold shape. Make tiny meatballs. Cover and set aside in refrigerator.

When chicken is finished cooking, debone and shred. Cover and set aside in refrigerator. Cool broth and skim off grease. Reheat broth and add chicken and meatballs. Simmer until meatballs are cooked through. (This may take 2 hours.) Chill overnight. Skim off fat again. Reheat.

Add a little water (not much), salt, pepper, bay leaves, spinach, 2 eggs (whisked before adding) and ½ cup Parmesan cheese. Stir. Add pasta beads. Extra cans of chicken broth are to be used when reheating soup. Dilute with broth for desired consistency. Undiluted mixture can be frozen, even with pasta added.

Homemade with Love

Once a national armory, Harpers Ferry was raided in 1859 by abolitionist John Brown to incite a slave rebellion. U. S. Army Colonel Robert E. Lee defeated the raiders, who later gained fame as the first martyrs of Emancipation. The structure now known as John Brown's Fort was the only armory building to escape destruction during the Civil War.

Mexican Tortilla Chicken Soup

1 tablespoon vegetable oil
1 red bell pepper, seeded and coarsely chopped
3 garlic cloves, minced
5 cups chicken broth
1 (16-ounce) package frozen whole-kernel corn
1 pound boneless chicken breasts or thighs, cut into small pieces
½ cup salsa
¼ cup chopped cilantro
1 cup crushed tortilla chips

In a Dutch oven, heat vegetable oil over medium heat. Add chopped red bell pepper and minced garlic. Cook for 3 minutes or until softened, stirring frequently. Stir in chicken broth, corn, chicken, and salsa. Bring to a boil. Reduce heat to low, cover, and simmer 5 minutes or until chicken is no longer pink inside. Stir in chopped cilantro and serve with crushed tortilla chips sprinkled on top.

Feeding the Flock—HCCLA

Parsley Soup

Serve this on one of the chilly rainy days of April. Put on your slicker and cut the parsley fresh from the garden.

½ cup flour
½ cup butter, melted
1 quart milk
Salt and pepper to taste
1½ teaspoons finely chopped onion
½ cup chopped parsley leaves

Stir flour in the melted butter in medium saucepan until smooth, and let sit to cool. Add milk slowly, stirring as it heats and thickens. Add salt, pepper, and onion. Just before serving, add the parsley and stir well.

A Dooryard Herb Cookbook

Kielbasa, Kale and Lentil Soup

1 (16-ounce) package kielbasa (Polish sausage)
1 medium onion, chopped
1 small red bell pepper, cut in 1-inch pieces
1 small yellow bell pepper, cut in 1-inch pieces
2 cups gently packed chopped fresh kale (1/4 pound) or fresh spinach
2 (19-ounce) cans Progresso® Lentil Soup
1 (10-ounce) can chicken broth

Peel and discard skin from sausage; cut sausage in half lengthwise, then cut into thin slices. In skillet, cook kielbasa over medium heat, stirring occasionally, until browned. Drain sausage on paper towels; set aside, reserving 1 tablespoon drippings in skillet.

In soup pot or Dutch oven, sauté onion, peppers, and kale in 1 tablespoon sausage drippings until softened (cover and simmer about 15 minutes, stirring occasionally). Stir in soup, broth, and sausage; bring to boil on high, then immediately reduce heat to low and simmer, covered, 15 minutes longer. Serve warm. Makes 8 servings.

Note: If colored peppers are unavailable, use green bell peppers. Diced potatoes may be added, if desired. If meat department sells the sausage individually, you can get by with 1/2 pound.

Nutrition Information: (1/8 of recipe) 330 cal; 180 cal from fat; 19g fat; 6g sat fat; 40mg chol; 2170mg sod; 23g carbo; 5g fiber.

The All or Nothing Cookbook

Bluefield radio station WHIS claims its broadcast of a murder trial in 1931 was the first ever in the U. S. The suspect was found guilty and sentenced to death. The case was appealed on grounds that the broadcast made a circus of the trial. In retrial the suspect was given life and subsequently served 20 years.

Mom-Mom's Potato Soup

3–4 medium potatoes, peeled and diced
1 teaspoon salt
2 (16-ounce) cans chicken broth
1 onion, chopped
3–4 strips bacon, fried, drained, and crumbled
1 cup thin white sauce
Salt and pepper to taste
½ stick butter

In pot of water to cover, add potatoes and salt. Cook until tender. Drain all but ¾ cup. Add chicken broth, chopped onion, and bacon bits. Cook for ½ hour, boiling. Add white sauce and salt and pepper to taste. Boil for an additional ½ hour. Add butter. Serve hot.

Mom-Mom's Cookbook

Editor's Extra: To make thin white sauce, heat 1 tablespoon butter till melted; add 1 tablespoon flour; stir in 1 cup milk; heat and stir till thickened and smooth.

Cauliflower Soup

4 medium potatoes, cubed
½ cup chopped onion
1 (16-ounce) package frozen cauliflower
1 (42-ounce) can chicken broth
½ teaspoon celery salt
⅛ teaspoon pepper
1 jar dried chipped beef, cut in thin strips
1 pint half-and-half

Boil potatoes, onion, and cauliflower in chicken broth with celery salt and pepper until potatoes are tender. Purée. Add small amounts of chicken broth, if necessary, to make the consistency of applesauce. Add beef and simmer 15 minutes. (Beef will provide salt enough for entire recipe.) Remove from heat and add half-and-half. Return to low heat to bring up to serving temperature, but do not allow to boil, as it will curdle. Serve with croutons or crusty bread.

West Virginia Country Cooking

Curried Butternut Squash Soup

4 tablespoons unsalted butter
2 cups finely chopped yellow onions
4–5 teaspoons curry powder
2 medium butternut squash (about 3 pounds)
3 cups chicken stock
2 apples, peeled, cored and chopped
1 cup apple juice
Salt and pepper
1 Granny Smith apple, unpeeled and shredded for garnish

Melt butter in pot. Add chopped onions and curry powder and cook, covered, over low heat until onions are tender (about 20 minutes). Meanwhile peel the squash, scrape out seeds, and chop the flesh. When onions are tender, pour in chicken stock, squash, and apples. Bring to boil. Reduce heat and simmer, partially covered, until squash and apples are very tender (about 20 minutes). Pour the soup through a strainer, reserving liquid, and transfer the solids to the bowl of a food processor fitted with a steel blade. Add 1 cup of cooking stock and process until smooth. Return puréed soup to pot and add apple juice and additional cooking liquid, about 2 cups, until soup is of the desired consistency. Season to taste with salt and pepper, simmering briefly to heat through. Serve immediately, garnished with shredded apple. Yields 4–6 portions.

A Gracious Plenty

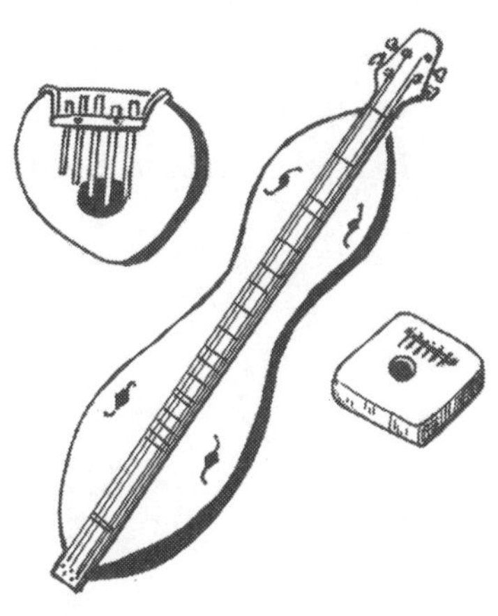

Corn Chowder

6 cups chicken broth
3 cups diced potatoes (about 4 medium)
1 cup diced onion (1 medium)
2 tablespoons butter
½ cup chopped celery
½ cup diced carrots
2 cups corn
½ teaspoon salt
¼ teaspoon pepper
1 cup milk
4 tablespoons flour
4 strips bacon, fried and crumbled

Combine broth, potatoes, onion, butter, celery, carrots, corn, salt, and pepper; boil until potatoes and carrots are tender. Mix milk and flour together and stir into broth. Add bacon. Simmer until thickened and raw flour taste is gone, about 10–15 minutes. Makes 8 cups.

West Virginia Country Cooking

Janet's Turkey Corn Chowder

1 onion, chopped, sautéed in ½ stick butter (or less)
2 cups chicken broth
3 cups diced cooked turkey or chicken
1 cup sliced celery
5 potatoes, cubed
1 large can whole-kernel corn
1 large can cream-style corn
1 quart milk
Parsley for garnish
Paprika for garnish

Combine onion, chicken broth, turkey or chicken, celery, and potatoes in large saucepan. Cook until potatoes are tender, then add both cans of corn and milk. Heat well, but don't boil. Before serving, sprinkle with parsley and paprika.

Take Two & Butter 'Em While They're Hot!

White Grass Chili

This is by far the most popular dish served at White Grass. We should have a sign reading "Over A Billion Bowls Served."

2½ cups dried or 2 (16-ounce) cans pinto beans
2 teaspoons salt
2 medium onions, chopped
4 cloves garlic, chopped
3 stalks celery, chopped
4 carrots, peeled and grated
1 large green pepper, chopped
2 tablespoons olive oil
1 cup raw bulgur
1 tablespoon ground cumin
1 teaspoon dried basil
1 teaspoon dried oregano
3 tablespoons chili powder
¼ teaspoon or a dash cayenne pepper
1 cup water
1 (16-ounce) can whole tomatoes, chopped
1 (16-ounce) can tomato purée
Salt and pepper to taste
Grated Jack or Cheddar cheese

If using dried beans, soak them overnight in 2 quarts water (plus a dash of baking soda). Rinse and cook in fresh water with salt. Cook until tender, about 1 hour. Reserve 1 cup broth.

In a large saucepan, sauté onions, garlic, celery, carrots, and green pepper in olive oil. Add bulgur, spices, herbs, and water. Mix well and add cooked beans, 1 cup of bean broth (or canned beans), tomatoes, and purée. Let simmer 45 minutes or until bulgur is softened. Season to taste. It may be necessary to add more water to determine thickness. Serve topped with grated Jack or Cheddar cheese. Serves 6.

White Grass Cafe Cross Country Cooking

Declared a state by President Abraham Lincoln, West Virginia is the only state to be designated by Presidential Proclamation.

Hot Dog Chili

1½ pounds hamburger
2 onions, chopped
1 can tomato paste
2 pints tomato juice
½ pint mustard
½ pint ketchup
1 teaspoon salt
1 teaspoon red pepper
1 teaspoon paprika
2 tablespoons chili powder

Fry hamburger and onions in medium saucepan until browned. Add remaining ingredients; boil until thick, stirring frequently.

Gypsy, West Virginia 100th Anniversary Cookbook

Stufato

(Italian Beef Stew)

1–2 pounds cubed beef
1 tablespoon olive oil
1 tablespoon butter
1 onion, chopped
1 garlic clove, chopped
1 small can tomato paste
1 bay leaf
2 tablespoons parsley
Salt and pepper to taste
Water to cover
1 can peas, drained (optional)
Steamed sliced carrots (optional)
Diced cooked potatoes (optional)

Wash beef cubes in cold water. Heat oil and butter in frying pan. Add chopped onion and garlic, and lightly brown. Add beef and lightly brown. Add tomato paste, bay leaf, parsley, and seasonings; cover with water and simmer on low, until meat is tender and sauce forms. You may add peas, carrots, and potatoes, if desired. Remove bay leaf before serving. As with any stew, a slow simmer will create wonderful flavors!

Recipe from Wisteria House Bed & Breakfast, Fayetteville
Good Morning West Virginia!

Meat Ball Stew and Egg Dumplings

1 pound ground beef
6 tablespoons sour cream, divided
¼ cup chopped onion
1 tablespoon parsley flakes
1 teaspoon salt
⅛ teaspoon pepper
1 can cream of celery soup
1 (16-ounce) can each: peas, green beans, and carrots or 1 can mixed vegetables, undrained
1 (15-ounce) can sliced potatoes, drained and rinsed, or 2 boiled, sliced potatoes
2 cups Bisquick® Baking Mix
2 eggs
2 tablespoons milk

Mix ground beef, 3 tablespoons sour cream, onion, and parsley flakes. Add salt and pepper. Shape into 1-inch balls. Brown on all sides on medium heat in large skillet.

Mix soup, 3 tablespoons sour cream, and vegetables. Pour over meat balls. Heat to boiling. Can add a small amount of milk if mixture seems too thick.

Stir last 3 ingredients into soft dough. Drop by spoonfuls onto hot mixture. Cook, uncovered, 10 minutes over low heat; cover and cook 10–15 minutes or until toothpick inserted in dough comes out clean.

West Virginia Librarians (bon) Appétit

Italian-Style One-Pot Stew

2 pounds lean stew beef
Water
1 (28-ounce) jar Ragú® sauce
10 ounces tomato paste
2 pounds potatoes
4–5 carrots
Salt
Pepper
Garlic salt (optional)

Cover stew beef with water in large Dutch oven or stockpot; cook until tender. Skim off foam as it cooks. Add Ragú sauce and tomato paste. Peel and quarter potatoes. Scrape and slice carrots. Add these to the beef and sauce. Season to taste. Cook until vegetables are tender. Serve with salad and garlic bread.

Tyrand Cooperative Ministries Cookbook

Irish Stew

2 pounds neck or shoulder of lamb
4 cups water
8 small onions
4 small carrots
8 medium potatoes
Salt and pepper

Cut meat into serving pieces, discarding excess fat. Place in saucepan with water almost to boiling point and simmer 1 hour. Add vegetables, coarsely chopped. Season and cook 1 hour longer without stirring. Serves 4.

More than Beans and Cornbread

BASE jumpers leap 876 feet into the New River Gorge every year on Bridge Day, West Virginia's largest one-day festival. BASE stands for the four types of fixed objects that are used for foot-launched dives: Building, Antenna, Span, and Earth.

Butch's Venison Stew

4 pounds cubed venison
10–12 large potatoes
3 onions
12–16 carrots
8 pieces celery
2 (46-ounce) cans tomatoes
2 (46-ounce) cans tomatoes with basil, garlic, and oregano
2 (46-ounce) cans tomato sauce
2 (6-ounce) cans tomato paste
1 (64-ounce) can V8 juice
1 hot pepper
2 pinches allspice
Salt and pepper to taste
Garlic salt to taste
1 stick butter

Cook venison in water until tender. Add potatoes and onions, peeled and cut in quarters, carrots cut in large pieces, celery cut in thirds. Add cans of tomato, tomato sauce, tomato paste, V8 juice, hot pepper, allspice, salt, pepper, garlic salt, and butter. Bake at 350° about 1 hour, or until all vegetables are done. Serves 12–14.

Elkins Manor Cookbook

Cathy's Pumpkin Stew

On Halloween night in Harpers Ferry, all the children and some brave grown-ups gather at "The Terrace," a huge and wonderfully ornate Victorian house on the hill. We feast on green spaghetti and this unusual stew served in a big golden pumpkin.

1 pumpkin (compatible with your oven size)
1 pound chicken, skinned
1 pound Italian sausage, cut into bite-size pieces
Carrots, potatoes, corn, onions, peas, beans
12 ounces of stewing tomatoes
1/4 cup raisins
Nuts (optional)
1/4 cup chopped fresh parsley
Salt and pepper to taste
Bay leaf

Prepare pumpkin to stuff. Cut lid and clean out contents. Lightly salt. Parboil chicken. Sauté sausage until browned. Parboil only carrots and potatoes. Stuff pumpkin with all ingredients; season to taste and place bay leaf on top. Place pumpkin on cookie sheet without lid and bake in a 350° oven approximately 2 hours or until pumpkin is soft, .

To serve, top with lid. Ladle each portion and serve with a wedge of "pumpkin squash." Consider any and all variations of the above. This is good served with corn bread, a tossed salad, and a dry wine.

A Dooryard Herb Cookbook

PHOTO © ROGER SPENCER PHOTOGRAPHY.

Dolly Sods Wilderness Area, in the Monongahela National Forest, has unique hiking trails—from Red Creek Trail with its beautiful rhododendrons and spectacular views, to the former beaver ponds and open plains of the Breathed Mountain Trail.

Autumn Fruit Salad

DRESSING:
$1\frac{1}{2}$ cups sugar
$\frac{1}{2}$ cup all-purpose flour
$1\frac{1}{2}$ cups water
1 teaspoon margarine
1 teaspoon vanilla

In saucepan, combine sugar and flour. Stir in water; bring to a boil. Cook and stir until mixture thickens. Remove from heat. Stir in margarine and vanilla. Cool to room temperature.

SALAD:
6 cups cubed unpeeled apples
2 cups halved red grapes
1 cup diced celery
1 cup walnuts

In large bowl, combine apples, grapes, celery, and walnuts. Add Dressing and toss gently. Refrigerate until serving. Serves 8–10.

Third Wednesday Homemakers Volume II

Fruit Salad

1 pound blue grapes
1 pound white grapes
1 large can fruit cocktail
1 can pineapple chunks
1 box vanilla cook and serve pudding
4 bananas, sliced
$1\frac{1}{2}$ cups small marshmallows
1 small jar maraschino cherries
$\frac{1}{2}$ cup chopped nuts

Cut grapes in halves. Drain fruit cocktail and pineapple; reserve juice. Mix pudding with reserved juice. Cook over low heat until thick. Stir constantly. Set aside and let cool completely. Mix all fruit together in large bowl with cooled pudding. Stir in marshmallows, cherries, and nuts.

Cooking for the New Era

Six Cup Salad

1 cup sour cream
1 cup shredded coconut
1 cup miniature marshmallows
1 cup mandarin oranges, drained
1 cup crushed pineapple, drained
1 cup chopped pecans
12 maraschino cherries (halved)

Combine all ingredients, except cherries, in a 2-quart bowl. Refrigerate 24 hours. Garnish with cherries.

Christ Reformed Church Historical Cookbook

Mama Pack's Frozen Fruit Salad

1 large can pineapple chunks
1 large can sweet white cherries
3 large bananas, sliced
1 cup small marshmallows
½ cup mayonnaise
½ cup whipping cream

Drain fruit and cut up in bite-size pieces. Mix all but whipping cream. Chill in freezer for about 30 minutes. Whip the cream and fold into the chilled mixture. Pour mixture into square pan; freeze. Cut in squares and serve on bed of lettuce.

Cookin' in a Coal Camp

Taffy Apple Salad

1 (8-ounce) can crushed pineapple, undrained
½ cup sugar
1 egg, beaten
1 tablespoon flour
2 tablespoons apple cider vinegar
8 ounces whipped topping
5 Granny Smith apples, chopped
1 cup chopped peanuts, divided

Combine pineapple, sugar, egg, flour, and vinegar in a saucepan; mix well. Cook over medium heat until thickened. Refrigerate until cooled.

Spoon whipped topping into a large bowl. Fold in pineapple mixture. Add apples and ¾ cup of the peanuts. Toss until well blended. Top with remaining ¼ cup peanuts. Refrigerate, covered, until ready to serve. Yields 12 servings.

Everything but the Entrée

Cranberry Waldorf Delight

1 (12-ounce) package fresh cranberries
1 (16-ounce) package miniature marshmallows
½ cup sugar
1 large apple, peeled, chopped
1 cup red seedless grapes, cut into halves
½ cup chopped walnuts
½ pint whipping cream
1 teaspoon vanilla extract or Grand Marnier®

Wash cranberries, discarding any that are soft. Finely chop the cranberries or grind in a blender or food processor container. Transfer to a bowl. Add marshmallows and sugar and mix well. Refrigerate, covered, for 8–10 hours. Fold the apple, grapes, and walnuts into the cranberry mixture; set aside.

Beat cream with vanilla in a chilled bowl with chilled beaters until soft peaks form. Fold whipped cream into fruit mixture. Refrigerate, covered, until ready to serve. Yields 10 servings.

Everything but the Entrée

Cranberry Apple Salad

Good for Thanksgiving and Christmas.

2 (1-pound) cans whole cranberries in sauce
2 cups boiling water
2 (3-ounce) packages strawberry gelatin
2 tablespoons lemon juice
½ teaspoon salt
1 cup mayonnaise
½ cup chopped walnuts
2 cups diced apples

Melt cranberry sauce over medium heat. Drain, saving the juice and berries separately. Mix together cranberry juice, boiling water, and gelatin. Stir until dissolved. Add lemon juice and salt. Chill until mixture mounds slightly on a spoon. Add mayonnaise; beat until fluffy and smooth. Fold in berries, nuts, and apples, and pour into a gelatin mold. Chill overnight. Makes 10–12 servings.

The Way Pocahontas County Cooks

Cranberry Salad

2 packages cherry Jell-O®
1 can crushed pineapple, drained
1 can whole cranberries, drained
1 cup chopped nuts
2 cups chopped apples
1 cup chopped celery

Make Jell-O according to package directions. When cool, add remaining ingredients. Pour into mold or bowl; chill until set.

Gypsy, West Virginia 100th Anniversary Cookbook

On May 31, 1910, the Supreme Court held that the Maryland-West Virginia boundary was the low-water mark of the south bank of the Potomac River.

Pineapple Orange Congealed Salad

1 (15 1/4-ounce) can crushed pineapple
1 (6-ounce) package orange gelatin
2 cups buttermilk
1 cup flaked coconut
1 cup chopped pecans
1 (12-ounce) carton whipped topping

Place pineapple in a saucepan. Bring to a boil, stirring constantly. Remove from heat. Add gelatin, stirring until completely dissolved. Stir in buttermilk, coconut, and pecans. Cool. Fold in whipped topping. Pour into a 9x13-inch dish. Chill until firm.

Our Daily Bread

Cherry Salad Supreme

1 package raspberry Jell-O®
2 cups boiling water, divided
1 (21-ounce) can cherry pie filling
1 package lemon Jell-O®
1 (3-ounce) package cream cheese, softened
1/2 cup mayonnaise
1 (8 1/4-ounce) can crushed pineapple, undrained
1/2 cup Cool Whip®
1 cup miniature marshmallows
1/4 cup chopped nuts

Dissolve raspberry Jell-O in 1 cup boiling water. Stir in pie filling; chill until set. Dissolve lemon Jell-O in 1 cup boiling water. Beat together cream cheese and mayonnaise; gradually add lemon Jell-O. Stir in undrained pineapple; fold in Cool Whip and marshmallows. Spread on top of set Jell-O; top with nuts.

Down Memory Lane

Pasta Primavera Salad

DRESSING:

¼ cup olive oil
½ tablespoon chopped garlic
½ tablespoon salt
1 teaspoon dried basil
1 tablespoon balsamic vinegar
¼ teaspoon black pepper

Simply mix all ingredients together; set aside.

SALAD:

1 (12-ounce) package dried pasta (your favorite type)
2–3 tablespoons water
1½ cups broccoli spears
1½ cups fresh mushrooms, halved
1½ cups sliced red bell pepper
1½ cups canned artichoke hearts
1 cup whole black olives, pitted
¼ cup chopped fresh basil

In a large saucepan, cook pasta in boiling water until tender, but still firm. Drain and rinse in cold water; set aside and let cool. In large deep skillet, heat water and sauté broccoli, mushrooms, and bell pepper for about 5 minutes or until tender-crisp. Remove and rinse in cold water; set aside and let cool.

In a large mixing bowl, mix together the reserved pasta and vegetables and pour Dressing over top. Add artichoke hearts, olives, and basil and mix together thoroughly. Serve immediately or chill for 1–2 hours, if desired.

A Gracious Plenty

Having enlisted at the age of 14, Chester Merriman of Romney was the youngest soldier of World War I.

Pasta Salad

SALAD:

1 package spiral pasta, cooked
¼ cup sliced radishes
¼ cup sweet pickle relish
¼ cup chopped celery
¼ cup chopped carrots
¼ cup chopped green pepper

Mix all Salad ingredients in large bowl. Set aside.

DRESSING:

½ cup mayonnaise
½ cup Miracle Whip® Salad Dressing
3 tablespoons sugar or substitute
Milk

In small bowl, mix Dressing ingredients, using enough milk for desired consistency; pour over Salad.

Heavenly Helpings

Corn Bread Bean Salad

1 box Jiffy® Corn Muffin Mix
1 can pinto beans, drained
1 onion, chopped
1 red pepper, chopped
½ cup salad dressing
¼ cup sweet pickle juice
1 medium tomato, chopped
Bacon bits

Bake Jiffy® Corn Muffin Mix according to package directions. Cool. Crumble in a 9x13-inch casserole or glass dish. Spread pinto beans over top; sprinkle chopped onion and chopped pepper on top of beans. Mix salad dressing and sweet pickle juice. Pour over pepper layer. Scatter chopped tomatoes on top, then sprinkle with bacon bits. Place in refrigerator until serving time.

Our Favorite Recipes

Vegetable Biriyani

This incredibly tasty salad is fabulous served warm or cold. It can stand on its own as an entrée or as an excellent side dish.

1½ cups basmati rice
½ teaspoon salt
4 bay leaves
3⅓ cups water, divided
2 large carrots, diced
1 medium onion, diced
½ cup raisins
1 cup chickpeas
½ cup chopped cilantro
1 cup frozen peas
1 tablespoon vegetable oil
4 cloves garlic, minced
1 tablespoon curry powder
¼ teaspoon cinnamon
¼ teaspoon ground cardamom
¼ teaspoon ground cloves
¼ teaspoon turmeric

In saucepan, place rice, salt, bay leaves, and 3 cups water. Cook over medium heat 15 minutes, then add carrots and onion and continue cooking until rice is tender. Spoon into a large bowl and add raisins, chickpeas, cilantro, and peas; let cool.

In a skillet, heat oil and sauté garlic for 1 or 2 minutes. Add spices, sauté another minute and add ⅓ cup water. Stir well and gently fold spices into rice until well mixed. Add a little cayenne, if you like heat. Serves 6 generously.

White Grass Cafe Cross Country Cooking

Vegetable Salad

2 cups broccoli flowerets
2 cups cauliflower flowerets
1 small red onion, thinly sliced
½ cup chopped green pepper
½ cup sliced carrot
½ cup sliced celery
½ cup mayonnaise
¼ cup salad oil
2 tablespoons vinegar
2–4 tablespoons sugar
½ teaspoon dry mustard

Combine broccoli, cauliflower, onion, green pepper, carrot, and celery. Stir together mayonnaise, oil, vinegar, sugar, and mustard. Stir into vegetable mixture. Cover and chill for 2–24 hours. Yields 8–10 servings.

Stout Memorial Culinary Treasures

Sunny Vegetable Salad

SALAD:
5 cups fresh broccoli flowerets
5 cups cauliflower flowerets
2 cups shredded Cheddar cheese
⅔ cup chopped onion
6 bacon strips, cooked and crumbled

In a large salad bowl, toss broccoli, cauliflower, cheese, onion, and bacon (reserve some to sprinkle on top).

DRESSING:
1 cup mayonnaise
½ cup sugar
2 tablespoons vinegar

In a small bowl, combine mayonnaise, sugar, and vinegar. Pour over salad, toss to coat. Cover and refrigerate for at least 1 hour. Sprinkle with bacon.

Our Favorite Recipes

Marinated Carrots

2 pounds raw carrots
1 medium green pepper, sliced
1 medium onion, sliced
1 can tomato soup, undiluted
½ soup can vegetable oil
1 cup sugar
½ cup cider vinegar
1 teaspoon salt
1 teaspoon pepper

Cut carrots into thin rounds; cook. Add sliced pepper and onion. Combine soup, oil, sugar, vinegar, salt, and pepper; pour over carrots while still warm. Refrigerate. Let stand overnight. May be used as an appetizer or a vegetable salad.

Gypsy, West Virginia 100th Anniversary Cookbook

Lima Bean Salad

2 packages frozen lima beans
2 cups sliced mushrooms
1 cup chopped red onion
½ cup chopped cooked ham
⅓ cup chopped ripe olives
¼ cup snipped parsley
1 (4-ounce) jar pimiento, drained
⅓ cup white wine vinegar
¼ cup oil
2 cloves garlic, minced
½ teaspoon sugar
½ teaspoon salt
½ teaspoon lemon juice
Dash of pepper

Cook lima beans according to package directions. Drain; rinse with cold water. Combine beans, mushrooms, onion, ham, olives, parsley, and pimiento. In screw-top jar, combine vinegar, oil, garlic, sugar, salt, lemon juice, and pepper. Shake to combine. Pour over bean mixture. Toss to coat. Chill 3–4 hours. Stir before serving. Serves 8–10.

Cookin' with the Stars

Marinate Slaw

1 medium cabbage
2 medium onions
2 medium green peppers
Salt and pepper to taste
1 cup sugar
1 cup white vinegar
1 cup Wesson oil

Shred cabbage. Into separate containers, thinly slice onions and peppers. In a large bowl make a layer of cabbage, then onions, then peppers; season to taste. Layer until all ingredients are gone.

In saucepan combine sugar, vinegar, and Wesson oil; boil until sugar is dissolved. Pour over cabbage mixture. Place in refrigerator, covered with foil, overnight. Toss when ready to use.

West Virginia Librarians (bon) Appétit

Nine-Day Slaw

1 medium head of cabbage, chopped
2 stalks celery, diced
1 medium onion, diced
1 green pepper, diced
2 cups sugar

Combine cabbage, celery, onion, and green pepper. Add sugar and blend well. Set aside.

SLAW DRESSING:
1 cup salad oil
1 cup vinegar
2 tablespoons salt

Combine oil, vinegar, and salt, and bring to a boil. Pour hot dressing over cabbage mixture; allow to cool and store in refrigerator. *Do not use for a day or two.* Will keep up to 9 days.

A Gracious Plenty

Sauerkraut Salad

Wonderful for picnics, covered-dish affairs, or just to have something "green" in the refrigerator to serve for dinner.

1 large (1-pound) can sauerkraut
1 cup diced celery
1 cup diced green pepper
½ cup diced onion
1 cup sugar
½ cup salad oil

Drain, but do not rinse, sauerkraut. Mix with celery, green pepper, and onion. Add sugar and oil. Mix well and chill overnight, stirring occasionally, if possible. If can't chill overnight, chill at least 3 hours before serving. Keeps well in refrigerator for up to 2 weeks.

More than Beans and Cornbread

Corned Beef Potato Salad

4 cups cubed, cooked potatoes
1 (12-ounce) can corned beef, cubed
½ cup diced dill pickle
½ cup chopped celery
¼ cup chopped onion
¼ cup salad oil
2 tablespoons wine vinegar
½ teaspoon salt
¼ teaspoon garlic powder
¼ teaspoon pepper
⅔ cup sour cream
2 tablespoons horseradish

In a large bowl, toss potatoes, meat, pickles, celery, and onion. In another bowl, mix oil, vinegar, salt, garlic powder, and pepper. Pour over meat/potato mixture and toss. Cover and refrigerate for at least 2 hours. Just before serving, mix sour cream and horseradish. Pour over salad mixture and toss. Season to taste. Makes 6 servings.

Cooking for the New Era

Chicken Salad with Grapes and Almonds

2½ cups chopped, cooked chicken
1 cup sliced scallions
1 cup thinly sliced celery
1 cup sliced almonds, lightly toasted
2 tablespoons pimento (optional)
2 cups mayonnaise
1 teaspoon basil
½ teaspoon thyme
¼ teaspoon garlic powder
1 teaspoon poultry seasoning
2 cups seedless grapes, halved

In a large bowl, combine chicken, scallions, celery, almonds, and pimento. Combine mayonnaise, basil, thyme, garlic powder, and poultry seasoning. Pour over chicken mixture and mix well. Gently fold in the grapes. Serve chilled in a bed of lettuce or stuffed into a pita pocket. Yields 6 servings.

A Taste of Fayette County

Chicken and Fruit Salad

1 (8-ounce) carton lemon, peach, or pineapple yogurt
¼ cup mayonnaise
½ teaspoon ground ginger
½ teaspoon lemon peel, finely shredded
2 cups cubed cooked chicken or turkey
3 cups cubed cantaloupe, watermelon, and/or honeydew
1 cup halved seedless red grapes
¾ cup sliced celery

In mixing bowl, stir together yogurt, mayonnaise, ginger, and lemon peel. Add remaining ingredients and mix well. Cover and refrigerate 2–4 hours. Serve on lettuce or purple kale-lined plates. Makes 6 servings.

United Methodist Ministers' Wives Cook Book

Nellie's Pickled Eggs

2 dozen eggs
4 cans beets (do not use pickled style)
$1\frac{1}{4}$ cups sugar
$1\frac{3}{4}$ cups vinegar

Boil eggs for 20 minutes, then cool and peel. Drain beets into saucepan and then set aside. Layer eggs and beets in large container with tight lid. Heat beet juice, sugar, and vinegar till it comes to a boil. Pour juice mixture over eggs and beets. Set aside to cool with lid partially on. Then put lid on firmly and place in refrigerator for 2 weeks. Take eggs out and slice or leave whole and serve.

A Taste of Fayette County

Poke Pickles

Gather and peel poke stalks. Make a pickle solution of 1 cup vinegar and 1 cup sugar; heat and stir to dissolve the sugar. Now add about 4 cups of peeled and sliced poke stalk. Heat to boiling and pack in a sterile quart jar. Let sit for about a week and I betcha' you can't eat just one!

In working up this recipe, I have added wild mustard or hot pepper seeds, but after much sampling, I like it best with just the vinegar-sugar solution. You might like to try a seasoning of your choice.

Bootstraps and Biscuits

The Greenbrier® resort in White Sulphur Springs frequently hosted presidents, even earning the distinction of being the "Summer White House."

Simply Scrumptious Salad Dressing

1/3 cup honey
1/3 cup olive or olive/canola oil
1/3 cup blackberry wine

Pour ingredients into a glass bottle with stopper or cap. Shake thoroughly. Best if allowed to stand in refrigerator several days, shaking frequently. Serve on bed of dark salad greens and sliced, fresh vegetables.

Carnegie Hall Cookbook

Buttermilk Horseradish Dressing

3/4 cup cultured buttermilk
2 tablespoons prepared horseradish
1 tablespoon sugar or honey
1/4 teaspoon salt
1 tablespoon vinegar
1/2 teaspoon prepared mustard

Combine all ingredients. Mix thoroughly and chill. Serve with cabbage, tossed green salads, or fresh fruit. Yields 1 cup.

Serving Our Best

PHOTO COURTESY OF MARY JANE BOHME.

West Virginia is home to two buildings constructed entirely of coal. Coal House, the only private residence in the world built entirely of coal, is located in White Sulphur Springs. The Williamson Coal House, shown here, houses the Tug Valley Chamber of Commerce.

Spicy Home Fries

2½ teaspoons vegetable oil
1 clove garlic, finely chopped
1 quart water
1 baking potato, peeled
½ cup chili powder
¼ teaspoon ground cumin
¼ teaspoon paprika
⅛ teaspoon ground red pepper
2 tablespoons thinly sliced onion

Preheat oven to 350°. Spray baking sheet with nonstick cooking spray. Combine oil and garlic in small bowl; let stand 15 minutes. Place water in medium saucepan; bring to a boil over high heat. Add potato; boil 12 minutes. Drain; let stand 10 minutes or until cool enough to handle.

Meanwhile, combine chili powder, cumin, paprika, and pepper in a small bowl until well blended. Cut potato into 20 slices. Place sliced onions on a baking sheet; arrange potato slices over onion. Brush potato slices with half of oil mixture. Sprinkle ½ the spice mixture over potato slices. Bake 40 minutes, turning once, and brushing with remaining oil and spice mixture. Makes 2 servings.

Dietary data: 172 calories per serving; exchanges 1½ starch; 1 fat.

Our Favorite Recipes

Sesame Potato Sticks

6–8 medium baking potatoes, peeled
¾ cup sesame seeds
½ cup butter, melted
½ cup Parmesan cheese
Seasoning salt

Preheat oven to 400°. Cut potatoes into sticks 1 inch thick. Sprinkle sesame seeds in a thin layer on waxed paper. Dip potato sticks in butter; coat 1 side of stick with sesame seeds. Place sticks on a well greased baking sheet. Sprinkle with Parmesan cheese and seasoning salt. Bake 35–40 minutes or until done. Yields 8 servings.

Almost Heaven

Gourmet Potatoes

12 medium potatoes, cooked and grated
1/4 cup margarine
2 cups Velveeta® cheese
1 cup grated Cheddar cheese
2 cups sour cream
1 small onion, chopped
2 teaspoons salt
1/2 teaspoon pepper
1 cup milk

Combine potatoes, margarine, Velveeta cheese, Cheddar cheese, sour cream, onion, salt, pepper, and milk. Place in crockpot. Heat on LOW for 2 hours or until thoroughly hot and bubbly.

More...Home Town Recipes

Fix-Ahead Mashed Potatoes

3 pounds (about 4 large) potatoes
1/2 teaspoon salt
3 tablespoons butter or margarine, divided
2/3 cup sour cream
2 (3-ounce) packages cream cheese, softened
1/4 cup milk
3/4 teaspoon salt
1/2 teaspoon paprika

Place potatoes in a saucepan; add water to cover and salt. Bring to a boil; cover. Reduce heat to medium and simmer 25 minutes or until potatoes are tender. Drain. Peel potatoes; place in a large mixing bowl and mash with a potato masher. Add 2 tablespoons butter, sour cream, cream cheese, milk, and salt, mixing until all ingredients are blended. Spoon mixture into a lightly greased 12x8x2-inch baking dish. Brush top of mixture with 1 tablespoon melted butter; sprinkle with paprika. Bake immediately, or cover and refrigerate. If refrigerated, let stand at room temperature 30 minutes before baking. Bake at 350°, uncovered, 30 minutes or until hot. Yields 6–8 servings.

Serving Our Best

Creamy Whipped Potatoes

5 pounds medium-size potatoes
2 teaspoons salt, divided
1 (8-ounce) container whipped cream cheese with chives
1 teaspoon garlic salt
1/4 teaspoon ground black pepper
6 tablespoons margarine or butter (3/4 stick)
2 cups heavy or whipping cream
1/4 cup sliced almonds
Paprika

Peel potatoes; cut each into quarters. In 5-quart saucepan over high heat, heat potatoes, 1 teaspoon salt, and enough water to cover to boiling. Reduce heat to low; cover and simmer 20 minutes or until potatoes are tender. Drain well.

Preheat oven to 375°. In large bowl, combine potatoes, cream cheese, garlic salt, pepper, 4 tablespoons margarine or butter and 1 teaspoon salt. Mash potatoes until smooth. Gradually add heavy cream, mixing well after each addition. Grease a 9x13-inch glass baking dish or shallow 3-quart casserole. Spoon potatoes into baking dish.

Dot potatoes with 2 tablespoons margarine or butter; sprinkle with sliced almonds and paprika. Bake 30 minutes or until top is golden. Makes 12 accompaniment servings.

Cookin' with the Colts

New England Scalloped Potatoes

4 cups raw potatoes, thinly sliced, divided
4 hard-cooked eggs, sliced
1 cup cubed ham
3 tablespoons chopped green pepper
3 tablespoons margarine
1 tablespoon chopped onion
3 tablespoons flour
1½ cups milk
½ teaspoon salt
6 tablespoons fine bread crumbs

Heat oven to 350°. Grease 8x12-inch shallow baking dish. Spread ½ of potatoes over bottom. Add eggs, ham, and green pepper. Cover with remaining potatoes. Melt margarine in small pan. Add onion. Stir in flour until well blended. Gradually add milk. Heat, stirring constantly, until blended and thickened. Add salt. Pour over potatoes. Sprinkle with bread crumbs. Bake, uncovered, 1¼–1½ hours until potatoes are fork-tender. Makes 6 servings.

Stout Memorial Culinary Treasures

Sinful Potatoes

1 pound Velveeta® cheese
2 pounds frozen hash browns, thawed
1 pint mayonnaise
¼ pound bacon, fried and crumbled

Melt cheese in double boiler. Mix with hash browns and mayonnaise. Top with crumbled bacon. Place in 9x13-inch greased baking dish. May mix and bake later, if desired. Bake at 350° for 45 minutes to 1 hour. Serves 10–12.

Third Wednesday Homemakers

Sweet Potato Casserole

3 pounds sweet potatoes
1/2 cup butter, melted
1/4 cup sugar
1 teaspoon vanilla
1/2 teaspoon cinnamon
2 eggs, well beaten

Cook and mash sweet potatoes; add remaining ingredients. Put in greased casserole. Top with Brown Sugar Topping and bake at 350° for 30 minutes.

BROWN SUGAR TOPPING:
1 cup packed brown sugar
1/2 teaspoon cinnamon
1/2 cup chopped nuts
1/3 cup butter, melted
1/3 cup flour

Combine all ingredients and sprinkle over sweet potato mixture.

Dutch Pantry Cookin'

Yam Casserole

3 cups cooked yams
1 cup sugar
1/2 teaspoon salt
1 teaspoon vanilla
2 eggs, beaten
6 1/2 tablespoons butter, divided
1/2 cup milk
1 cup brown sugar
1/3 cup flour
1/3 cup chopped pecans

Beat yams, sugar, salt, vanilla, eggs, 4 tablespoons butter, and milk with mixer until smooth. Pour yam mixture in a greased baking dish (do not cover). Mix brown sugar, flour, pecans, and 2 1/2 tablespoons butter. Pour over yams. Bake at 350° for 35 minutes.

Homemade with Love

Broccoli Casserole

2 cups water
2 cups Minute® Rice
2 cans cream of mushroom soup
2 (10-ounce) boxes frozen chopped broccoli
1 onion, chopped
1 stick margarine, cut into pieces
1 large jar Cheez Whiz®

Mix all ingredients in a large bowl. Pour into a 9x13-inch baking dish. Bake at 300° for 1 hour.

Treasured Recipes

Broccoli Casserole

1 can cream of mushroom soup
2 tablespoons chopped onion
2 medium eggs, well beaten
3 tablespoons lemon juice
1 cup mayonnaise
2 (10-ounce) boxes frozen chopped broccoli, cooked and drained
1½ cups shredded sharp Cheddar cheese, divided
¼ cup bread crumbs

Combine soup, onion, eggs, juice, and mayonnaise, and beat until well blended. Put layer of cooked broccoli in bottom of buttered 1½-quart casserole. Spoon a layer of soup mixture over broccoli. Sprinkle with a layer of cheese. Repeat layers reserving ½ cup of cheese. Bake at 350° for 20 minutes. Combine remaining ½ cup of cheese with bread crumbs. Sprinkle over top and bake for 10 minutes more.

Feeding the Flock—MOPs of Westminister

In 1862, President Abraham Lincoln signed the Morrill Act, offering land grants of 30,000 acres of federally owned land to each state that agreed to establish a college to teach agriculture and the "mechanic arts" (engineering). The State of West Virginia established the "Agricultural College of West Virginia" on February 7, 1867. The name was changed to West Virginia University in 1868.

Italian Zucchini Crescent Pie

This recipe is great for picnics or to go with ham, pork chops, etc.

4 cups thinly sliced unpeeled zucchini
1 cup chopped onions
½ cup margarine or butter
2 tablespoons parsley flakes
¼ teaspoon garlic powder
¼ teaspoon oregano
½ teaspoon salt
½ teaspoon pepper
¼ teaspoon basil leaves
2 eggs, well beaten
8 ounces shredded mozzarella cheese
1 (8-count) can crescent rolls
2 teaspoons mustard

Heat oven to 375°. In 10-inch skillet, cook zucchini and onions in margarine until tender (about 10 minutes). Stir in parsley and seasonings. In large bowl, blend eggs and cheese. Stir in vegetable mixture. Separate dough into 8 triangles. Place in ungreased 11-inch quiche pan. Press over bottom and up sides to form crust. Spread crust with mustard. Pour vegetable mixture evenly into crust. Bake at 375° for 18–20 minutes, or until knife inserted near center comes out clean. Let stand 10 minutes before serving.

Note: For extra cheesy flavor; use 12 ounces mozzarella instead of 8 ounces.

Dutch Pantry Cookin'

Zucchini Tiela

SAUCE:

$2\frac{1}{2}$ pounds ground chuck
2 cloves garlic, minced
1 small onion, finely chopped
$4\frac{1}{2}$ cups tomato sauce
2 tablespoons grated Italian cheese
1 tablespoon parsley
$1\frac{1}{2}$ teaspoons basil
Salt and pepper to taste

Brown ground chuck, garlic, and onion. Add tomato sauce, grated cheese, parsley, basil, and salt and pepper. Simmer Sauce 1 hour.

VEGETABLE MIXTURE:

8 medium potatoes, sliced
4 medium zucchini, sliced
2 green peppers, cut in thin strips
1 large onion, sliced
2 cups Italian bread crumbs
$\frac{1}{2}$ cup grated Italian cheese

Grease a deep casserole dish; put a layer of Sauce in dish. Place a layer of potatoes on Sauce; spread bread crumbs and cheese on potatoes. Add layer of zucchini, pepper, onions; add Sauce and continue layering until all ingredients are used. Place a layer of Sauce on top and bake 1 hour at 350° or until potatoes are done.

Treasures from Heaven

A marble monument of William Anderson "Devil Anse" Hatfield stands over his grave in the Hatfield Family Cemetery, located in the city of Sarah Ann south of Logan. Anse was the leader of the Hatfield family during the famous Hatfield-McCoy Feud.

Squash Casserole

1 package Pepperidge Farm® Corn Bread Stuffing Mix
1 stick margarine, melted
2 cups cooked, mashed summer yellow squash
1 can cream of chicken soup
2 medium carrots, grated
1 small jar pimentos
1 small onion, chopped fine
1 cup sour cream

Mix stuffing mix and melted margarine; put ½ in bottom of 1½-quart casserole; reserve remainder for topping. Mix remaining ingredients and cover stuffing mix, then sprinkle remaining stuffing mix on top. Bake 30–45 minutes at 350° or until bubbly.

Our Best Home Cooking

Special Eggplant

1 garlic clove, minced
1 large onion, chopped
1 tablespoon oil
2 cans tomatoes
2 teaspoons sugar
½ teaspoon oregano
½ teaspoon basil
¼ teaspoon salt
2 eggs
2 tablespoons water
1 large eggplant
1 cup bread crumbs
½ cup Parmesan cheese
8 ounces shredded mozzarella cheese

Cook garlic and onion in oil until tender. Add tomatoes, sugar, oregano, basil, and salt. Reduce heat; cook, covered, 30 minutes. Mix eggs and water. Slice eggplant into ½-inch slices. Dip in egg mixture and roll in bread crumbs. Cook slices in oil until brown. Place in greased 9x13-inch baking dish; cover with tomato mixture. Top with cheeses. Bake at 350° for 25–30 minutes. Serves 6.

Third Wednesday Homemakers Volume II

Cabbage for a King

½ cup chopped onion
3 tablespoons butter or margarine, divided
2 tablespoons flour
2 cups canned tomatoes
½ teaspoon Worcestershire sauce
¾ teaspoon salt
½ teaspoon sugar
¼ teaspoon pepper
6 cups (1 large head) chopped cabbage
3 slices bread, cubed
½ pound cheese, cubed

Sauté onion in 2 tablespoons butter until tender. Blend in flour until smooth. Add tomatoes, Worcestershire sauce, salt, sugar, and pepper. Cook cabbage in salted, boiling water 5 minutes; drain. Lightly brown bread crumbs in remaining tablespoon butter; remove from skillet and mix with cheese cubes. Arrange in layers, cabbage, tomato mixture, bread and cheese mixture in a 2-quart casserole. Bake at 375° for 30 minutes.

Third Wednesday Homemakers

Cabbage Patch Supper

1 cup sliced onions
¼ cup sliced celery
2 tablespoons butter
¼ cup flour
1½ teaspoons chili powder
1½ teaspoons salt
1 (1-pound) can tomatoes or 1 pint home-canned tomatoes
1 can kidney beans, drained
2 cups sliced cabbage
1 package weiners, cut into 2-inch pieces

Cook onions and celery in butter until tender. Combine flour and seasonings; blend into onion mixture. Stir in tomatoes and beans, then cabbage. Cover and cook slowly, stirring carefully for 15 minutes. Add weiners and cook 10 minutes longer.

Note: For convenience, use electric skillet and serve directly from skillet.

The Way Pocahontas County Cooks

Cabbage Casserole

1 small head cabbage
1 pound ground beef
½ cup chopped onion
½ cup uncooked rice
½ teaspoon salt
¼ teaspoon pepper
1 can tomato soup
1½ cups water
¼ cup grated Parmesan cheese

Chop cabbage into medium-size pieces. Spread in bottom of greased 9x13x2-inch pan. Brown meat and onion in a large skillet, breaking up meat as it cooks. Stir in rice, salt, and pepper. Spoon mixture over cabbage. In saucepan, heat tomato soup and water to boiling. Pour over all ingredients. Sprinkle with cheese. Cover casserole tightly with foil. Bake for 1½ hours in a 350° oven. Fluff lightly with fork before serving.

Heavenly Helpings

Jalapeño Spinach

1 medium onion, chopped
½ cup butter
1 (8-ounce) package cream cheese, cut into cubes
2 (10-ounce) packages frozen chopped spinach
1 teaspoon chopped jalapeño pepper
1 cup fresh bread crumbs
¼ cup butter, melted

Sauté onion in ½ cup butter in a large skillet until tender. Add cream cheese, stirring until melted. Remove from heat.

Cook spinach according to package directions; drain. Add spinach and jalapeño pepper to onion mixture, blending well. Spoon spinach mixture into a greased 1-quart baking dish. Combine bread crumbs and ¼ cup melted butter in a bowl. Sprinkle over the top. Bake at 350° for 30 minutes or until heated through. Yields 4–6 servings.

Note: Recipe may be doubled. May substitute 20 ounces fresh spinach leaves for frozen spinach.

Everything but the Entrée

Spinach and Bacon Bake

2 slices bacon, crisp and crumbled, reserve drippings
½ cup chopped onion
½ cup chopped celery
1 can cream of mushroom soup
1 (3-ounce) package softened cream cheese
2 (10-ounce) packages spinach, thawed and drained
½ cup croutons
1 tablespoon margarine, melted

Cook onion and celery in bacon drippings. Stir in soup and cream cheese; heat until cheese melts. Stir in spinach and bacon. Pour into casserole. Toss croutons with margarine; sprinkle over all. Bake, uncovered, at 325° for 45–50 minutes. Can be mixed ahead and baked later. Serves 10.

Cookin' with the Stars

Spanakopita

Don't be intimidated by working with filo dough! It's not as scary as the instructions on the box say. This is a fabulous and relatively easy dish.

2 medium onions, chopped
1 tablespoon butter
1½ cups ricotta or cottage cheese
2 cups crumbled feta cheese
2 (10-ounce) packages frozen chopped spinach, thawed and water squeezed out
6 eggs
1 teaspoon dried basil
1 teaspoon dried dill weed
1 teaspoon dried oregano
½ teaspoon salt
⅛ teaspoon black pepper
1 (1-pound) package filo dough, thawed
1 cup (2 sticks) butter, melted

Sauté onions in 1 tablespoon butter until soft. In a large bowl, mix cottage cheese, feta, spinach, eggs, herbs, salt, and pepper. Add onions and mix well.

Open filo and take out 2 sheets at a time, laying in a 9x13-inch pan and brushing with butter, generously. Stack 8 sheets of filo, then spoon on half of the filling and spread over the pan. Continue to layer filo in "two's," being sure to brush them with butter. Place 4 sheets down, and spoon remainder of the filling. Pile the rest of the sheets on top and tuck in around the edges. Bake at 400° for 1 hour or until golden. Let this dish sit for at least 15 minutes before cutting.

White Grass Cafe Cross Country Cooking

Ricotta Stuffed Peppers

1 pound whole milk ricotta cheese
2 or 3 eggs
¼ cup Romano cheese
1 teaspoon Italian seasoning
1 teaspoon garlic powder (or 2–3 cloves garlic, crushed)
1 teaspoon seasoned salt
1 teaspoon black pepper
6 or so leaves of sweet basil, cut in small pieces
1 cup seasoned bread crumbs
6 medium-size green peppers, cleaned and cut in half (or stuff them whole)
Spaghetti sauce

In a medium-size bowl, combine ricotta cheese, eggs, Romano cheese, Italian seasoning, garlic powder (or crushed garlic), seasoned salt, pepper, and basil, and mix well. Add bread crumbs. Preheat oven to 350°. Spray a shallow baking dish with nonstick spray. Stuff each pepper with ricotta mixture and place in baking dish. Bake for about 15 minutes. Remove from oven and cover with spaghetti sauce. Return to oven for an additional 30–40 minutes or until done.

Recipes for You & Your Best Friends

Tomatoes Supreme

6 medium tomatoes, sliced
1 small onion, thinly sliced
1 cup seasoned croutons
½ cup grated Parmesan cheese
1½ teaspoons basil
1 teaspoon salt
1¼ teaspoons pepper
3 tablespoons butter

Layer tomatoes, onion, and croutons in shallow buttered casserole dish. Sprinkle with cheese, basil, and seasonings. Dot with butter. Bake, uncovered, at 350° for 30 minutes.

United Methodist Ministers' Wives Cook Book

Crusty Baked Tomatoes

4 medium tomatoes
Seasoning salt
Dijon-style mustard
6 tablespoons butter, melted
½ cup herb dressing mix
½ cup grated Parmesan cheese
½ cup sliced fresh mushrooms

Preheat oven to 350°. Cut tomatoes in half. Sprinkle cut side with seasoning salt; spread with mustard. Combine butter, dressing mix and cheese. Top tomatoes with mushrooms and crumb mixture. Bake until crumbs are brown and tomatoes are tender, about 30 minutes. Yields 8 servings.

Almost Heaven

Mom-Mom's Fried Green Tomatoes

3–4 large firm green tomatoes
1 egg, beaten
Flour
Salt and pepper to taste
Oil or bacon drippings for frying
Milk

Cut tomatoes to ¼-inch thickness. Dip into egg then into flour, salt and pepper mixture. Place tomato slices in hot oil in skillet. Fry until you get a nice golden brown color on both sides; don't burn. Place a brown paper bag on a platter; drain tomatoes on bag. Meanwhile, add a little milk to skillet. With a wooden spoon, scrape bottom of pan to release browned flavorings. Add some flour to milk mixture. Over low heat, stir until thickened and smooth. Place tomatoes on plate and spoon gravy over top.

Mom-Mom's Cookbook

Tarragon Carrots

Sometimes by March, the first tarragon is up in the garden, and we are anxious to use these new sprigs.

1/4 cup plus 2 tablespoons butter
6 large carrots, shredded
1/2 teaspoon dried tarragon or 1 teaspoon minced fresh tarragon
1/4 teaspoon coarse salt
Freshly ground black pepper

Melt butter in large skillet. Add carrots and cook, stirring constantly, 3–5 minutes until thoroughly heated. Sprinkle with tarragon, salt, and pepper.

A Dooryard Herb Cookbook

Festive Carrot Ring

2 cups mashed carrots
1 cup cracker crumbs
1 cup milk
3/4 cup grated Cheddar cheese
1 cup soft butter
1/4 cup grated onion
1 teaspoon salt
1/2 teaspoon pepper
1/8 teaspoon cayenne pepper
3 eggs

Combine carrots, crumbs, milk, cheese, butter, onion, and seasonings. Beat eggs until fluffy. Fold in carrot mixture. Pour into greased 1 1/2-quart ring mold. Bake at 350° for 40–45 minutes. Serve green peas in the center. Serves many.

Stout Memorial Culinary Treasures

Governor Cecil Underwood holds a unique place in West Virginia history as both the state's youngest and oldest governor to take office. He was elected in 1956 at the age of 34, then re-elected in 1996 at the age of 74.

Glazed Apple Slices and Carrots

1 large onion, sliced
1/4 cup butter or margarine
4 or 5 medium carrots
2 1/2 cups apple slices
1/4 cup sugar
Dash of nutmeg

Sauté onion in butter. Peel carrots (leave whole or halve, length and crosswise, cutting each carrot into 4 pieces). Add carrots, apple slices, sugar, and nutmeg to onion. Cover; cook slowly about 1 hour or until carrots are tender (add a little water, if necessary). Turn several times during cooking. Serve with baked ham or roast pork.

For the Love of Kids

Baked Corn

2 cups corn
3 eggs, well beaten
1/4 teaspoon pepper
1 tablespoon sugar
2 tablespoons melted butter
2 cups light cream
Dash of nutmeg
1/4 cup flour
1 teaspoon salt

Combine corn and eggs. Add remaining ingredients. Place in greased casserole dish. Bake in 350° oven for 1 hour.

Tyrand Cooperative Ministries Cookbook

Corn Pudding

1 (8 1/2-ounce) package corn muffin mix
1 (15-ounce) can cream-style corn
1 (15-ounce) can whole-kernel corn
1 (8-ounce) carton sour cream
1 stick margarine, melted
2 eggs

Stir together all ingredients and pour into a greased baking dish. Bake at 350° for 1 hour or until golden brown.

Heavenly Helpings

Garden Casserole

2 pounds eggplant, peeled
5 teaspoons salt, divided
¼ cup olive oil
2 medium onions, finely chopped
2 cloves garlic (or more as desired)
2 medium zucchini, sliced ½ inch thick
5 medium tomatoes, peeled and chopped
2 celery ribs, sliced
¼ cup fresh minced parsley
¼ cup fresh minced basil (or 1 tablespoon dried basil)
½ teaspoon black pepper
½ cup grated Romano cheese (more, if desired)
1 cup dry Italian bread crumbs
2 tablespoons butter or margarine, melted
1 cup shredded mozzarella cheese (more, if desired)

Cut eggplant into ½-inch slices; sprinkle both sides using 3 teaspoons salt. Place in a deep dish and let stand for 30 minutes. Rinse with cold water, drain and dry on paper towels. Cut into ½-inch cubes and sauté in olive oil until lightly browned (about 5 minutes). Add onions, garlic, and zucchini, and sauté another 3 minutes or so. Add tomatoes, celery, parsley, basil, pepper, and remaining salt, and bring to a boil. Reduce heat and simmer for 10 minutes. Remove from heat and stir in Romano cheese. Pour into a greased 9x13-inch baking dish. Combine bread crumbs and butter and sprinkle over vegetables. Bake uncovered in a 350° oven for 15 minutes. Remove from oven and sprinkle with mozzarella cheese. Return to oven for 5 minutes or until cheese is melted. Makes about 12 servings.

Recipes for You & Your Best Friends

In Mingo County on September 10, 1938, the Mingo Oak, the largest and oldest white oak tree in the United States, was declared dead and felled with ceremony. Its age was estimated at 582 years.

Garden Medley

½ cup cornmeal
½ cup flour
Salt and pepper to taste
1 yellow squash, sliced
1 zucchini, sliced
1 green tomato, sliced
1 cucumber, sliced
1 potato, sliced
1 onion, sliced
1 hot pepper, sliced
Oil

Combine cornmeal, flour, and salt and pepper. Roll or shake vegetable slices in cornmeal/flour mixture. Fry in hot oil until brown. Remove vegetables with slotted spatula; drain.

Home Cookin'

Mexican Beans

8 slices bacon
1 pound pinto beans
Water
1 cup chopped onions
1 cup chopped celery
2 cloves fresh garlic, minced
1 teaspoon salt
½ teaspoon pepper

Fry bacon crisp and drain on paper towels. Wash pinto beans and place in large pot or crockpot. Fill almost to top with water. Crumble bacon and put in with beans, using bacon grease also. Add onion, celery, garlic, salt, and pepper. Cook until beans are done.

Our Daily Bread

The 1888 election for governor between Democrat Aretas Brooks Fleming and Republican Nathan Goff, Jr., was decided by just over 100 votes. Fleming, the losing candidate, disputed the vote counts in several counties and appealed to the legislature to choose him as the rightful winner. The legislature failed to act by the end of Gov. Emanuel Willis Wilson's term on March 4, 1889, and both Goff and Fleming were sworn in as governor. As president of the state senate, Robert S. Carr also claimed the governorship. The state Supreme Court decided Wilson should remain governor until the matter was settled. In January 1890, the legislature chose Fleming.

Baked Beans

6 slices bacon
1 cup chopped onion
2 (31-ounce) cans pork and beans
2 medium Granny Smith or Rome Beauty apples, cut in bite-size pieces
½ cup ketchup
¼ cup packed brown sugar or light molasses
4 teaspoons mustard seed
3½–4 teaspoons curry powder
2 teaspoons Worcestershire sauce

Fry bacon slices and put in refrigerator to cool. Sauté onion in bacon grease. Mix all ingredients, except bacon, together and pour into 9x13-inch baking pan. Bake at 350° until desired consistency. After beans come out of oven, crumble bacon slices on top.

Heavenly Helpings

Baked Bean Casserole

1 can kidney beans, drained
1 can green beans, drained
1 can butter beans, drained
1 can baked beans, undrained
1 cup brown sugar
½ cup chopped onions
3–4 strips fried bacon, crumbled
1 (6-ounce) can tomato paste

Place beans in casserole; add all other ingredients. Mix well. Bake at 350° for 45–55 minutes.

Cookin' with the Colts

Barbecue Butter Beans

3 (15½-ounce) cans butter beans, half the broth drained
1 (28-ounce) can whole tomatoes, drained and chopped
½ cup prepared yellow mustard
1 teaspoon dry mustard
2 cups brown sugar
10 slices bacon
1 green pepper, chopped
1 medium onion, chopped

Combine beans, tomatoes, mustards, and brown sugar in a 3-quart casserole dish or pan. Fry bacon until crisp; crumble and set aside. Sauté pepper and onion in a little bacon drippings. Add sautéed vegetables to bean mixture. Sprinkle crumbled bacon on top. Bake at 350° for 30 minutes. Makes 6–8 servings.

Elkins Manor Cookbook

Savory Beans

1 pound dried beans
1 large onion, chopped
1 green pepper, chopped
2 tablespoons oil
¼ pound bacon, diced, then browned and drained
2 teaspoons salt
2 tablespoons brown sugar
1 tablespoon mustard
1 (16-ounce) can diced tomatoes
½ teaspoon pepper sauce (more, if desired)
2 teaspoons Worcestershire sauce

Place beans in large saucepan and cover with water. Bring to boil on high, then reduce heat and simmer about 1 hour, or until tender. Sauté onion and green pepper in oil for 5 minutes, then add to beans. Add bacon, salt, brown sugar, mustard, tomatoes, pepper sauce, and Worcestershire. Simmer for 1 hour, adding water during cooking, if necessary. Serves 6–8.

West Virginia Country Cooking

West Virginia Reunion Beans

1 pound hot sausage
1 can lima beans, drained
1 can kidney beans, drained
1 can pork and beans, undrained
1 can stewed tomatoes, undrained
1 cup ketchup
⅓ cup brown sugar (more, if desired)
1 red pepper, diced
1 onion, diced

Put sausage in skillet and crumble. Cook until done, then drain. Put cooked sausage along with remaining ingredients in slow cooker (crockpot) and cook for 4–5 hours on LOW.

Cooking for the New Era

Ramp Casserole

An excellent recipe for ramp, a wild leek—an Appalachian spring delicacy—that looks like a scallion but tastes stronger.

4–5 potatoes, diced
8–10 ramps, stems and all
½ pound pork sausage
3 eggs, beaten
1 cup American cheese, diced
1 cup milk

Cook potatoes until barely tender. Chop ramps, stems and all, and steam with potatoes last few minutes of cooking time. Meanwhile, fry and separate pork sausage. Drain sausage; combine with eggs, cheese, and milk. Bake in uncovered casserole for 30 minutes at 350°. Serves 6–8.

Best Taste of Fairmont

West Virginia is well-known for its many festivals and events celebrating the ramp. The ramp, sometimes called wild leek, is a wild onion native to North America. Though the bulb resembles a scallion, the flat, broad leaves of the ramp distinguish them.

Taste Tempting Mushrooms

Who can resist the luscious mixture of melted cheese, butter, and cream over mushrooms?

½ cup butter, divided
3 (8-ounce) packages, sliced, fresh mushrooms
1½ cups herb-seasoned stuffing mix
2 cups shredded Cheddar and mozzarella mixture, divided
½ cup half-and-half

Melt ¼ cup of butter in a large skillet on medium heat; cook mushrooms until tender, stirring occasionally. Stir in stuffing mix. Spoon half of mushroom mixture into greased 8-inch baking dish. Sprinkle with 1 cup cheese. Repeat layers of remaining mushroom mixture, then remaining cheese. Dot top with remaining ¼ cup butter. Pour cream evenly over all.

Bake, uncovered, at 325° for 30 minutes or until hot and bubbly. When done, you will see a thin layer of melted butter over surface; that is how it is supposed to be. The butter will be absorbed as mixture cools. Serve with Marinated Beef Steaks (page 127) for a special treat. Makes 6–8 servings.

Enjoy at Your Own Risk! Cookbook

PASTA, RICE, ETC.

PHOTO © MICHAEL RIBAS PHOTOGRAPHY.

Outdoor advertising has its origin in Wheeling about 1908 when the Block Brothers Tobacco Company painted bridges and barns (like this restored barn) with the wording: "Chew Mail Pouch Tobacco, Treat Yourself to the Best."

Homemade Noodles

4 eggs
2–3 drops of yellow food coloring
1 teaspoon salt
3–4 cups flour
Chicken broth

Beat well eggs, food coloring, and salt. Add flour to make dough, about like biscuits. Roll out on floured board; cut into narrow strips and drop into boiling chicken broth. Cook about 25–30 minutes or until done.

Gypsy, West Virginia 100th Anniversary Cookbook

Chicken Noodles

2 eggs
7 tablespoons milk
1 teaspoon baking powder
½ teaspoon salt
Flour (enough to make stiff dough)
2–3 quarts chicken broth

In mixing bowl, combine eggs, milk, baking powder, and salt. Add flour, a cupful at a time, until dough is like pie dough. Cut dough into 2 pieces and roll thin as pie crust. Roll up like jellyroll and cut in thin slices (strips). Unroll; sprinkle with extra flour and let set for at least 3 hours. In Dutch oven, boil 2–3 quarts chicken broth; add noodles slowly, stirring constantly. When all noodles have been added to broth, cook on low heat until done, about 15 minutes. Stir occasionally so noodles don't stick.

Treasured Recipes

West Virginia has a mean altitude of 1,500 feet, giving it the highest average altitude east of the Mississippi.

Fresh Vegetable Lasagna

2 tablespoons oil
3 small zucchini, sliced and quartered
3 large carrots, sliced in rounds
2 medium red peppers, sliced
4 green onions, sliced
1 (28-ounce) can Italian tomatoes, quartered
1 (28-ounce) can tomato purée
Salt and pepper to taste
15 uncooked lasagna noodles
1 (16-ounce) carton skimmed ricotta cheese
1 cup grated Parmesan cheese
1 pound grated mozzarella cheese
2 cups water

Place oil in large frying pan; when hot, add zucchini, carrots, peppers, onions, and tomatoes and stir-fry for 5 minutes. Stir in tomato purée and salt and pepper. Remove from heat. Spray 10½ x 15-inch baking dish with nonstick spray. Place 1 layer of uncooked noodles in pan; add layers of vegetables and remaining ingredients, except water, alternating with noodles. After assembly is complete, add water. Cover with foil sprayed with non-stick spray. Bake at 350° for 1½ hours. Allow to set for ½ hour before cutting.

Treasures from Heaven

Lasagna

1 pound ground meat
2–3 (8-ounce) cans tomato sauce
2 (6-ounce) cans tomato paste
2 teaspoons Italian seasoning
1 teaspoon oregano
½ teaspoon garlic salt
9 lasagna noodles
3 cups cottage cheese
2 eggs
1 teaspoon salt
¼ teaspoon pepper
2 tablespoons parsley flakes
1 pound mozzarella cheese

Brown meat and drain. Add tomato sauce and paste, Italian seasoning, oregano, and garlic salt, and simmer for 30 minutes. Cook noodles in large pan until tender; drain. In separate bowl, mix remaining ingredients except mozzarella cheese.

In a 9x13-inch baking pan, make layers (2 or 3) of noodles, cottage cheese sauce, mozzarella cheese, and meat sauce. Repeat until all ingredients are used. Bake at 375° for 35 minutes.

Cookin' with the Colts

Meaty Manicotti

½ pound ground chuck
½ cup chopped onion
1 clove garlic, minced
½ teaspoon salt
¼ teaspoon oregano
1 slice bread, diced
1 tablespoon parsley flakes
1 (15½-ounce) jar spaghetti sauce, divided
½ cup grated Romano cheese
½ pound grated mozzarella cheese
1 egg, slightly beaten
8 manicotti shells, parboiled

Brown meat, onion, and garlic in skillet. Spoon off excess fat. Stir in salt, oregano, bread, parsley, ¼ cup spaghetti sauce, and Romano cheese. Cool slightly. Mix in mozzarella cheese and egg. Fill manicotti shells with meat mixture. Spread 1 cup spaghetti sauce in bottom of 12x7-inch baking dish. Arrange shells and cover with remaining sauce. Cover with foil. Bake at 350° for 30 minutes. Remove foil. Sprinkle with additional grated cheese. Bake, uncovered, 10 minutes. Serves 4.

Cookin' with the Stars

Pasta with Artichoke Sauce

1 (6-ounce) jar marinated artichoke hearts
8 ounces fresh mushrooms, sliced
1 small onion, chopped
1 clove garlic, minced
1½ cups chopped, fresh tomatoes
2 tablespoons chopped, fresh parsley
Salt and pepper to taste
4 ounces thin spaghetti, cooked and drained
Parmesan cheese

Drain artichoke hearts and reserve juice; coarsely chop artichokes and set aside. Heat reserved marinade in skillet and sauté mushrooms, onion, and garlic until tender. Stir in chopped artichokes, tomatoes, and parsley. Cook on low heat about 15 minutes, stirring occasionally. Season to taste. Spoon over warm cooked spaghetti. Sprinkle with Parmesan and serve. Makes 6 servings.

Enjoy at Your Own Risk! Cookbook

Pasta with Artichoke Hearts

Olive oil
1 small onion, chopped
3 cloves garlic, minced
Basil, divided
Oregano, divided
8 ounces mushrooms, quartered
1 can artichoke hearts (in water), chopped into bite-size pieces
1 can whole, pitted black olives, halved
3 sun-dried tomatoes, chopped
1 pound ziti (small tube shaped pasta)
Parmesan or Romano cheese, grated

Pour olive oil in frying pan, using enough to coat bottom. Add onion and garlic. Sauté over medium heat, about 5 minutes, until onion starts to become clear. Sprinkle with basil and oregano. Add a little more olive oil. Add mushrooms, artichoke hearts, olives, and sun-dried tomatoes. Stir to coat and continue to cook over medium heat until lightly sautéed, about 5–10 minutes. Sprinkle again with basil and oregano.

Meanwhile, cook pasta according to package directions. Drain. Pour pasta into a large bowl. Pour artichoke mixture over pasta and toss. Sprinkle with Parmesan or Romano cheese and serve.

Recipes for You & Your Best Friends

Broccoli, Tomato, Pasta Bake

8 ounces pasta (shells, rigatoni or macaroni)
1 onion, chopped
1 small red pepper, chopped
1 clove garlic
1 tablespoon oil
1 (14-ounce) can tomatoes
1 teaspoon dried basil
Salt and pepper to taste
1 pound broccoli with stalks trimmed off
8 ounces natural yogurt
4 ounces cream cheese
2 eggs, beaten
2 ounces grated Cheddar cheese

Cook the pasta in plenty of boiling water until tender. Sauté onion, pepper, and garlic in oil until softened, but not brown. Add tomatoes and basil and simmer until the sauce thickens. Season to taste. Steam broccoli just until tender. Place a layer of tomato sauce on bottom of a large, well-greased, oven-proof dish. Cover with a layer of pasta, then broccoli and a final layer of pasta.

For the topping, beat together yogurt, cream cheese, eggs, and salt and pepper to taste until smooth. Pour mixture over pasta and sprinkle with grated cheese. Bake for 25–30 minutes at 400° until golden brown. Serves 4.

Carnegie Hall Cookbook

Summer Linguine

This is a crowd pleaser. The fresh basil makes all the difference.

4 large tomatoes, chopped
1 pound Brie cheese, coarsely chopped
5 cloves garlic, peeled, minced
1 cup chopped fresh basil
1 cup olive oil
½ teaspoon salt
½ teaspoon pepper
6 quarts water
⅛ teaspoon olive oil
1 tablespoon salt
1½ pounds uncooked linguine
¼ cup freshly grated Parmesan cheese
Freshly ground pepper to taste

Combine tomatoes, Brie cheese, garlic, basil, 1 cup olive oil, ½ teaspoon salt, and ½ teaspoon pepper in bowl; mix well. Let stand, covered, for 1 hour or longer.

Bring water to a boil in large saucepan. Stir in ⅛ teaspoon olive oil and 1 tablespoon salt. Add linguine. Cook for 8–10 minutes or until firm; drain. Toss hot linguine with tomato mixture in bowl. Brie will melt into pasta. Sprinkle with Parmesan cheese and fresh pepper. Yields 6 servings.

The Best of Wheeling

Macaroni Cheese Deluxe

1 (7-ounce) package elbow macaroni
2 cups small curd cream-style cottage cheese
1 cup dairy sour cream
1 slightly beaten egg
¾ teaspoon salt
Dash pepper
8 ounces sharp American cheese

Cook macaroni and drain well. Mix with remaining ingredients. Bake in greased casserole at 350° for 45 minutes.

The Way Pocahontas County Cooks

Stuffed Spaghetti Chicken Parmesan

9 ounces uncooked spaghetti
1 cup ricotta cheese
1 cup shredded mozzarella cheese, divided
2 tablespoons grated Parmesan cheese
1/2 teaspoon dried Italian seasoning
1/2 teaspoon garlic powder
1 (28-ounce) jar spaghetti sauce, divided
4 frozen, breaded chicken cutlets
1 (14.5-ounce) can Italian seasoned, diced tomatoes
1 (4.5-ounce) jar sliced mushrooms, drained
1 tablespoon chopped parsley

Preheat oven to 375°. Cook spaghetti according to package directions; drain and set aside. Coat 9-inch baking dish with cooking spray. Combine ricotta cheese, 1/2 cup mozzarella cheese, Parmesan cheese, Italian seasoning, and garlic powder. Set aside. Toss spaghetti with 2 cups spaghetti sauce. Use 1/2 the remaining sauce to coat bottom of dish. Place 1/2 the spaghetti in the baking dish. Spread with cheese mixture. Top with remaining spaghetti. Arrange chicken cutlets on top of spaghetti and pour remaining spaghetti sauce, diced tomatoes, and sliced mushrooms over chicken. Sprinkle remaining 1/2 cup mozzarella cheese over top. Bake uncovered until cheese melts and spaghetti is heated through, about 25 minutes.

Our Favorite Recipes

On June 20, 1863, West Virginia became the 35th State in the Union. The area was part of Virginia until the Civil War. However, the inhabitants were loyal to the Union and formed a separate state after Virginia became part of the Confederacy. Kanawha was the originally suggested name but at the new state's Constitutional Convention meeting, the name was changed to West Virginia. June 20 is now annually observed as West Virginia Day, a legal holiday in the State.

Pizza Casserole

1 pound ground beef
1 (16-ounce) can pizza sauce
1 (4-ounce) can sliced mushrooms, undrained
1 tablespoon oregano
1 tablespoon garlic salt
1 small onion, chopped
1 package sliced pepperoni
2 cups rotini, cooked and drained, or 2 cups twisted macaroni
2/3 cup milk
8 ounces shredded mozzarella cheese

Brown ground beef and drain. Stir in pizza sauce, undrained mushrooms, oregano, garlic salt, onion, and pepperoni. Bring to boil and remove from heat. Combine rotini with milk. In a greased 2-quart casserole, layer 1/2 of the rotini mixture, 1/2 meat mixture, and 1/2 cheese; repeat layers and cover. Bake at 350° for 25–30 minutes.

United Methodist Ministers' Wives Cook Book

Pizza Rice Casserole

3 cups cooked rice
2 cups spaghetti or pizza sauce
1 pound ground beef, browned
1 cup sliced mushrooms
12–15 slices pepperoni
1/2 cup diced green onions
1/4 cup diced green pepper
Other pizza toppings, if desired
1 teaspoon dried basil
2 cups mozzarella cheese

In a 9x13-inch baking dish which has been sprayed with cooking spray, press the cooked rice. Pour sauce over rice. Layer ground beef, mushrooms, pepperoni, onions, and pepper as well as any additional toppings. Sprinkle with basil. Cover with cheese. Bake at 350° for 25–30 minutes.

Our Favorite Recipes

Reuben Casserole

½ cup chopped onion
2 tablespoons butter
2 cans cream of mushroom soup
½ cup mayonnaise
2 teaspoons mustard
1 pint sauerkraut, drained
8 ounces noodles, cooked and drained
1 (12-ounce) can corned beef, shredded
1 cup Swiss cheese, shredded
1 cup bread crumbs, buttered

Sauté onions in butter until tender. Mix soup, mayonnaise, mustard, and onions. Layer sauerkraut, noodles, and corned beef in oblong baking pan. Pour soup mixture over top. Sprinkle cheese on top and cover with bread crumbs. Bake at 350° for 45 minutes.

For the Love of Kids

Hominy Chili Casserole

1 (15-ounce) can chili with beans
1 (15½-ounce) can golden hominy, drained
1 small onion, finely chopped
1 (2.2-ounce) can sliced ripe olives, drained, divided
1 cup shredded sharp Cheddar cheese

Combine chili, hominy, onions, and half of olives. Spoon into a lightly greased 1½-quart casserole. Bake at 350° for 25 minutes. Sprinkle cheese and remaining olives over top. Bake 5 more minutes. Serves 4.

Cookin' with the Stars

On Oct. 23, 1998, J. R. House, quarterback for Nitro High School, broke the national high school career passing record with 14,457 yards passing, breaking the old record of 12,104 yards. The previous record was set by Tim Couch, who played high school football in eastern Kentucky from 1992-95.

Chinese Egg Rolls

½ head cabbage, shredded
½ head lettuce, shredded
1 small onion, chopped
½ cup chopped celery
½ cup chopped green pepper
¼ cup oil
½ pound shrimp, cooked
½ pound pork, cubed and cooked
1 can sliced water chestnuts
½ pound bean sprouts
1 package egg roll skins
1 egg yolk, beaten

Steam cabbage, lettuce, onion, celery, and green pepper until soft but not mushy; set aside. In deep skillet, add oil to stir-fry shrimp and pork for 3 minutes. Add water chestnuts and cook 5 minutes. Add cabbage mixture and stir, then add bean sprouts and cook until soft. Place small amount of mixture onto center of egg roll skin. Fold envelope-style (corners together) and seal with a slight amount of egg yolk. Deep fry until brown, or fry in ½ inch of oil until brown on each side.

Third Wednesday Homemakers

Cheesy Pineapple Bake

2 cups sugar
1 cup flour
1 teaspoon cinnamon
4 (15-ounce) cans pineapple chunks, drained
1½ cups grated Cheddar cheese, divided
½ cup butter, melted
3 dozen butter-flavored crackers, crushed

Preheat oven to 375°. Mix sugar, flour, and cinnamon. Add pineapple and ¾ cup of cheese, mixing well until coated. Pour into a buttered 9x13-inch pan. Pour remaining cheese on top of casserole. Melt butter slowly and add crackers. Cover top of casserole with cracker crumbs. Bake 45 minutes. Yields 10–12 servings.

Almost Heaven

Sauerkraut Relish

1/2 cup chopped celery
1/2 cup chopped carrots
1/4 cup chopped onion
1/2 cup chopped green pepper
1 (16-ounce) can sauerkraut
1/2 cup sugar

Finely chop all vegetables. Mix with remaining ingredients. Put in jars or bowl and refrigerate 12 hours. Serve with...anything.

Home Cookin'

Tomato Chutney

2 pounds tomatoes, peeled, coarsely chopped
1 pound tart apples, peeled, cored, chopped
2 medium onions, chopped
1 cup cider vinegar
1 tablespoon salt
1 cup packed brown sugar
1 cup golden raisins
1 clove garlic, minced
1/2 teaspoon ground cinnamon
1/2 teaspoon dry mustard
1/4 teaspoon cayenne pepper
1/8 teaspoon ground allspice
1/8 teaspoon ground ginger
1/8 teaspoon ground cloves

Combine all the ingredients in a large saucepan or Dutch oven; bring to a boil. Reduce heat and simmer, uncovered, for about 1 1/2–2 hours or until mixture thickens, stirring frequently. Pack hot chutney into hot sterilized jars, leaving 1/4-inch head space. Adjust caps. Process for 10 minutes in a boiling water bath. Yields 3 pints.

Dutch Pantry Cookin' Volume II

MEATS

PHOTO © ROGER SPENCER PHOTOGRAPHY.

The restored Pioneer Farm on Bowers Ridge at Twin Falls Resort State Park in Wyoming County appears much like the farms of the 1830s, providing a glimpse into the lives and times of the people who settled the Twin Falls area.

Delicious Beef Roast

1 (1 3/8-ounce) package dry onion soup mix
1 (5- to 6-pound) chuck, sirloin or shoulder roast
1 can cream of mushroom soup
1 1/3 cups water
1/2 teaspoon pepper
5 medium potatoes, cut in chunks
5 carrots, cut in 2-inch pieces

Sprinkle dry soup mix in bottom of Dutch oven. Add roast, cream of mushroom soup, water, and pepper. Bring to boil; cover and simmer 2 hours. Add vegetables and cook 45 minutes or until tender. Serves 10–12.

Third Wednesday Homemakers

Holiday Beef Rib Roast with Currant Sauce

2 garlic cloves, crushed
1 teaspoon salt
1 teaspoon cracked black pepper
1 teaspoon dried thyme leaves
1 (4-pound) rib roast
1 1/2 teaspoons dry mustard dissolved in 1 teaspoon water
1 (12-ounce) jar brown beef gravy
1/4 cup currant or grape jelly

Heat oven to 350°. Combine garlic, salt, pepper, and thyme. Press evenly into surface of roast. Place roast on rack in shallow roasting pan. Do not add water or cover. Roast for 18–22 minutes per pound for rare to medium. If using a meat thermometer, remove roast at 135° internal temperature for rare and 155° for medium. Let stand 15 minutes before carving. (As roast stands, the internal temperature should continue to rise to 140° for rare and 160° for medium.)

While the roast stands, in a small saucepan, combine dry mustard and water, brown beef gravy, and jelly. Cook over medium heat for 5 minutes or until bubbly, stirring occasionally. Carve roast into slices and serve with sauce. Makes 8–10 servings.

A Gracious Plenty

Prime Rib of Beef Au Jus

1 whole rib eye (14 ounces to 1 pound per person)
1 small bottle Kitchen Bouquet or Gravy Master
Salt to taste
Pepper to taste
2 cans beef consommé
Dash of Worcestershire sauce
½ cup dry red wine
Small amount of water
Mushrooms, sliced
Shallots, sliced

Place rib eye in a large roasting pan and rub with Kitchen Bouquet, salt, and pepper. Pour beef consommé, Worcestershire sauce, red wine, and a small amount of water over beef. Cover with mushrooms and shallots. Place in preheated oven at 500° for ½ hour. Reduce heat to 375° for approximately 2 more hours. Use roasting meat charts for weight and time. Baste every 15 minutes.

Serving Our Best

London Broil Marinade

2–3 pounds London Broil or other steak
¼ cup soy sauce
1 tablespoon Worcestershire sauce
¾ teaspoon salt
1 clove garlic, crushed, or garlic powder
1 tablespoon lemon juice
¼ teaspoon ground pepper
1 teaspoon dry mustard
3 tablespoons wine vinegar

Score steak lightly. Combine remaining ingredients and marinate steak in mixture for at least 24 hours (can freeze meat in marinade). Broil until the desired doneness. Serve immediately.

United Methodist Ministers' Wives Cook Book

Towns in West Virginia named after cities in other countries include Athens, Berlin, Cairo, Calcutta, Geneva, Ghent, Glasgow, Killarney, Lima, London, Moscow, Odessa, Ottawa, Palermo, Rangoon, Santiago, Shanghai, Vienna and Wellington.

Steak and Peppers Italian

1½ pounds beef tenderloin or strip steaks
1 medium onion, quartered, thinly sliced
1 medium red bell pepper, cut into strips
1 medium yellow pepper, cut into strips
1 (14-ounce) can Italian-style stewed tomatoes
1 (8-ounce) can tomato sauce with garlic
Black pepper to taste

Cut beef into strips as for stir-fry. Heat nonstick skillet or wok; cook onion and peppers 5 minutes, using some of tomato liquid, if needed to keep vegetables from sticking. Add beef; cook and stir until meat is no longer pink in center; stir in remaining ingredients. Cover and simmer on low 20 minutes. Good served over cooked pasta or with Pasta Alfredo as a side dish. Makes 6 servings.

Note: May change beef to chicken or pork tenderloin.

Nutrition Information: (1/6 of recipe) 370 cal; 240 cal from fat; 26g fat; 12g sat fat; 80mg chol; 430mg sod; 11g carbo; 2g fiber.

The All or Nothing Cookbook

Deviled Swiss Steak

1 tablespoon dry mustard
½ cup flour
1½ pounds top round steak
Salt and pepper to taste
1 cup sliced onion
1 carrot, diced
1½ cups diced tomatoes
2 tablespoons Worcestershire sauce
1 tablespoon brown sugar

Mix dry mustard with flour; pound into 1-inch thick pieces of steak. Season with salt and pepper. Brown on both sides in a little fat. Place in small roaster. Add sliced onion, carrot, tomatoes, Worcestershire sauce, and brown sugar. Cover and bake at 325° for 1–1½ hours. Serves 6.

Dutch Pantry Cookin'

Marinated Beef Steaks

1/2 cup olive oil
3/4 teaspoon seasoned salt
3/4 teaspoon lemon pepper seasoning
3/4 teaspoon dried oregano
1/4 teaspoon garlic powder
4–6 beef tenderloin steaks (about 3/4 inch thick)

Combine oil, salt, lemon pepper, oregano, and garlic powder in shallow glass dish large enough to hold steaks in single layer. Stir oil mixture well and add steaks. Cover and marinate at least 4 hours, up to overnight in refrigerator, turning steaks occasionally. Remove steaks from marinade. Discard marinade. Grill or broil steaks until done. Serve hot. Makes 4–6 servings.

Enjoy at Your Own Risk! Cookbook

Chicken-Fried Steak

1 cup dry bread crumbs
1/2 teaspoon salt
1/4 teaspoon freshly ground black pepper
8 thin slices round steak or minute steak (approximately 1 pound)
1 large egg, beaten
1/4 cup vegetable oil
2 tablespoons flour
1 cup water or milk
Additional salt and pepper to taste

On a plate, mix bread crumbs with salt and pepper. Dip steak into beaten egg, then bread crumbs. Heat oil in heavy skillet and add meat. Brown over low heat 10–15 minutes on each side. Place on a warm platter and keep hot. Make a gravy by adding flour to pan drippings. Stir over medium heat until light brown. With a whisk, stir in water or milk until thickened. Add more liquid, if too thick. Add salt and pepper to taste. Return steaks to pan. Simmer until ready to serve. Makes 4 servings.

More than Beans and Cornbread

Hamburger Stroganoff

1 pound ground beef
½ cup chopped onion
¼ cup butter or margarine
2 tablespoons flour
1 teaspoon salt
1 clove garlic, minced
¼ teaspoon pepper
1 (4-ounce) can mushroom pieces, drained
1 (10½-ounce) can cream of chicken soup
1 cup dairy sour cream

In large skillet, cook and stir meat and onion in butter until meat is brown and onion is tender. Stir in flour, salt, garlic, pepper, and mushrooms; cook 5 minutes, stirring constantly. Stir in soup; heat to boiling, stirring constantly. Reduce heat; simmer uncovered 10 minutes. Stir in sour cream; heat thoroughly. Serve over hot buttered noodles. Yields 4 servings.

Casseroles, Meats and Fish...Cookies

The Greenbrier's Beef Stroganoff

2 pounds beef tenderloin, cut in thin strips
1 teaspoon paprika
1 teaspoon salt
1 teaspoon pepper
½ cup butter, divided
⅓ cup peeled, chopped shallots
1 cup sliced mushrooms
2 tablespoons flour
½ cup dry white wine
½ cup beef stock
½ cup sour cream

Sprinkle meat with paprika, salt, and pepper. Melt ¼ cup butter in a 9-inch skillet and brown meat quickly over high heat. Remove meat and set aside in a warm place. Melt the remaining ¼ cup butter in the skillet; add shallots and cook until brown. Add mushrooms and sauté until all liquid has evaporated. Add flour and mix well. Gradually add wine and beef stock. Bring mixture to a boil, stirring constantly, then simmer for 30 minutes. Remove sauce from heat and fold in sour cream. Add the meat to the sauce. Heat to just below boiling and serve immediately. Serves 6.

Christ Reformed Church Historical Cookbook

Sweet and Sour Meatballs

This is a very versatile dish. It's very good for covered-dish dinners. Finger-size strips of chicken or shrimp can be substituted for the meatballs.

MEATBALLS:
5 thin bread slices, cubed
½ cup milk
1 egg
2 pounds ground beef
⅛ teaspoon pepper
⅛ teaspoon garlic salt
2 tablespoons oil

Combine and form into meatballs. Fry lightly in oil and remove from skillet. Remove any excess oil and make Sauce.

SAUCE:
1½ cups water (or juice from pineapple)
1 tablespoon cornstarch
½ cup sweet gherkin chunks
2 (8-ounce) cans tomato sauce
½ cup white vinegar
½ cup sugar (may be eliminated if you use pineapple juice)
1 (13½-ounce) can pineapple chunks, drained

Combine water (or juice) and cornstarch until smooth, add remaining ingredients, bring to a boil, and add meatballs (or chicken or shrimp), carefully, so they don't break apart.

2 small green peppers, sliced
Large carrot, sliced diagonally
1–2 ribs celery, sliced diagonally
1 tablespoon oil

Sauté peppers, carrot, and celery in oil. Add to above mixture. Serve over rice.

Casseroles, Meats and Fish...Cookies

Meat Balls

3 pounds hamburger
1 onion, diced
½ cup canned milk
4 hamburger buns, crumbled fine
½ cup sugar
2 eggs
Salt
Pepper

Combine all ingredients; mix well. Make meat mixture into small balls. Put meat balls in skillet and cook until brown and done.

TOMATO SAUCE:
2 (6-ounce) cans tomato paste
5 (6-ounce) cans water
Sugar, salt, and pepper to taste

Combine tomato paste and water. Stir until blended. Add sugar, salt, and pepper to taste. Pour Tomato Sauce over meat balls and simmer for 30 minutes to 1 hour.

Treasured Recipes

Eula's Meatballs

MEATBALLS:
2 pounds ground chuck
1 cup cornflake crumbs
⅓ cup dry parsley
2 eggs, beaten
2 tablespoons soy sauce
¼ teaspoon pepper
½ teaspoon garlic salt
½ cup ketchup
2 tablespoons instant onion flakes

In large bowl mix all ingredients; make into balls and brown in large skillet.

SAUCE:
2 tablespoons brown sugar
1 (12-ounce) bottle Heinz® Chili Sauce
1 (16-ounce) can jellied cranberry sauce
1 tablespoon lemon juice

In medium-size bowl combine brown sugar, chili sauce, cranberry sauce and lemon juice. Pour sauce over meatballs in ovenproof casserole dish. Bake for 50 minutes at 300°.

Cookin' with the Colts

Porcupine Beef

1 pound ground beef
½ cup uncooked instant rice
2 eggs, beaten
1 (1½-ounce) envelope dry onion soup
¼ cup chopped green pepper
1 (14½-ounce) can stewed tomatoes
1 (12-ounce) can beer
2 teaspoons chili powder
3 tablespoons flour

Mix together ground beef, rice, eggs, dry soup mix, and pepper. Shape into 6 large balls. Combine tomatoes, beer, and chili powder in a large skillet or 3-quart baking dish. Heat to a boil over medium heat or in a 350° oven. Carefully drop meatballs into hot tomato mixture. Cover and simmer or bake for 45–55 minutes. Lift out meatballs and thicken sauce with 3 tablespoons flour mixed with water; cook another 5 minutes. Replace meatballs and serve. Makes 6 servings.

Generations

Hawaiian Burgers

2 pounds ground beef
3 tablespoons dry Italian dressing
⅛ teaspoon pepper
1 can pineapple rings, drained, reserve juice
¾ cup barbecue sauce
¼ cup brown sugar
¼ cup honey
1 teaspoon lemon juice
8 slices bacon

Mix ground beef, Italian dressing, and pepper. Blend well. Make into 8 patties. Mix pineapple juice, BBQ sauce, brown sugar, honey, and lemon juice. Set aside for awhile. On each patty, first place a slice of bacon, then a slice of pineapple. Secure with toothpicks. Place burgers into a dish that has a lid. Pour BBQ mixture over patties. Marinate for 24 hours in refrigerator. Flip container at least once or whenever you are near the refrigerator. Grill or broil patties and discard the marinade sauce.

Homemade with Love

Barbecued Meat Loaf

1½ pounds ground chuck
1 cup bread crumbs
1 small onion, finely chopped
1 egg, beaten
1 teaspoon salt
¼ teaspoon pepper
2 (8-ounce) cans tomato sauce
½ cup water
3 tablespoons vinegar
3 tablespoons brown sugar
3 tablespoons Worcestershire sauce

Combine first 6 ingredients. Combine remaining ingredients for sauce. Add ½ cup tomato sauce mixture to meat mixture, mixing well. Place in baking pan and shape into loaf. Pour remaining tomato sauce mixture over loaf. Bake at 350° for 1 hour and 15 minutes, basting often with the sauce. Serves 6–8.

Stout Memorial Culinary Treasures

Italian Meat Loaf and Noodles

SAUCE:
2 tablespoons vegetable oil
½ cup chopped onions
2 (6-ounce) cans tomato paste
2 (6-ounce) cans water

Combine Sauce ingredients and simmer for 20 minutes.

MEAT LOAF:
1½ pounds ground beef
1 egg
1 cup soft bread crumbs
2 teaspoons salt
¼ teaspoon pepper
1 teaspoon oregano
¼ teaspoon basil
1 pound noodles, cooked and drained

Mix beef, egg, bread crumbs, salt, pepper, oregano, and basil in large bowl. Add 1 cup prepared Sauce and blend well. Form into loaf shape and place in 6x10-inch or larger baking dish. Bake in moderate oven (375°) for 50 minutes. Serve Meat Loaf on platter lined with cooked noodles and top with Sauce from baking pan. Serves 6.

Just Plain Country

Aunt Florence's Stuffed Peppers

1 small box instant rice
3 pounds ground chuck
2 (14-ounce) bottles ketchup, divided
12–14 green peppers

Prepare rice as directed on package. Mix with ground chuck. Add about 1½ bottles ketchup. Mix well. Cut tops off peppers and clean out insides. Rinse and drain well. Stuff peppers with meat mixture. Place in roaster and top with remaining ketchup. Bake at 350° for 2 hours.

Our Daily Bread

Shepherd's Pie

2½ pounds potatoes, peeled and cooked
1–1½ cups sour cream
1 teaspoon salt
¼ teaspoon pepper
1 package frozen mixed vegetables (may use frozen vegetable of your choice)
2 pounds ground beef (chuck)
½ cup chopped onion
1 medium green pepper (or red pepper), chopped
1 teaspoon garlic powder
1 (10¾-ounce) can cream of mushroom soup, undiluted
½ cup milk
½ cup shredded Cheddar cheese

Mash potatoes, adding sour cream, salt, and pepper. Set aside. Cook frozen vegetables according to directions on package. In a large skillet cook beef, onions, and pepper until meat is brown and onions and pepper are tender. Drain mixture. Stir garlic powder into meat mixture. Add cream of mushroom soup, milk, and vegetables to meat. Mix well. Spread meat mixture into a 9x13x2-inch baking dish. Spread mashed potatoes over mixture. Bake for 30–35 minutes or until heated through. In the last 5 minutes of baking, sprinkle shredded cheese over potatoes and return to oven until cheese is melted. Serves 8–10.

Just Plain Country

Potato Patch Casserole

CHEESE SAUCE:

3 tablespoons butter
3 tablespoons flour
1/3 teaspoon salt
1/4 teaspoon pepper
1 1/2 cups milk
1/2 pound processed cheese, cubed

Melt butter over low heat; blend in flour, salt, and pepper. Cook over low heat; stir until smooth and bubbly. Remove from heat. Stir in milk. Return to heat and bring to a boil, stirring constantly; cook until thick. Stir in cheese and heat until melted.

MEATBALLS:

1 pound ground beef
1/2 cup chopped onion
1 egg, beaten
1/4 cup bread crumbs
1 teaspoon salt
1/4 teaspoon pepper
1/4 teaspoon celery salt
1/4 teaspoon garlic

Combine beef, onion, egg, bread crumbs, and seasonings; mix well, shape into meatballs, and brown in large saucepan.

POTATO MIXTURE:

5 cups sliced potatoes
1 (10-ounce) package peas and carrots, partially thawed
1 teaspoon salt
Pepper

Combine potatoes, peas and carrots, salt, and pepper. Arrange Meatballs in large greased casserole. Add Potato Mixture; cover with Cheese Sauce. Bake at 375° for 45 minutes or until potatoes are tender.

Cooking for the New Era

West Virginia was the first state to have a sales tax. It became effective July 1, 1921.

Fiesta Casserole

1 pound ground beef
2 tablespoons cooking oil
1 large onion, chopped
1 clove garlic, minced
1 (1-pound, 12-ounce) can tomatoes
1 (16-ounce) can mild enchilada sauce
1 (15½-ounce) can kidney beans, undrained
2 teaspoons salt
¼ teaspoon pepper
Chili powder to taste
1 (11-ounce) package corn tortillas
Cheddar cheese, at least 1 cup

In large skillet, brown ground beef, leaving in chunks, with oil, onion, and garlic. Add tomatoes, enchilada sauce, kidney beans, salt, pepper, and chili powder to meat mixture. Heat to boiling. Place corn tortillas, overlapping, in a long baking dish. Add layer of meat sauce. Continue these layers until you have used most of sauce. Have meat sauce on top layer and sprinkle with Cheddar cheese. I think the more cheese, the better. Bake for 30 minutes in a 400° oven. Cool before serving. Yields 8 servings.

Note: May be made ahead of time and heated when ready.

Treat Yourself to the Best Cookbook

Dad's Company Casserole

1 (8-ounce) package medium noodles
2 tablespoons butter
1½ pounds ground meat
1 teaspoon salt
Pepper to taste
¼ teaspoon garlic powder
1 (8-ounce) can tomato sauce
1 cup cottage cheese
1 cup sour cream
6 green onions, chopped
¾ cup grated sharp cheese

Cook noodles in boiling water until tender. Drain and rinse with cold water. Melt butter in skillet; add meat and cook. Add salt, pepper, garlic powder, and tomato sauce; simmer gently for 5 minutes. Remove from heat. Combine cottage cheese, sour cream, onions, and noodles. Layer noodles and meat in casserole dish. Top with cheese. Bake at 350° for 30 minutes.

Homemade with Love

Railroad Special

(Corn Bread Pie)

1 pound ground beef
1 large onion, chopped
1 can tomato soup
2 cups water
1 teaspoon salt
¾ teaspoon pepper
1 tablespoon chili powder
1 cup whole-kernel corn, drained
½ cup chopped green pepper

Brown beef and onion in skillet; add soup, water, seasonings, corn, and green pepper. Mix well. Let simmer 15 minutes. Fill casserole or 12x6x2-inch pan, leaving room for Topping.

TOPPING:

¾ cup cornmeal
1 tablespoon sugar
1 tablespoon flour
½ teaspoon salt
1½ teaspoons baking powder
1 egg
½ cup milk

Sift together cornmeal, sugar, flour, salt, and baking powder. Stir together with egg and milk. Top meat mixture; bake at 350° for 45 minutes or until done.

The Way Pocahontas County Cooks

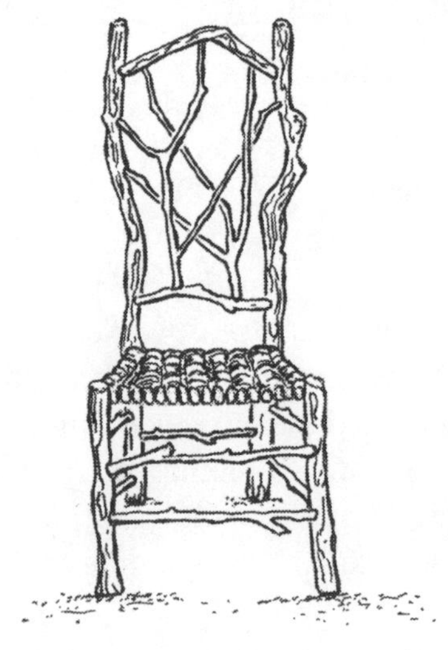

Taco Skillet Dinner

1 pound ground beef
1 (15-ounce) can black or kidney beans, drained
1 packet taco seasoning
¾ cup water
1 cup shredded Cheddar cheese
2 small tomatoes, diced
1 snack-size bag tortilla chips, coarsely crushed (1 cup)

In 10-inch skillet, brown beef; drain. Stir in beans, taco seasoning, and water; bring to boiling on high. Immediately reduce heat to low and simmer, stirring occasionally, for 10 minutes. Turn off heat; sprinkle evenly with cheese, then tomatoes and chips. Serve immediately. Makes 6 servings.

Note: May add 8-ounce can of whole corn or 11-ounce can of Mexicorn with beans. May sauté zucchini or yellow squash with beef.

Nutrition Information: (1/6 of recipe) 350 cal; 190 cal from fat; 21g fat; 10g sat fat; 70mg chol; 570mg sod; 17g carbo; 6g fiber.

The All or Nothing Cookbook

Veal Parmesan

8 breaded veal steaks
2 quarts tomato juice
2 tablespoons chopped onion
1 teaspoon salt
¼ teaspoon pepper
½ teaspoon garlic powder
½ cup sugar
2 teaspoons Worcestershire sauce
½ teaspoon oregano
1 teaspoon Italian seasoning
Pinch of baking soda
8 ounces mozzarella cheese
¼ cup Parmesan cheese

Brown veal steaks in skillet. Mix remaining ingredients, except cheeses, in saucepan; simmer 30 minutes. Lay steaks in a shallow baking dish; cover steaks with sauce. Top with mozzarella and Parmesan cheeses. Bake at 350° for 30 minutes. Good served with noodles.

Down Memory Lane

BBQ Beef Ribs

3 tablespoons oil
2 tablespoons lemon juice
Dash dry mustard
3 tablespoons chili sauce
Dash pepper
1½–2 pounds baby beef ribs

Combine oil, lemon juice, mustard, chili sauce, and pepper; set aside. Place ribs in a single layer in a shallow roasting pan. Roast ribs at 450° for 20 minutes, turning once. Remove ribs and brush with basting sauce on both sides. Return to oven. Continue baking about 20 minutes longer or until ribs are tender. Baste with remaining sauce while baking. If ribs start getting too dark, cover with aluminum foil and reduce heat to 400° for the last 10 minutes of baking.

Dutch Pantry Cookin' Volume II

Barbecued Beef Liver

1 pound beef liver
Salt and pepper
1 cup sliced onion
2 tablespoons butter
1 tablespoon vinegar
1 tablespoon Worcestershire sauce
1 teaspoon sugar
⅛ teaspoon pepper
1 teaspoon prepared mustard
⅛ teaspoon chili powder
¼ cup ketchup
1 tablespoon water

Arrange half of liver in bottom of covered casserole. Sprinkle lightly with salt and pepper. Sauté onions until lightly browned in skillet. Place half over liver. Combine remaining ingredients. Spoon half of sauce over liver-onion mixture. Arrange another layer of liver and onions. Cover pan. Bake covered for 25 minutes at 325° for 45 minutes. Pour remaining sauce over liver. Bake, uncovered, for 10 minutes.

Cooking for the New Era

Spare Ribs with Plum Sauce

5–6 pounds pork spare ribs
3/4 cup soy sauce
3/4 cup plum jam
3/4 cup honey
2–3 cloves garlic, minced

Cut ribs into serving pieces and place bone-side-down on a rack in a shallow roasting pan. Cover and bake at 350° for 1 hour or until ribs are tender; drain. Combine soy sauce, plum jam, honey, and minced garlic. Brush over the ribs and return to oven uncovered for 30 minutes, brushing occasionally with the sauce.

Feeding the Flock—HCCLA

Special Indoor Barbecued Spare Ribs with Sauce

1 large onion, chopped
1/4 cup Wesson® oil
1 (6-ounce) can tomato paste
1/2 cup water
1 beef bouillon cube
1/4 cup Worcestershire sauce
1/4 cup soy sauce
1/4 cup white vinegar
2 tablespoons honey
2 teaspoons Tabasco® sauce
2 teaspoons salt
1 1/2 teaspoons liquid smoke
1 large clove garlic, minced
1 teaspoon dry mustard
4–5 pounds pork spare ribs

In small saucepan, sauté onion in oil until transparent. Add remaining ingredients, except spare ribs; mix well. Simmer 15 minutes. Pour over spare ribs in large glass baking dish; let stand 1 hour, turning occasionally. Arrange on shallow rack or broiler pan; bake at 350° for about 1 1/2–2 hours. Turn ribs and baste with remaining barbecue sauce 2 or 3 times during baking. Cut into portions to serve. Makes 4 servings.

Down Memory Lane

Pork Chop Skillet

4 loin chops
½ teaspoon salt
⅛ teaspoon pepper
¼ teaspoon garlic powder
2 cups chopped celery
½ cup sliced onion
1 medium apple, peeled and sliced
1 cup beef bouillon

Sprinkle chops with salt, pepper, and garlic powder. Brown chops and remove from pan. Add celery and onion slices and cook until slightly softened. Arrange chops over vegetables and top with apple slices and bouillon. Cover skillet and simmer 45 minutes or until chops are tender.

Just Plain Country

Mom's Stuffed Pork Chops

4–6 pork chops
3 cups bread crumbs
2 tablespoons chopped onion
½ teaspoon salt
½ teaspoon pepper
2 tablespoons parsley flakes
2 tablespoons chopped celery
¾ tablespoon sage
¼ cup milk
¼ cup broth
1 egg, beaten

Brown chops quickly. Place chops in single layer in casserole dish. Mix remaining ingredients together and mound the stuffing on top of each chop. Cover and bake at 350° for 1 hour. Serves 3–4.

Third Wednesday Homemakers

Covering fifty acres and producing 48,000 implements a day, the Kelly Axe Factory, located in Charleston, was once the largest axe factory in the world.

Ham Loaf

BASTING SAUCE:

½ cup brown sugar
½ cup hot water
1½ tablespoons mustard
2½ tablespoons vinegar

Combine all ingredients until brown sugar is dissolved.

HAM LOAF:

1 pound ground, smoked ham
1 pound ground pork
3 cups bread crumbs
1 cup milk
⅛ teaspoon pepper
2 eggs, beaten

Combine all ingredients; form into loaf and place in loaf pan or oblong baking pan. Baste Ham Loaf with Basting Sauce before and 2 or 3 times during baking. Bake in 350° oven for 1½ hours.

Our Best Home Cooking

Spicy Venison Roast

1 large venison roast
1 teaspoon salt and pepper, to taste
2 cans tomato soup
2 cups water
2½ teaspoons hot pepper
3 bay leaves
1 tablespoon brown sugar
2 tablespoons vinegar
1 large onion, chopped
3 medium potatoes, sliced

Put roast in roasting pan and season with salt and pepper. Add tomato soup and water combined with hot pepper. Add bay leaves; sprinkle with brown sugar and vinegar. Bake 1½ hours at 375°, covered. Remove cover and add onion and potatoes. Cover and bake 30 minutes longer. Turn roast and brown other side. Serves 6–8.

Pocahontas County Hunter's Cookbook

Deer Patties

2 pounds ground deer tenderloin
1 pound ground pork sausage
2 tablespoons very fine bread crumbs
2 tablespoons grated onion (optional)
2 teaspoons salt
1 egg, lightly beaten
1/2 teaspoon turmeric
1/4 teaspoon chili powder
1/4 teaspoon garlic salt (optional)
1/8 teaspoon pepper
1/2 cup margarine or bacon fat
1/3 cup water

Blend first 10 ingredients, leaving out garlic or onion, if you prefer, and shape into patties. Place in skillet in margarine or bacon fat and brown. When browned; add water and cover. Simmer 45 minutes. Serves 4–6.

Pocahontas County Hunter's Cookbook

Trail Bologna

2 pounds ground venison
1/2 cup water
1 1/2 teaspoons liquid smoke
1/8 teaspoon garlic powder
Little pinch of pepper
1 1/2 tablespoons Morton® Tender Quick

Mix all together, rolling a log 1 1/2 inches thick. Separate into 2 logs and wrap in wax paper. Refrigerate 24 hours. Put on cookie sheet. Bake at 300° for 3–5 hours.

Pocahontas County Hunter's Cookbook

Movies shot wholly or in part in West Virginia include: *The Deer Hunter* (1978, in Weirton), *Pudd'n'head Wilson* (1984, in Harpers Ferry), *Reckless* (1984, in Weirton), *Sweet Dreams* (1985, in Martinsburg) and *Matewan* (1987, in Thurmond).

Deviled Hot Dogs

½ cup finely chopped onion
2 tablespoons chopped green pepper
2 tablespoons oil
1 pound (8–10) frankfurters
¾ cup ketchup
2 tablespoons brown sugar
2 tablespoons prepared mustard
1 tablespoon Worcestershire sauce
1 teaspoon salt

Cook onion and pepper in hot oil until tender. Score frankfurters diagonally. Add with remaining ingredients to onion mixture. Cover and simmer 8–10 minutes. Makes 5 servings.

Elkins Manor Cookbook

T-Ball Hot Dog Sauce

2 pounds hamburger meat
4 medium onions, chopped
1½ cups sugar
½ cup vinegar
1 large bottle ketchup
¼ cup mustard
1 can tomato juice and 1 quart water (or 2 quarts homemade tomato juice)
½ small box chili powder
Salt and pepper to taste
Bread crumbs

Brown hamburger and onions in large saucepan. Add remaining ingredients, except bread crumbs. Cook 1 hour, then thicken with bread crumbs. Serve on buns over hot dogs. Serves 1 T-Ball team.

Generations

Ground Hog

The cleanest meat one can find.

After the ground hog is skinned, remove every bit of fat from the meat. Cut meat into pieces, wash, and drain. Use only the meaty pieces if you like. The good pieces of 2 ground hogs make a nice platter of meat.

Parboil the meat in plain salt water and ½ teaspoon baking soda. In the parboiling, watch the pot, as it is bad to foam up and run over. Drain and wash meat.

Put meat in large cooking pot; add 2 quartered onions and 2 or 3 carrots. Boil gently until meat is tender. Remove meat, roll in flour and brown in heavy skillet in margarine or butter, adding salt and pepper, and if desired, any other seasoning you might use on any meat.

Pocahontas County Hunter's Cookbook

PHOTO BY DAVID FATTALEH, COURTESY OF WEST VIRGINIA DIVISION OF TOURISM.

New River Gorge Bridge near Fayetteville is the second highest steel bridge in the U.S. Every October on Bridge Day, the road is closed and individuals parachute and bungee jump 876 feet off the bridge.

Swiss Baked Chicken Breasts

¼ cup butter or margarine, melted
8 chicken breast halves, deboned and skinned
2 tablespoons chopped chives
1 (6-ounce) package sliced Swiss cheese
1 (10¾-ounce) can cream of chicken soup, undiluted
¼ cup dry white wine
1 cup herb-seasoned stuffing crumbs, crushed

Preheat oven to 350°. Melt butter in a small saucepan. Set aside. Arrange chicken in a buttered 9x13x2-inch baking dish. Sprinkle chives over chicken. Place ½ slice of Swiss cheese on each chicken breast half. Mix together soup and wine. Spread sauce evenly over chicken. Sprinkle top with crushed stuffing mix. Drizzle butter over crumbs. Bake for 45–55 minutes, uncovered. Yields 8 servings.

Almost Heaven

Chicken Cordon Bleu

2 whole chicken breasts, split, deboned, and skinned
⅛ teaspoon salt
⅛ teaspoon pepper
1 egg, beaten
½ cup milk
2 (1-ounce) slices cooked ham
2 (1-ounce) slices Swiss cheese
½ cup all-purpose flour
⅔ cup fine bread crumbs
2 tablespoons grated Parmesan cheese
¼ cup butter or margarine

Place each breast on sheet of waxed paper. Flatten with meat mallet to ¼-inch thickness. Sprinkle with salt and pepper. Combine egg and milk. Dip both sides of breast in mixture. Place piece of ham and cheese in center of each breast. Fold over and close with toothpicks. Dredge in flour, dip in remaining milk mixture and coat well with bread crumbs mixed with Parmesan cheese. Cover and chill for 1 hour or longer. Melt butter in heavy skillet, brown on both sides. Remove to a lightly greased 9-inch-square pan. Bake, uncovered, at 350° for 40–45 minutes.

More...Home Town Recipes

Breast of Chicken Veronique

9 tablespoons butter, divided
3 large chicken breasts, split
18 medium mushrooms, quartered (caps only)
3 tablespoons flour
1½ cups half-and-half
¾ cup white wine
1 cup diced ham
Salt and pepper to taste
1½ cups seedless grapes

Melt 6 tablespoons butter in large heavy pan and brown chicken breasts. Remove to casserole. Melt 3 tablespoons butter in same pan and sauté mushrooms over high heat for 3 minutes. Remove with slotted spoon and scatter over chicken. Reduce heat and stir flour into skillet. Cook the roux 1 minute. Gradually add half-and-half and wine, stirring constantly. Cook until thick. Add diced ham. Season with salt and pepper and pour sauce over chicken. Bake covered in a 350° oven 35–40 minutes. Uncover and scatter grapes over chicken and bake another 10 minutes. Yields 6 servings.

Variation: You may add some herbs to the sauce; approximately ¼–½ teaspoon thyme, rosemary, and tarragon mixed, or alone. This can be prepared ahead and refrigerated, but grapes should not be added until the last 10 minutes of cooking.

Treat Yourself to the Best Cookbook

Chicken Pecan

½ pound Ritz® Crackers, crushed
½ cup grated real Parmesan cheese
¼ cup dried parsley
½ pound crushed pecans
Flour
4–6 boneless, skinless chicken breasts
1 egg, beaten
Olive oil

Preheat oven to 400°. Mix Ritz® Crackers, Parmesan cheese, parsley, and pecans together well for pecan breading. Flour chicken breasts, dip in beaten egg, then in pecan breading. Sauté chicken in oven-proof pan in olive oil until golden brown, then finish cooking in oven for 20 minutes.

POULETTE MUSHROOM SAUCE:
Mushrooms to taste
Butter and garlic for sautéing
Chicken stock to taste
Flour or cornstarch to thicken

Lightly sauté mushrooms in butter and garlic. Add chicken stock and thicken to taste with flour or cornstarch.

Recipe from Richard's Country Inn, Huttonsville
Good Morning West Virginia!

No Peek Chicken

1½ cups raw quick cooking rice
6 chicken breasts
1 can cream of chicken soup
1 can cream of celery soup
1 package onion soup mix

Place rice in pan lined with foil long enough to fold over and seal. Add chicken. Combine soups and pour over chicken. Sprinkle with onion soup mix. Seal foil. Bake 2 hours at 300°.

Somebody's Cookbook

Rosemary Chicken

4 chicken breasts with ribs and skin
½ cup water
3 tablespoons butter or margarine
1 chicken bouillon cube
1 small bay leaf, cracked
1 teaspoon garlic salt
¼ teaspoon crushed dried rosemary
Dash of seasoned pepper

Arrange chicken in shallow baking pan, bone-side-up. In small saucepan, heat all remaining ingredients together until butter melts and bouillon dissolves. Pour mixture evenly over chicken and bake, uncovered, at 350° for 45–55 minutes or until chicken is tender and no longer pink in center. Serve chicken with sauce spooned over. Very good with mashed potatoes with some of the sauce over them as well. Makes 4 servings.

Note: You can do up to 6 chicken breasts with the same amount of sauce.

Enjoy at Your Own Risk! Cookbook

Jenny's Crockpot Chicken

8 boneless chicken breasts
1 envelope dry Italian salad dressing
2 tablespoons margarine, melted

Place chicken breast in crockpot. Shake Italian dressing on chicken breast and pour melted margarine on top. Cook on HIGH 4–5¼ hours.

SAUCE:
1 can cream of mushroom soup
1 (8-ounce) package cream cheese, cut into small chunks
½ cup apple juice
1 tablespoon finely chopped onion

Mix all Sauce ingredients and pour over chicken breasts. Cook another 30–40 minutes more and serve on rice.

United Methodist Ministers' Wives Cook Book

Gourmet Breasts of Chicken

4 boneless, skinless chicken breasts
Salt and pepper
4 slices Swiss cheese
1 beaten egg
2 tablespoons water
1 cup crushed potato chips
¼ cup butter
1 teaspoon rosemary

Pound breasts flat and sprinkle with salt and pepper. Place a slice of cheese on each breast; roll jellyroll-fashion and fasten with toothpick. Dip into egg batter (made with egg and water) and roll in crushed potato chips. Combine butter and rosemary; spread on top of each breast. Bake, covered, at 350° for 1 hour. Serves 4.

Treasures from Heaven

Bonnie's Ceylonese Chicken

This could soon become a favorite dish at your house. Make extra paste and keep it in the freezer for a fast (but great) dinner for another night.

1 medium onion
5 cloves garlic
3 tablespoons grated fresh ginger
1 teaspoon cinnamon
1 teaspoon crushed red peppers
⅓ cup chopped fresh cilantro
1 tablespoon curry powder
1 teaspoon salt
6 boneless, skinless chicken breasts
2 tablespoons vegetable oil
1 (14-ounce) can coconut milk
1 cup chicken broth
1 teaspoon turmeric

Using a food processor, blend onion, garlic, ginger, cinnamon, peppers, cilantro, curry, and salt. Rub paste over chicken and marinate at least 2 hours.

In a large skillet, sear chicken in oil over high heat about 2 minutes. Remove chicken and add coconut milk and broth to the skillet. Stir in turmeric and return chicken to the skillet. Simmer for 15–20 minutes, until chicken is fully cooked. Serve over rice (basmati is an excellent choice).

White Grass Cafe Cross Country Cooking

Sweet and Sour Chicken

1 (8-ounce) bottle Catalina dressing
1 (8-ounce) jar apricot preserves
1 package Lipton® Onion Soup Mix
1 small can pineapple chunks
6 boneless chicken breasts
1 (10-ounce) package broccoli spears, thawed
1 can cooked potatoes
Cooked rice

Mix together dressing, preserves, soup mix, and pineapple chunks. Marinate chicken in sauce for 2 hours. Bake at 350° for 1½ hours. Add broccoli spears and potatoes; pour over chicken. Bake 10 minutes; serve over cooked rice.

Down Memory Lane

Chicken Enchiladas

½ cup chopped onion
1 tablespoon butter
2 cans cream of chicken soup
1 soup can milk
1 or 2 chopped jalapeño peppers
1 (12-count) package flour tortillas
3 cups chopped, cooked chicken
2 cups grated Cheddar cheese (mild or sharp), divided

Sauté onion in butter. Add soup, milk, and jalapeño peppers. Heat through. Fill tortillas with chicken and cheese (reserving some for topping). Place small amount soup mixture in a 9x13-inch pan. Place filled tortillas on mixture. Pour remaining soup mixture on top. Sprinkle with reserved cheese. Bake 30–40 minutes at 350°, uncovered.

Our Best Home Cooking

West Virginia's Memorial Tunnel, located about 25 miles south of Charleston, opened on November 8, 1954, and was the first in the nation to be monitored by television.

Hot Chicken Salad

2 cups cubed cooked chicken
2 cups diced celery
½ cup slivered almonds
2 tablespoons minced onion
2 tablespoons lemon juice
1 small green pepper, diced
1 teaspoon salt
1 cup mayonnaise
½ cup light cream
¾ cup crushed potato chips
¾ cup shredded Cheddar cheese
Paprika

Mix chicken, celery, almonds, onion, lemon juice, green pepper, salt, mayonnaise, and cream. Place in a greased 1½-quart casserole dish. Place crushed potato chips all over the top. Sprinkle cheese over potato chips and add paprika to taste. Bake in a 350° oven until brown, approximately 30 minutes.

Just Plain Country

Country-Kitchen Casserole

1 pound Velveeta® cheese, cubed
1 cup milk
½ cup mayonnaise
5 ounces spaghetti, cooked and drained
1 tablespoon chopped chives or onions
2 cups chopped, cooked chicken
1 (10-ounce) package frozen peas and carrots, cooked, drained

Heat cheese, milk, and mayonnaise over low heat. Stir until sauce is smooth. Add remaining ingredients. Mix well. Pour into 2-quart buttered casserole dish. Bake at 350° for 30–40 minutes.

Stout Memorial Culinary Treasures

Famous West Virginians include: George Brett, Pearl S. Buck, Jack Canfield, Bob Denver, Little Jimmy Dickens, Sam Huff, Stonewall Jackson, Don Knotts, Kathy Mattea, Randy Moss, Brad Paisley, Ed Rabel, Mary Lou Retton, John D. Rockefeller IV, Soupy Sales, Booker T. Washington, Jerry West, and Charles Elwood "Chuck" Yeager.

West Virginia Casserole

This makes a great meal if served with mashed potatoes and gravy and a vegetable.

2 boxes Stove Top® Stuffing Mix, divided
2 cups bite-size pieces cooked chicken or turkey
1 can cream of chicken soup
1 can cream of mushroom soup

Follow the directions on the box to prepare 1 box of stuffing mix. Place in a casserole dish or 9x13-inch pan. Add chicken or turkey. Mix the 2 soups and pour over mixture. Mix the second box of stuffing mix, but do not heat. Spread over top of layered mixture. Bake, uncovered, at 350° for 35 minutes.

West Virginia Librarians (bon) Appétit

Rice Krispies Chicken Casserole

2 cups cubed cooked chicken
1 cup cooked rice
1 teaspoon minced onion
1 teaspoon salt
1 can cream of chicken soup
¼ cup milk
1 cup diced celery
¾ cup mayonnaise
1 teaspoon lemon juice
1 can water chestnuts, diced

Combine all ingredients; mix well. Put in a greased 11-inch casserole. Put Topping on mixture and bake in 350° oven for 30 minutes.

TOPPING:
½ stick margarine, melted
1½ cups Rice Krispies®
½ cup chopped pecans (optional)

Mix margarine, Rice Krispies, and nuts well. Spread on top of casserole before baking.

Cookin' in a Coal Camp

Chicken Pie

I used to watch my grandmother toss this together effortlessly. She had about 12 inches of counter space to work with, and she'd be covered with flour when she was finished.

Boil a 3-pound chicken until done; debone and cook the broth down to 2 cups. Cook up some vegetables (green beans, peas, corn, carrots . . . whatever you have) along with 2 white potatoes. Combine vegetables, chicken, 2 chopped hard-boiled eggs, the broth, and 3 tablespoons flour dissolved in a little cold water. Place in a baking dish and top with biscuits or a vented pastry crust. Bake at 400° about 20–25 minutes, until bubbly and browned. Put it on the table after everyone's seated.

Take Two & Butter 'Em While They're Hot!

Mini Chicken Pies

1 (3-ounce) package cream cheese, softened
2 tablespoons mayonnaise
3/4 cup cooked and chopped chicken
1/8 cup finely chopped green bell pepper
1/8 cup finely chopped red bell pepper
1/4 cup chopped onion
1/2 cup shredded Cheddar cheese
1 (7-ounce) can Mexican-style corn, drained
1 can refrigerated large flaky biscuits
Sesame seeds

Heat oven to 375°. Lightly grease 8 muffin cups. In a medium bowl, blend cream cheese and mayonnaise until smooth. Stir in chicken, green and red bell peppers, onion, Cheddar cheese, and corn. Separate biscuits and then divide into 2 parts by removing the top 1/3 of each biscuit. Place bottom 2/3 of biscuit into greased muffin cups. Firmly press in bottom and up the sides forming a 1/4-inch rim. Spoon 1/3 cup of chicken mixture into each cup. Top each with remaining 1/3 biscuit, stretching slightly to fit. Press edges to seal. Sprinkle with sesame seeds. Bake for 15–20 minutes or until golden brown.

Feeding the Flock—HCCLA

Chicken, Carrots and Ramps

2 tablespoons butter
1 (3-ounce) chicken, cut into 8 serving pieces
1 pound carrots
1 cup water
½ teaspoon dried thyme leaves
¼ teaspoon salt
⅛ teaspoon black pepper
1 cup chopped ramps* (white bulbs and green tops), divided
1 tablespoon all-purpose flour

In 12-inch skillet melt butter over medium heat. Add chicken and brown on all sides, about 20 minutes. Meanwhile, peel carrots and cut into 2½ x ½-inch sticks. When chicken pieces are browned, spoon off all fat from skillet, reserving 1 tablespoon in small cup. Add carrots, water, thyme, salt, pepper, and ½ cup ramps to chicken in skillet. Stir carefully to mix; cover skillet. Cook over low heat until chicken is tender, about 15 minutes. Stir flour into reserved fat in cup. Push chicken and vegetables to one side in skillet. Stir flour mixture and remaining ramps into pan juices; cook until thickened and bubbly. Spoon sauce over chicken and serve hot. Makes 4 servings.

Elkins Manor Cookbook

Editors' Extra: *Ramps, also known as wild leeks, resemble scallions. Substitutions are leeks, scallions or green onions.

Chicken Stew with Dumplings

1 (4- to 5-pound) chicken, cut up
½ cup diced celery
1 bay leaf
2 teaspoons salt
⅛ teaspoon pepper
2 tablespoons parsley
1 clove garlic, diced
1 whole onion, chopped

Wash chicken; combine with all ingredients in large pot. Cover with water. Bring to a boil, then lower heat and simmer, covered, 3–4 hours or until tender. Thicken, if desired, then add Dumplings on top. Cover. Cook as directed.

DUMPLINGS:
2 cups all-purpose flour
3 teaspoons baking powder
1 teaspoon salt
¼ cup shortening
1 cup milk

As soon as stew is done, sift flour, baking powder, and salt into bowl. Drop in shortening. Cut in until blended. Add milk and mix with a fork until it forms a dough. (Don't overmix.) Form Dumplings (tablespoon size); drop into stew. Cover pot; simmer 12–15 minutes. Serve hot.

Mom-Mom's Cookbook

Mrs. Minnie Buckingham Harper was the first African-American woman to become a member of a legislative body in the United States. In 1928 she was appointed by the Governor to the House of Delegates to fill the vacancy caused by the death of her husband.

Chicken and Dumplings

1 (3½-pound) chicken, cut up
1½ quarts water
Salt and freshly ground pepper to taste
1 small onion, quartered
1 small carrot, cut into chunks
2 celery stalks with leaves, cut into chunks
3 tablespoons butter or chicken fat
¼ cup all-purpose flour
⅛ teaspoon paprika
½ cup half-and-half
White pepper to taste
Dumplings
Parsley for garnish

Wash chicken and pat dry with paper towels. Place chicken in large pot. Add water, salt, pepper, onion, carrot, and celery, and simmer, covered, 45 minutes to 1 hour or until chicken is tender. Remove from broth; strain and reserve broth. Cool chicken until able to handle, then discard skin and bones; dice meat; refrigerate.

In a large, heavy saucepan, heat butter or chicken fat. Stir in flour and paprika. Gradually add 3 cups reserved chicken broth, stirring until thickened and smooth. Cook 2 minutes. Add half-and-half and white pepper. Taste and adjust seasonings. Return diced chicken to broth. Prepare Dumplings.

DUMPLINGS:
1½ cups all-purpose flour
½ teaspoon salt
3 teaspoons baking powder
1 tablespoon shortening, melted
⅓ cup milk

In a medium bowl, combine flour, salt, and baking powder. Blend in shortening and milk; mix well.

Dip a teaspoon into cold water; spoon teaspoonfuls of batter on top of simmering chicken mixture. Cook, covered, 15 minutes, *without lifting lid.* Sprinkle with parsley and serve immediately. Makes 6 servings.

More than Beans and Cornbread

Turkey Breast with Lemon Caper Sauce

This is wonderful for company. Must start a day in advance.

MARINADE:
1 cup parsley
5 large cloves garlic
1½ cups fresh lemon juice
1 cup vegetable oil
4 teaspoons crushed rosemary
1½ teaspoons salt
Freshly ground pepper to taste

Process parsley and garlic in food processor until chopped. Add lemon juice, oil, rosemary, salt, and pepper. Process constantly for 3 minutes.

1 (5- to 6-pound) bone-in turkey breast
Salt and pepper to taste
6 tablespoons chilled unsalted butter, divided
¼ cup drained capers
Wild rice

Rinse turkey and pat dry. Combine with Marinade in plastic food storage bag; mix to coat well. Marinate in refrigerator overnight.

Let stand until room temperature. Drain turkey, reserving Marinade. Place turkey in roasting pan. Sprinkle with salt and pepper to taste. Roast at 400° for 30 minutes. Reserve ⅔ cup of the Marinade (for caper sauce). Roast turkey for 1 hour longer, basting with remaining marinade. Cool turkey while making caper sauce.

To make caper sauce, bring reserved ⅔ cup Marinade to a boil in saucepan; remove from heat. Whisk in 2 tablespoons butter. Cook over low heat for several minutes, whisking in remaining butter 1 tablespoon at a time. Stir in capers.

Cut turkey into thin slices. Serve over wild rice with caper sauce. Yields 12 servings.

The Best of Wheeling

Turkey Bake

3 cups cubed turkey
1 package frozen peas, cooked and drained
1 cup shredded sharp Cheddar cheese, divided
¼ cup chopped onion
½ teaspoon salt
Dash of pepper
½ cup mayonnaise
6 slices tomato
¾ cup crushed potato chips

Combine turkey, peas, ½ cup cheese, onion, salt, pepper, and mayonnaise. Mix well. Spoon into greased 10x6x2-inch baking dish. Place tomato slices on top. Bake at 350° for 25 minutes. Combine remaining ½ cup cheese and potato chips; mix well and sprinkle over casserole. Bake an additional 5 minutes or until cheese melts. Serves 6.

Best Taste of Fairmont

Marinated Turkey Breasts

1 turkey breast
1 cup soy sauce
¼ cup oil
1 tablespoon honey
Garlic to taste
1 tablespoon dry mustard
1 tablespoon ginger

Debone turkey breast and slice in 1-inch slices. Mix remaining ingredients well for the marinade and pour over turkey slices. After marinating overnight, grill on both sides.

Our Best Home Cooking

Weirton is the only city in the United States that extends from one state border to another. Located in the Northern Panhandle, the city extends from the Ohio border eastward to the Pennsylvania border.

Roast Wild Turkey with Chestnut Stuffing

1 (16- to 18-pound) turkey
2 teaspoons salt
1½ teaspoons pepper
2 tablespoons allspice
4 stalks celery, sliced thin
½ cup bacon drippings

Preheat oven to 400°. Wash turkey and pat dry with paper towels. Rub the turkey inside and out with salt, pepper, and allspice. Put celery in body cavity and tie turkey's legs together. Fasten neck skin to back with a skewer. Fold wing tips onto back. Place turkey on a rack in a large, shallow roasting pan and brush with bacon drippings. Roast uncovered at 400° for 25 minutes. Baste frequently with bacon drippings.

STUFFING:
½ cup chopped onion
2 garlic cloves, peeled, chopped, crushed
½ cup butter
½ cup sausage meat
10 slices bread, toasted, coarsely crumbled
2 cups chopped roasted chestnuts
½ cup brandy

Sauté onion and garlic in melted butter in a skillet until transparent. Add sausage meat and brown well. In a large bowl, combine toasted bread, chestnuts, and sausage mixture. Sprinkle with brandy and toss to combine well. Set aside until ready to use.

Take turkey from oven, untie legs, and discard celery. Fill body cavity loosely with Stuffing and close with skewers.

Skim off about ½ the fat from the drippings. Place turkey in center of pan, breast-side-up, and cover loosely with foil. Roast uncovered at 325° for 5½–6 hours, basting frequently with pan drippings. Turkey is done when the thigh joint moves easily in its socket and the thickest part of the drumstick feels very soft when pressed between protected fingers. A meat thermometer inserted in the thickest part of the thigh should register about 185°. Transfer turkey to a platter and keep warm.

(continued)

(continued)

SAUCE:

1 cup turkey drippings
1 cup dry white wine
2 tablespoons cornstarch
⅓ cup brandy
Salt and pepper to taste

Skim off and discard fat from drippings in roasting pan. Measure 1 cup of the drippings and pour into a saucepan. Add wine and simmer 10 minutes. In a small bowl combine cornstarch and the ⅓ cup brandy; add cornstarch mixture to simmering mixture. Cook, stirring constantly, until thickened. Season to taste with salt and pepper. Arrange slices of turkey with stuffing. Serve with Sauce.

Pocahontas County Hunter's Cookbook

Chestnut Stuffing

½ cup chopped onion
½ cup chopped celery
1 cup cooked, peeled, and ground chestnuts
2 cups broth
1 tablespoon fresh sage
2 teaspoons salt, if needed
Cornbread, cubed and dried

Sauté onion and celery; add chestnuts, broth, and seasoning. Add cornbread to make it the consistency you want. Stuff your meat or bake in a pan at 350° for 30 minutes.

Note: To prepare chestnuts, place in a pan, cover with cold water. Bring to a boil and boil for about 5 minutes. Let them cool in the pan of hot water to continue the cooking. Cut them apart, remove each side with the point of a knife. Place in blender with water, and chop. Drain the water. These can be used in lots of recipes like meat loaf, stews, Jerusalem artichoke salad, and, most especially, stuffings.

Bootstraps and Biscuits

On October 23, 1870, the first brick street in the world was laid on Summers Street in Charleston by a private citizen at his own expense.

Cornish Hens with Wild Rice Stuffing

1/4 cup minced celery
1/4 cup minced shallots or onion
2 tablespoons minced green pepper
2 tablespoons butter or margarine
1 1/3 cups chicken broth
2 tablespoons minced, fresh parsley
1 teaspoon herb seasoning
2/3 cup wild rice (uncooked)
2 (1- to 1 1/4-pound) Cornish hens
Salt and pepper
1/4 cup butter or margarine
1/2 cup red currant jelly
1/4 cup brandy

Sauté celery, shallots, and green pepper in 2 tablespoons butter in a medium saucepan. Stir in the next 3 ingredients. Bring to a boil and add wild rice. Cover and reduce heat to medium low; cook about 25 minutes.

Remove giblets from hens and reserve for another use. Rinse hens with cold water and pat dry; sprinkle cavity with salt and pepper. Stuff hens lightly with rice mixture. Close cavities and secure with wooden picks; truss. Place hens, breast-side-up, in a shallow baking pan. Melt 1/4 cup butter in a saucepan; brush hens with butter, reserving any remaining butter in saucepan.

Bake hens at 375° for 30 minutes. Combine jelly and brandy in saucepan with remaining butter; cook over low heat, stirring often, until jelly melts. Brush hens with jelly mixture. Bake 30–40 additional minutes, depending on size of hens, basting every 10 minutes with jelly mixture. Yields 2 servings.

Carnegie Hall Cookbook

PHOTO BY STEPHEN SHALUTA, COURTESY OF WEST VIRGINIA DIVISION OF TOURISM.

U.S. men's team takes a wild and wonderful ride during the 2001 World Rafting Championships held on the New and Gauley rivers in Fayette and Nicholas counties. This was the first time the event was held in North America.

SAUCE:

6 tablespoons butter
6 tablespoons flour
½ teaspoon salt
2⅓ cups milk
⅔ cup dry white wine
10 ounces Swiss cheese, grated

Melt butter in large saucepan, add flour and salt, and cook until bubbly. Remove from heat and slowly add milk, stirring constantly. Add wine. Return to heat and add Swiss cheese and heat until thickened.

1 pound fresh scallops (bay or halved sea scallops)
12 ounces medium shrimp, peeled and deveined
8 ounces fresh mushrooms, cleaned and sliced
3 tablespoons butter
Melted butter
¼ cup dried bread crumbs
Parmesan cheese

Preheat oven to 350°. In large frying pan, sauté scallops, shrimp, and mushrooms in 3 tablespoons butter until shrimp are just pink and mushrooms look moist. Put scallops, shrimp, and mushrooms into greased 4-quart casserole dish. Top with Sauce and stir. Add enough melted butter to moisten ¼ cup bread crumbs. Sprinkle crumbs over casserole. Top with Parmesan cheese to taste. Bake 20–30 minutes until cheese bubbles. Yields 4–6 servings.

Almost Heaven

Pocahontas County has been called the "Birthplace of Rivers," since no streams flow into the county, but the headwaters of eight rivers can be found within its boundaries: Greenbrier, Cherry, Elk, Gauley, Cheat, Tygart Valley, Williams and Cranberry rivers.

Shrimp and Crab Étouffée

Excellent Cajun cuisine, this is one of our most special dishes at White Grass. It looks involved, but is definitely worth it.

1 large onion
6 green onions
1 large green bell pepper
1 large red bell pepper
3 ribs celery
3/4 cup chopped parsley
6 cloves garlic
1/2 stick butter
3 tablespoons flour
1 1/2 pounds large raw shrimp, shells on
6 cups water
1 tablespoon seafood seasoning
1/2 teaspoon cayenne pepper
2 teaspoons salt
1/2 teaspoon ground black pepper
1/2 teaspoon ground white pepper
1 tablespoon vegetable bouillon
1 pound crab meat

In a food processor, finely chop onions, peppers, celery, parsley, and garlic.

Melt butter in a large pot over medium-high heat. Add flour to make a roux and stir constantly until it becomes peanut butter colored. (Be careful not to burn the roux.) Add the chopped vegetables and let them cook until soft, about 30 minutes. Remember to stir occasionally so they don't stick.

In the meantime, peel and devein shrimp. Save shells and make a stock by boiling them in water and seafood seasoning for 8–10 minutes, then strain.

When the veggies are done, add stock and stir. Simmer, then add remaining seasonings. You may want to adjust them to your own taste. About 15 minutes before you are ready to eat, add crab and shrimp. Cook until shrimp are pink and tender; don't overcook—they will get tough. This dish goes best over hot fluffy rice. Serves 6.

White Grass Cafe Cross Country Cooking

My Own Shrimp Sauce

¾ cup ketchup
1 tablespoon horseradish
1 tablespoon Worcestershire sauce
2 teaspoons lemon juice
Dash Tabasco®
Salt to taste

Combine and mix well. This will keep for several weeks in a tightly covered jar in the refrigerator.

Casseroles, Meats and Fish...Cookies

Shrimp and Green Noodle Casserole

6 green onions, chopped
4 tablespoons melted butter, divided
3 pounds raw shrimp
1 (16-ounce) package vermicelli
1 cup mayonnaise
1 cup sour cream
1 can cream of mushroom soup
1½ teaspoons prepared mustard
3 tablespoons dry vermouth
6 ounces white Cheddar cheese
1 (10-ounce) box spinach, cooked

Sauté onions in 2 tablespoons butter. Cook, peel, and drain shrimp. Cook, drain, and toss noodles with remaining melted butter. Place noodles in buttered casserole. Cover with shrimp and green onions. Mix mayonnaise, sour cream, soup, mustard, vermouth, cheese, and spinach together. Pour over onions and shrimp. Bake at 350° for 30–40 minutes. Makes 10–12 servings. Freezes well.

A Gracious Plenty

The Greenbrier® resort secretly housed a government relocation facility buried some 720 feet into its hillside until its whereabouts were exposed in a May 1992 *Washington Post* article. Planned during the Eisenhower administration, the bunker was built to accommodate the U.S. Senate and House of Representatives, in the event of nuclear war.

Grilled Swordfish

½ cup butter or margarine
¼ cup fresh lemon juice
1 teaspoon White Wine Worcestershire Sauce*
½ teaspoon seasoned salt
½ teaspoon seasoned pepper
2–4 swordfish steaks (4 if small)

In saucepan, combine all but fish steaks. Heat until butter is melted. Place steaks in glass dish large enough to hold in single layer. Pour sauce over fish. Cover and marinate 1 hour in refrigerator. Turn steaks, spooning some sauce over the just-turned-up side and marinate 1 hour longer. Cook on grill over hot coals or broil until done, turning once, basting with sauce once. Serve hot. Makes 2–4 servings.

*White Wine Worcestershire Sauce is also called Worcestershire for Chicken.

Enjoy at Your Own Risk! Cookbook

Cheese Baked Fish

2 tablespoons butter or margarine
3 tablespoons flour
¾ teaspoon salt
⅛ teaspoon nutmeg
½ teaspoon dry mustard
1 cup hot milk
¾ teaspoon lemon juice
½ cup shredded Cheddar cheese
2 pounds fish fillets (haddock, perch, flounder or sole)

Melt margarine or butter and blend in dry ingredients. Stir in milk and cook until thickened, stirring constantly. Add lemon juice and cheese. Stir until cheese melts. Place fish in greased baking dish and cover with cheese sauce. Bake at 375° for 40 minutes. Serves 6.

More than Beans and Cornbread

Chile Trout

Having a trout farm just down the road, we've come up with some great ways to prepare this wonderful delicate fish. This is probably the most popular.

1 onion, chopped
1 tablespoon oil
1 roasted red pepper
2 dried Ancho chiles, soaked in water till soft
4 cloves garlic
1 bunch fresh cilantro
3 tablespoons fresh lime juice
1/4 teaspoon salt
6 whole trout, filleted
2 limes, cut into wedges

Purée onion, oil, pepper, chiles, garlic, and cilantro in a food processor; add lime juice and salt. Rub paste over fish. Bake at 450° for 10–15 minutes, or until fish is flaky. Don't overbake. Serve with lime wedges.

Note: This chile paste works well with catfish, or any other white fish and can also be made ahead of time and stored in the fridge or freezer.

White Grass Cafe Cross Country Cooking

Crusty Corn Trout

4 cleaned and boned trout
1/3 cup flour
1 egg
1 tablespoon water
1 cup yellow cornmeal
1/4 cup ground nuts (peanuts, walnuts, etc.)
1 teaspoon salt
1/4 teaspoon pepper
1/4 teaspoon paprika
1/4 teaspoon ground cumin
Vegetable oil

Roll trout in flour. Beat egg with water. Mix cornmeal, ground nuts, salt, pepper, paprika, and cumin. Dip floured trout into egg mixture and then into cornmeal. Heat about 1 inch of oil in deep skillet. Cook trout 5 minutes on each side. Fish flakes when done. Makes 4 servings.

Generations

Crispy Oven Catfish

4 catfish fillets
1 cup mayonnaise
1½ teaspoons Mexican seasoning
⅔ cup Parmesan cheese
¼ cup cornmeal
¼ cup hot salsa

Preheat oven to 450°. Brush fish with mayonnaise and Mexican seasoning. Coat fish with Parmesan cheese and cornmeal. Spray broiler pan with cooking spray; arrange fish on broiler. Bake 12–15 minutes or until fish flakes easily with fork. Serves 4. Serve with hot salsa.

Third Wednesday Homemakers Volume II

Tuna Casserole

2 cups stuffing mix, divided
1 (13-ounce) can tuna or 2 small cans tuna
1 can cream of mushroom soup
1 cup finely chopped celery
½ cup mayonnaise
1 cup sour cream
1 tablespoon lemon juice
1 can sliced mushrooms, drained
½ cup chopped onion
½ cup chopped green pepper
1 teaspoon salt
1 teaspoon pepper
1 teaspoon garlic powder
1 cup shredded Cheddar cheese

Combine 1½ cups stuffing mix and all remaining ingredients, except cheese; place in greased 9x13-inch baking dish. Top with cheese and bake in a 350° oven for 30 minutes. Sprinkle remaining ½ cup stuffing mix on top and bake for 10 minutes longer.

Just Plain Country

The first long-span, wire-cable suspension bridge in the United States was completed in Wheeling in November 1849. From 1849 until 1851, the 1,100-foot Wheeling Bridge was the longest bridge in the world. It was blown down by high winds in 1854.

Salmon Patties

1 can pink salmon, drained, reserve liquid
1/2 cup crushed saltine crackers
1/4 cup cornmeal
1 large egg, slightly beaten
1/4 teaspoon salt
1/4 teaspoon pepper
1/2 cup diced celery
1/2 cup diced onion

Drain salmon, reserving liquid; remove skin and bones; flake and set aside. Combine cracker crumbs with reserved liquid; let stand 5 minutes or until all liquid is absorbed. Stir in salmon, cornmeal, egg, salt, pepper, celery, and onion. Shape into 6 patties. Fry in hot oil over medium heat until browned on both sides.

Just Plain Country

The youngest person ever elected by popular vote to the U. S. Senate was Rush D. Holt. Holt, born in Weston, was dubbed the "boy senator" because, even though he was elected in 1934 at age 29, by law he couldn't take office until he turned thirty in 1935. His son, Rush Jr., was elected to Congress from New Jersey in 1998.

CAKES

PHOTO © MICHAEL RIBAS PHOTOGRAPHY.

The West Virginia State Capital was moved to Charleston from Wheeling in 1870. However, Charleston lacked a railroad and other advantages essential for a state capital, so five years later, the legislature moved it back to Wheeling. Finally, in 1885, the capital returned to Charleston, where it has remained.

Costmary Pound Cake

Large light green costmary leaves are abundant in May. Often eight inches long, they were called Bibleleaf and once used as a fragrant bookmark. Costmary has a rich fruity-mint flavor that makes a refreshing tea, too. Try this delicious variation of pound cake.

8 large costmary leaves, divided
4 cups sifted flour
1 teaspoon salt
4 teaspoons baking powder
1½ cups butter
3 cups sugar
8 eggs
1 cup milk
2 teaspoons vanilla

Preheat oven to 325°. Line 2 (4½x8-inch) loaf pans with wax paper. Place 4 costmary leaves on the bottom of each pan. Sift flour, salt, and baking powder together. Cream butter and sugar very well. Add eggs 1 at a time to butter and sugar and continue creaming. Add flour mixture alternately with milk and vanilla. Stir only until blended. Pour batter in pans over the leaves. Bake for 1 hour. Remove from pans and discard costmary leaves.

A Dooryard Herb Cookbook

Mrs. Shingleton's Buttermilk Pound Cake

3 cups sugar
½ cup shortening
1 cup butter
4 eggs
1 teaspoon vanilla
½ teaspoon baking soda
½ teaspoon salt
3 cups flour
1 cup buttermilk
1 cup chopped pecans

Preheat oven to 325°. Grease and flour a 10-inch tube pan. Cream together sugar, shortening, and butter until light and fluffy. Add eggs, 1 at a time, beating after each. Add vanilla. Sift baking soda, salt, and flour together. Add sifted dry ingredients alternately with buttermilk to creamed mixture, beating after each addition.

Line greased and floured pan with chopped nuts. Pour cake batter on top of nuts. Bake for 1½ hours. Cool cake in pan for 10 minutes. Remove from pan and cool on rack. Yields 10–12 servings.

Almost Heaven

The Best Lemon Pound Cake

1 box Duncan Hines® Deluxe Lemon Supreme Cake Mix
1 small box lemon instant pudding and pie filling mix
4 eggs
1 cup water
1/3 cup oil
1/2 can Duncan Hines® Creamy Homestyle Lemon Frosting

Preheat oven to 350°. Grease and flour a 10-inch Bundt pan. Combine cake mix, pudding mix, eggs, water, and oil in large mixing bowl. Beat at medium speed with electric mixer for 2 minutes. Pour into pan. Bake for 50–60 minutes or until toothpick inserted in center comes out clean. Cool in pan for 25 minutes. Invert onto cake plate. Cool completely. Heat frosting in a small saucepan over medium heat, stirring constantly, until thin (or microwave 10–15 seconds). Do not overheat. Drizzle over cake.

Elkins Manor Cookbook

Real Pound Cake

1 teaspoon baking soda
2 teaspoons cream of tartar
1 pound (4 cups) flour
1 pound (2 cups) sugar
1/2 pound (1 cup) butter
1 pound (6) eggs, separated, divided
3/4 cup milk

Sift baking soda and cream of tartar into flour. Cream butter and sugar. Beat egg whites until soft peaks form, then add 1/4 of them to creamed mixture. Add 1/4 of beaten yolks. Add flour, milk, remaining yolks, and lastly the remaining whites, in that order. Fold into a greased and floured tube or Bundt pan. Bake at 325° for 1 1/4 hours. Test for doneness by inserting toothpick in thickest part of cake and it should come out clean.

West Virginia Country Cooking

West Virginia Jam Cake

This makes a magnificent cake—something to be proud to take to a reunion.

2 cups sugar
1 cup shortening
3 eggs
1 cup buttermilk
1 cup berry jam
3 cups sifted flour
1 teaspoon baking soda
1 cup chopped black walnuts
1 cup raisins
1 large apple, grated
½ cup chopped dates (optional)
1 cup ground coconut

Cream sugar and shortening; add eggs and beat well. Add buttermilk and jam alternately with sifted flour and baking soda; beat well. Add nuts, fruits, and coconut; stir until well distributed throughout batter. Bake in 3 (9-inch) greased cake pans for 30–40 minutes at 350°.

FROSTING:
2 cups sugar
2 tablespoons flour
½ cup milk
½ cup butter or margarine
1 cup chopped nuts
1 cup chopped raisins
1 cup grated apples
1 cup grated coconut
Maraschino cherries (optional)

Mix sugar and flour together in saucepan; add milk and butter and cook about 2 minutes, stirring occasionally. Remove from heat and beat till thickened; add nuts, fruit, and coconut. Spread between layers and on top and sides of cake. Decorate with maraschino cherries, if desired.

Note: If black walnuts are not available, use pecans or other nuts and add ½ teaspoon black walnut flavoring.

Keaton Mills Family Cookbook

Jam Cake

This is a very old recipe.

1 cup butter
2 cups sugar
4 eggs
2 1/2 cups blackberry jam
3 cups flour
1 teaspoon baking soda
1 teaspoon salt
1 teaspoon ground cloves
1 teaspoon nutmeg
1 teaspoon cinnamon
1 cup buttermilk

Cream butter and sugar; add eggs and blackberry jam. Beat thoroughly. Sift flour, measure, and resift with baking soda, salt, and spices; add alternately with milk to the first mixture. Beat well; pour into well-greased tube cake pan. Bake for about 55 minutes at 350°.

The Way Pocahontas County Cooks

Blackberry Cake

1/2 cup butter, softened
2 cups sugar
4 eggs
1/2 cup sour milk
2 teaspoons baking soda
4 cups flour
2 teaspoons cinnamon
1 teaspoon ground cloves
1 teaspoon nutmeg
2 cups cooked or canned blackberries

Cream butter and sugar; add well beaten eggs and milk to which baking soda has been added. Add flour and spices. Add berries and bake in 2 greased cake pans at 350° for 30–40 minutes, or fluted pan for 1 hour.

Gypsy, West Virginia 100th Anniversary Cookbook

Blackberry Cake

CAKE:

2½ cups flour
1 teaspoon salt
2 teaspoons baking powder
1 teaspoon baking soda
1 teaspoon cinnamon
1 teaspoon nutmeg
⅔ cup butter
3 eggs
1¼ cups sugar
1 teaspoon vanilla
1 cup blackberry juice
1 cup blackberries

Preheat oven to 350°. Sift together flour, salt, baking powder, baking soda, cinnamon, and nutmeg into a large bowl. Set aside. Cream together butter and eggs. Mix in sugar and vanilla. Alternate, adding flour mixture and blackberry juice to creamed mixture until well blended. Stir in blackberries. Pour into a greased and floured 9x13-inch cake pan. Bake at 350° for 30–35 minutes or until toothpick inserted in center of cake comes out clean. Remove from oven and cool on a wire rack.

CARAMEL FROSTING:

½ cup butter
1 cup firmly packed brown sugar
¼ teaspoon salt
¼ cup milk
2½ cups powdered sugar, sifted
½ teaspoon vanilla

Melt butter in a saucepan over low heat. Blend in brown sugar and salt. Cook over low heat 2 minutes, stirring constantly. Add milk and continue stirring until mixture comes to a boil. Remove from heat. Blend in sifted powdered sugar gradually. Add vanilla and mix. Thin with cream, if necessary. Spread on cooled Blackberry Cake.

Recipes for You & Your Best Friends

Luella's Blueberry Cake with Lemon Butter Sauce

This old-timey (sauce) recipe originally called for one cup butter and vinegar instead of lemon juice. If you're watching your fat intake, the cake tastes good by itself.

CAKE:

1 tablespoon butter
1 cup sugar
1 egg
2 cups flour
2 teaspoons baking powder
½ teaspoon salt
1 cup milk
2 cups fresh blueberries

Grease and flour a 9-inch-square cake pan. Cream butter and sugar. Add beaten egg into creamed mixture. Combine dry ingredients and add to egg mixture alternately with milk. Coat berries with a small amount of flour, then add to mixture. Bake at 375° for about 30 minutes.

LEMON BUTTER SAUCE:

2–4 tablespoons butter
¾ cup sugar
3 tablespoons cornstarch
1 cup water, divided
Juice of 2 lemons
Grated lemon rind
1 teaspoon vanilla

Melt butter and stir in sugar. Add ½ cup water, lemon juice and rind to melted butter mixture. Mix cornstarch with remaining water until dissolved. Add to melted butter mixture. Boil until clear. Take off heat and add vanilla. Pour over cake as you serve.

Take Two & Butter 'Em While They're Hot!

William Tompkins used natural gas to evaporate salt brine in 1841, thus becoming the first person in the United States to use natural gas for industrial purposes. The world's greatest gas well, "Big Moses" in Tyler County, was drilled in 1894. It produces 100 million cubic feet of gas per day.

Applesauce Cake

2/3 cup shortening, softened
1 1/4 cups sugar
1 cup brown sugar
3 eggs
1 3/4 cups unsweetened applesauce
3 cups flour, sifted
1/3 teaspoon baking powder
1 3/4 teaspoons baking soda
1 1/4 teaspoons cinnamon
1/2 teaspoon ground cloves
3/4 teaspoon allspice
1/4 teaspoon nutmeg
1 3/4 teaspoons salt
1/2 cup water or orange juice
1 1/2 cups raisins and dates, chopped
1 1/2 cups chopped walnuts

Cream shortening and sugars, then add eggs and applesauce; mix well. Sift dry ingredients, including spices; add alternately with water to applesauce mixture. Blend fruit and nuts into batter and bake in a greased 9x13-inch baking pan at 350° for 55–60 minutes.

Cakes...Cakes...and more Cakes

Apple Cake

2 cups sugar
2 teaspoons cinnamon
4 cups chopped apples
1 cup vegetable oil
2 teaspoons vanilla
2 eggs
1 teaspoon salt
3 cups flour
2 teaspoons baking soda
1 cup chopped nuts or dates

Pour sugar and cinnamon over apples. Let stand 1 hour. Mix vegetable oil, vanilla, eggs, and salt. Beat until creamy. Mix in flour, baking soda, and nuts or dates. Add apple mixture. Pour into a greased 9x13-inch baking pan.

GLAZE:
2 teaspoons flour
1 1/4 teaspoons cinnamon
1/4 cup butter, softened

Mix flour, cinnamon, and softened butter. Crumble together; sprinkle on top of cake. Bake at 350° for 40–45 minutes.

More...Home Town Recipes

Apple Cake in a Jar

2/3 cup shortening
2 2/3 cups sugar
4 eggs
1 teaspoon cinnamon
2 teaspoons baking soda
1/2 teaspoon baking powder
1 1/2 teaspoons salt
3 cups all-purpose flour
2/3 cup water
3 cups peeled, grated apples
2/3 cup raisins
2/3 cup chopped nuts (optional)

Mix ingredients together in order given. Sterilize 7–9 wide-mouth jars and lids (pints). Grease jars with shortening. Fill to 1/2 full and bake 45 minutes at 350°. As soon as cakes are done, remove jars 1 at a time from oven. Wipe rim of jars clean with a damp cloth and put on hot sterilized lid. Screw down lid. Cool. Cakes have a one-year shelf life.

Our Favorite Recipes

Gedeckter Birnenkuchen

(Covered Pear Cake)

5 1/2 ounces butter or margarine
1/2 cup sugar
3 eggs
1 1/3 cups flour
3/4 cup milk
4 tablespoons oats
3 teaspoons baking powder
1 tablespoon rum
1 tablespoon cocoa
1 teaspoon cinnamon
1 teaspoon nutmeg
2 1/2 pounds fresh pears (soft), or 1 large can pears

GLAZE:
Powdered sugar
Lemon juice

Mix together butter and sugar; add eggs, flour, milk, oats, and remaining ingredients except pears. The dough must be smooth. Butter a springform pan and place 2/3 of the dough on the bottom of the pan. Place pears (if using fresh pears, peel and core but do not cook) on top and cover with remaining dough. Preheat oven to 375° and bake cake for 1 hour. Let cool and cover with a mixture of powdered sugar and lemon juice.

West Virginia Librarians (bon) Appétit

Mandarin Orange Cake

CAKE:

1 package yellow cake mix
1 (11-ounce) can mandarin oranges
4 eggs
¼ cup oil

Combine cake mix, mandarin oranges, eggs, and oil. Beat 2 minutes at highest speed of electric mixer. Reduce speed to low; beat 1 minute. Pour batter into greased and floured 9x13-inch pan. Bake at 350° for 30 minutes. Cool completely.

TOPPING:

1 (12-ounce) carton Cool Whip®
1 (5½-ounce) package vanilla instant pudding
1 (20-ounce) can crushed pineapple, drained (reserve juice)

Combine all ingredients except reserved juice; beat 2 minutes at medium speed with electric mixer. Let stand 5 minutes; add enough pineapple juice for spreading consistency, if needed. Spread mixture over cool cake and chill at least 2 hours before serving. Store in refrigerator.

Down Memory Lane

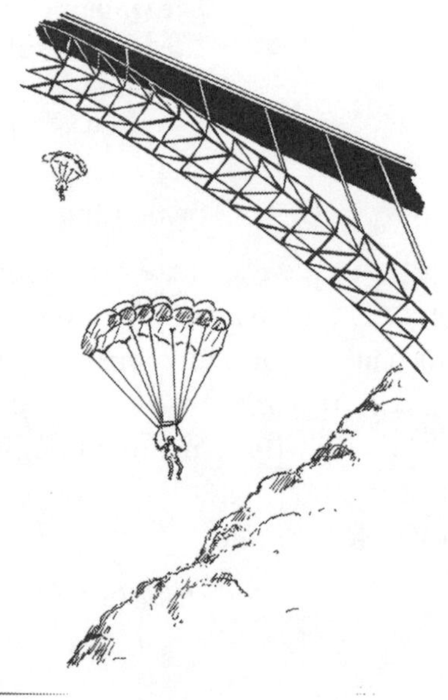

Banana Pineapple Cake

2 cups sugar
3 cups flour
1 teaspoon cinnamon
1 teaspoon baking soda
1 teaspoon salt
1½ teaspoons vanilla
2 cups diced bananas
1 (8-ounce) can crushed pineapple
1 cup oil
½ cup water

Preheat oven to 350°. In large bowl mix sugar, flour, cinnamon, baking soda, and salt. Add vanilla, bananas, pineapple, oil, and water. Mix well. *Do not beat.* Pour into greased and floured 10-inch tube pan. Bake for 1 hour and 20 minutes. Cool well before removing from pan.

More...Home Town Recipes

Banana Cake

½ cup shortening
1½ cups sugar
2 egg whites, beaten until fluffy
2 egg yolks
2 cups flour
¼ teaspoon baking powder
¾ teaspoon baking soda
½ teaspoon salt
¼ cup buttermilk
1 cup mashed bananas (about 3 medium)
1 teaspoon vanilla
½ cup chopped nuts

Cream shortening and sugar. Add egg whites and beat well, then add egg yolks. Sift flour, baking powder, baking soda, and salt together and then add to egg mixture. Mix in buttermilk, bananas, and vanilla. Add nuts and mix well. Pour into greased and floured cake pan. Bake at 350° for 30–35 minutes.

West Virginia Country Cooking

Banana Split Cake

1 (2-layer) banana cake mix
2 cups Cool Whip®, thawed, divided
1 cup fresh strawberries, sliced
1 (8¼-ounce) can crushed pineapple, well drained
1 (11- to 12-ounce) container fudge ice cream topping
½ cup chopped peanuts
Bananas for garnish
Lemon juice

Prepare banana cake mix according to package directions. Bake in 2 (8-inch) greased cake pans. Set aside to cool. Divide Cool Whip in half. Fold strawberries into half of Cool Whip and pineapple in other half. Heat and stir fudge topping until warm (not hot). Split cake layers in half. Place half on plate and cover with strawberry mixture. Place another half cake layer on top and cover with half of fudge mixture and half of peanuts. Place another half cake layer on top of peanuts and cover with pineapple mixture. Place last half cake layer on top and cover with remaining fudge and peanuts. Garnish with banana slices that have been dipped in lemon juice.

Heavenly Helpings

Hawaiian Splendor Sponge Cake

This is a very easy and moist cake to make.

2 cups flour
1½ cups sugar
1 teaspoon baking soda
¼ teaspoon salt
1 (20-ounce) can crushed pineapple, undrained
2 eggs, lightly beaten

Preheat oven to 350°. In large bowl, combine flour, sugar, baking soda, and salt. Add undrained pineapple and eggs. Stir until combined. Pour batter into a greased 9x13-inch baking pan. Bake in preheated oven 30 minutes or until wooden pick inserted in center comes out clean. Cool in pan on wire rack 10 minutes. Spread Golden Frosting over hot cake in pan. Serves 12.

GOLDEN FROSTING:

¾ cup sugar
¾ cup evaporated milk
½ cup butter or margarine
1 teaspoon vanilla extract
½ cup chopped nuts
½ cup flaked coconut

In saucepan combine sugar, evaporated milk, butter or margarine, and vanilla extract. Bring to a boil; boil 7 minutes, stirring, until mixture is thick. Stir in chopped nuts and flaked coconut.

A Gracious Plenty

Key Lime Cake

1 (18.25-ounce) package lemon supreme cake mix
1 (3.4-ounce) lemon instant pudding mix
4 eggs
½ cup water
¾ cup key lime juice, divided
½ cup oil
2 cups sifted powdered sugar
Whipped cream

Combine cake mix, pudding mix, eggs, water, ½ cup lime juice, and oil. Beat 2 minutes and pour into greased and floured 9x13x2-inch pan. Bake at 350° for 35 minutes. Combine sugar and ¼ cup juice. Drizzle juice mix over the cake. Chill and serve with whipped cream.

Best Taste of Fairmont

Lemon Cake

1 box lemon Jell-O®
1 cup hot water
1 box lemon cake mix
¾ cup oil
4 eggs
1 cup powdered sugar
1½ teaspoons lemon juice

Dissolve Jell-O in hot water until clear. Mix cake mix, oil, and Jell-O mixture together. Add eggs 1 at a time. Pour into lightly greased 9x13-inch pan. Bake in a 350° oven for 35 minutes. While still hot, prick with fork. Glaze with powdered sugar dissolved in lemon juice to make light glaze.

Our Best Home Cooking

West Virginia Gold Cake

2 sticks margarine
2 cups sugar
5 eggs
1 tablespoon each: vanilla, lemon, and orange extract
½ teaspoon almond extract
2 cups flour

Cream margarine with sugar until light and fluffy. Add eggs, 1 at a time. Add vanilla, lemon, orange, and almond extracts. Add flour gradually. Bake in greased and floured 9-inch cake pan for 1 hour at 350°. Cool 10 minutes before removing from pan.

Serving Our Best

The first bareknuckle world heavyweight boxing championship was held on June 1, 1880, near Colliers. Paddy Ryan won an undisputed title by knocking out Joe Goss of England in the 85th round.

Mother's Easter Cake

1 package yellow cake mix
1 (20-ounce) can crushed pineapple, in juice
¾ cup sugar
2 (3½-ounce) packages vanilla instant pudding
3 cups milk
1 cup Dream Whip® or Cool Whip®
1 cup coconut, toasted

Bake cake in greased 9x13-inch pan according to directions. When cake is done, prick with fork at 1-inch intervals. Combine pineapple with juice and sugar. Cook over medium heat until thick and syrupy. Stir occasionally. Pour pineapple mixture over cake and spread evenly. Cool completely. Combine pudding mix with milk; blend until thick. Spread over cake. Spread prepared Dream Whip or Cool Whip over cake. Refrigerate for 24 hours. Before serving, sprinkle with toasted coconut.

Heavenly Helpings

Honey Bun Cake

1 yellow cake mix
4 eggs
¾ cup oil
1 (8-ounce) carton sour cream
½ cup sugar
1 cup brown sugar
1 teaspoon cinnamon

Combine cake mix, eggs, oil, sour cream, and ½ cup sugar. Pour into greased 9x13-inch pan. Mix brown sugar and cinnamon and sprinkle over cake, then swirl. Bake at 350° for 1 hour.

ICING:
1 cup powdered sugar
5 tablespoons milk
½ teaspoon vanilla

Mix Icing ingredients and pour over cake while still hot.

Feeding the Flock—MOPs of Westminister

Peanut Butter Sheet Cake

½ cup peanut butter
½ cup oil
1 stick margarine
1 cup water
2 cups sugar
2 cups flour
½ cup milk
2 eggs, beaten
1 teaspoon baking soda
1 teaspoon vanilla

Boil together peanut butter, oil, margarine, and water. Remove from heat and add sugar, flour, milk, eggs, baking soda, and vanilla. (This is a very thin batter.) Pour into greased 9x13-inch pan and bake 20–25 minutes in 375° oven. Begin Peanut Butter Frosting.

PEANUT BUTTER FROSTING:
½ cup peanut butter
⅓ cup milk
1 stick margarine
1 pound powdered sugar
1 teaspoon vanilla

Boil together the peanut butter, milk, and margarine. Remove from heat and add powdered sugar and vanilla. Beat until smooth and spread on cake which has cooled slightly.

Cakes...Cakes...and more Cakes

West Virginia Black Walnut Cake

½ cup butter
½ cup vegetable shortening
2 cups sugar
5 eggs, separated
1 cup buttermilk
1 teaspoon baking soda
2 cups all-purpose flour
1 teaspoon vanilla
1½ cups chopped black walnuts
1 (3-ounce) can flaked coconut
½ teaspoon cream of tartar

Cream butter and shortening. Gradually add sugar and beat well. Add egg yolks; beat well. Combine buttermilk and baking soda; add flour to creamed mixture alternately with buttermilk. Stir in vanilla. Add walnuts and coconut. Beat egg whites and cream of tartar until stiff peaks form. Fold into batter. Bake in 3 greased and floured round cake pans at 350° for 30 minutes. Frost with Cream Cheese Frosting and decorate with chopped walnuts.

CREAM CHEESE FROSTING:

1 (8-ounce) package cream cheese, softened
1 (3-ounce) package cream cheese, softened
¾ cup butter
6¾ cups powdered sugar
1½ teaspoons vanilla
Walnuts for garnish

In mixer bowl, cream both packages of cream cheese and butter. Add sugar and vanilla. Beat well. Frost cake and decorate with walnuts.

Cooking for the New Era

West Virginia's smallest church is located south of Buckhannon. The building, about 10 feet by 12 feet, was constructed by community volunteers in memory of Randy Brown, a young boy who passed away. You'll need to duck your head upon entering!

West Virginia Apple Black Walnut Cake

4 cups coarsely chopped raw apples
2 cups sugar
1 teaspoon salt
2 cups sifted all-purpose flour
2 teaspoons baking soda
1 teaspoon cinnamon
½ teaspoon nutmeg
3 eggs
¾ cup vegetable oil
2 teaspoons vanilla
1 cup chopped black walnuts

Combine apples and sugar; let stand. Sift together flour, salt, baking soda, and spices. Beat eggs slightly, then beat in oil and vanilla. Stir in apple mixture alternately with dry ingredients. Add walnuts. Pour into greased and floured 9x13x2-inch baking pan. Bake at 350° for about an hour or until done. Cool, then cover with Lemon Butter Frosting.

LEMON BUTTER FROSTING:

4 tablespoons butter or margarine, softened
3 cups confectioners' (powdered) sugar
2 tablespoons lemon juice
1 teaspoon lemon extract
Few grains of salt
1 or 2 tablespoons cold water

Cream butter; add sugar gradually, creaming thoroughly. Beat in lemon juice, lemon extract, salt and enough water to make of spreading consistency. Spread on cool cake. Makes about 3½ cups frosting.

More than Beans and Cornbread

The 7' 2" bronze and metal Coal Miners Statue stands as an everlasting tribute to coal miners—past, present and future—on the front lawn of the Boone County Courthouse in Madison. The Coal River Council of the Holmes Safety Association raised funds to erect the statue as a memorial to an industry that originated in Boone County.

Chocolate Cake

1 stick margarine, softened
1 cup sugar
4 eggs
1 (16-ounce) can Hershey's® Chocolate Syrup
1 cup cake flour
Pinch of salt
½ teaspoon baking powder
1 teaspoon vanilla

Cream margarine with sugar. Add eggs, 1 at a time, and chocolate syrup, cake flour, salt, baking powder, and vanilla. Stir well. Bake in a 9x13-inch greased and floured pan for 30–40 minutes at 350°.

TOPPING:
1 cup sugar
1 stick margarine
⅓ cup cream
½ cup chocolate chips

Bring sugar, margarine, and cream to boil. Boil for 60 seconds and remove from heat. Add chocolate chips and beat with electric mixer until smooth. Pour hot Topping over hot cake.

Just Plain Country

Black Forest Cake

½ cup butter, softened
1½ cups firmly packed light brown sugar
3 eggs
4 squares unsweetened chocolate, melted and cooled
1 teaspoon vanilla
1¼ cups flour
1 teaspoon baking powder
½ teaspoon baking soda
1 cup milk
2 cups heavy cream
2 tablespoons sugar
1 (21-ounce) can cherry pie filling, drained

Preheat oven to 375°. Grease and flour 3 (9-inch) round cake pans. In a large mixing bowl, cream butter and brown sugar for approximately 5 minutes or until completely combined. Beat in eggs, 1 at a time. Beat in chocolate and vanilla. Sift flour, baking powder, and baking soda together. Beat into chocolate mixture alternately with the milk. Spread batter into prepared baking pans. Bake 15–17 minutes or until toothpick comes out clean when tested. Turn onto cake rack to cool.

In a large bowl, beat cream with 2 tablespoons sugar until stiff peaks form. Spread ¾ cup whipped cream on first layer, top with second layer and spread with ¾ cup more whipped cream. Place third layer on top of cream. Reserve 1 cup whipped cream. Frost cake with remaining whipped cream. Use reserved whipped cream to form a decorative border around the outer edge of the cake top. Place cherries on top of cake inside the ring created by the whipped cream.

Feeding the Flock—HCCLA

The world's largest sycamore tree is located on the Back Fork of the Elk River in Webster Springs.

Texas Sheet Cake

4 tablespoons cocoa
2 sticks margarine
1 cup water
2 cups flour
2 cups sugar
½ teaspoon salt
1 teaspoon baking soda
2 eggs
½ cup sour cream

Bring cocoa, margarine, and water to boil. Remove from heat and add flour, sugar, salt, baking soda, eggs, and sour cream. Pour into lightly greased 10x15x1-inch jellyroll pan and bake at 375° for 20–22 minutes. Immediately start icing.

ICING:
1 stick margarine
4 tablespoons cocoa
6 tablespoons milk
1 cup nuts
1 pound powdered sugar
1 teaspoon vanilla

Bring margarine, cocoa, and milk to boil. Remove from heat and add nuts, powdered sugar, and vanilla. Mix well and spread on cake that has cooled 5 minutes.

Cakes...Cakes...and more Cakes

Coal Miner's Daughter's Cake

This recipe is from Dolly Parton and appeared in an issue of Country Music Magazine.

1 box German chocolate cake mix
1 can condensed milk (nonfat may be used)
1 jar caramel topping
1 cup Cool Whip®

Bake cake according to package directions in sheet cake pan. While cake is warm, poke holes halfway into cake about 1 inch apart using end of wooden spoon. Pour condensed milk into holes. Pour caramel over cake and refrigerate. When completely cooled, top with Cool Whip. If desired it can be topped with crushed Heath candy bars.

Christ Reformed Church Historical Cookbook

Milky Way Cake

CAKE:

2 sticks butter, divided
8 Milky Way® Bars
2 cups sugar
4 eggs
2½ cups flour
½ teaspoon baking soda
1 cup buttermilk
1½ cups pecans
½ teaspoon vanilla

Melt 1 stick butter and 8 Milky Way Bars in double boiler. Beat until smooth. In a bowl, cream 1 stick butter and sugar. Add 1 egg at a time, beating well after each addition. In another bowl, sift flour and baking soda. Add this alternately with buttermilk to the creamed mixture. Add candy mixture, pecans, and vanilla. Bake in greased and floured Bundt pan at 325° for about 1½ hours, or in a 9x13-inch pan for 1 hour.

ICING:

3 Milky Way® Bars
1 stick butter
2 tablespoons milk
¾ box powdered sugar

Melt Milky Way Bars, butter, and milk in double boiler. Gradually add powdered sugar, beating until smooth. Pour over cake.

West Virginia Librarians (bon) Appétit

Custard Devil's Food Cake

CUSTARD:

3 ounces unsweetened chocolate
1/2 cup milk
1 egg, beaten
2/3 cup sugar

Cook over medium heat until thick and set aside.

CAKE:

1/2 cup shortening or butter
1 cup sugar
1 egg
2 cups cake flour
1/4 teaspoon salt
1 teaspoon baking soda
1 cup milk
1 teaspoon vanilla

Cream shortening and sugar. Add egg. Sift together flour, salt, and baking soda, then add alternately with milk. Add vanilla. Mix in cooled Custard. Pour into 2 greased and floured 8-inch cake pans. Bake at 350° for 25–30 minutes. Cool and frost, if desired.

West Virginia Country Cooking

Cream Cheese Frosting

3 ounces cream cheese, softened
1/2 cup butter, softened
2 cups powdered sugar
1 teaspoon vanilla

Mix cream cheese and butter; add sugar and vanilla and mix until smooth. Spread on cooled cake.

West Virginia Country Cooking

West Virginia leads the nation in underground coal production. Coal occurs in 53 of West Virginia's 55 counties. Surface mines account for over 50 million tons of production each year.

Bavarian Cream Cake

1 envelope unflavored gelatin
½ cup cold water
4 eggs, separated
1 pint milk
1 cup sugar
2 tablespoons flour
Pinch salt
1 teaspoon vanilla extract
1 teaspoon almond extract
1½ pints whipping cream
1 angel food cake, torn into chunks
Additional whipped cream for garnish
Coconut, almonds, strawberries, bananas, peaches for garnish (optional)

Dissolve gelatin in cold water. To make custard, combine egg yolks, milk, sugar, flour, and salt in top of double boiler and cook until it thickens on spoon. While hot, dissolve the gelatin and water mixture in the custard and stir until well distributed through the custard. Cool. When cold, add vanilla and almond extract.

Beat egg whites until stiff and dry, then fold into the custard. Beat the whipping cream and fold into mixture. Rinse an angel food cake pan with cold water and leave a few drops in it; pour ⅓ of custard on bottom. When it is thick enough, drop bits of angel food cake into it. Completely cover this layer of custard with cake (approximately half the cake). Cover cake with another ⅓ custard. Repeat cake layer and remaining ⅓ custard. Set this in the refrigerator overnight, or make in the morning to serve at night. Turn mold out onto plate.

After it is firm, you may "ice" it with whipped cream, which has been sweetened with sugar to taste. This may be topped with coconut, almonds, strawberries, bananas, or peaches, if desired.

Cookin' in a Coal Camp

Chocolate Bavarian Torte

1 package devil's food cake mix (without pudding)
1 (8-ounce) package cream cheese, softened
2/3 cup packed brown sugar
1 teaspoon vanilla
1/8 teaspoon salt
2 cups whipping cream, whipped
2 tablespoons grated semisweet chocolate

Mix and bake cake according to package directions using 2 (9-inch) greased cake pans. Cool in pans for 15 minutes. Remove from pans and cool completely on wire rack. In mixing bowl, beat cream cheese, sugar, vanilla, and salt until fluffy. Fold in whipped cream. Split each cake into 2 horizontal layers (making 4 layers); place 1 on serving plate. Spread with 1/4 of cream mixture. Sprinkle with 1/4 of chocolate. Repeat layers. Cover and refrigerate 8 hours or overnight.

Treasured Recipes

Italian Creme Cake

1 stick margarine, softened
1/2 cup shortening
2 cups sugar
5 eggs, separated
2 cups flour
1 teaspoon baking soda
1 cup buttermilk
1 teaspoon vanilla
1 small can coconut
1 cup nuts (optional)

Cream margarine and shortening; add sugar and beat until smooth. Add egg yolks and beat again. Alternately add flour, baking soda, and buttermilk. Mix well. Fold in stiffly beaten egg whites, coconut, and nuts, if using. Bake in 3 (8-inch) greased pans at 350° for 25 minutes.

FROSTING:

1 (8-ounce) package cream cheese, softened
1 (1-pound) box powdered sugar
1/2 cup margarine, softened
1 teaspoon vanilla
1/2 cup chopped nuts

Mix cream cheese, powdered sugar, margarine, vanilla, and chopped nuts. Mix until smooth. Spread on cooled cake.

More...Home Town Recipes

French Cream Cake

FIRST LAYER:

1 cup flour
1 stick butter, melted
1 cup chopped nuts (reserve a few for topping)

Mix flour, butter, and nuts. Pat into 9x13-inch pan. Bake 10–12 minutes. Let cool.

SECOND LAYER:

1 (8-ounce) package cream cheese, softened
1 cup powdered sugar
1 large container Cool Whip®, divided

Blend cream cheese and sugar; fold in ½ of Cool Whip. Spread over crust.

THIRD LAYER:

2 small boxes chocolate instant pudding
3 cups milk
1 teaspoon vanilla

Mix pudding, milk, and vanilla. Spread over Second Layer. Spread remaining Cool Whip on top and sprinkle with nuts.

A Taste of Fayette County

ESPN's sports show, "*Scholastic,*" once picked the Dots of Poca High School in Poca as the best sports team nickname in America. The team nickname (Poca Dots) was suggested by a sportswriter for the Charleston Gazette in 1928.

Mom's Shortcake

Prepare biscuit dough as suggested on Bisquick® box, adding about 1/4 cup sugar to every 2 cups of dough; knead, and divide in half. Generously butter a cookie sheet and your hands. Spread half the dough very thinly on the cookie sheet, then spread on more butter. Butter your hands again and spread out the remaining dough on top of the first. Bake 8–10 minutes at 450°. Serve with sliced, sweetened strawberries, and whipped cream or milk.

Cakes...Cakes...and more Cakes

Gumdrop Cake

1 cup margarine
2 cups sugar
2 eggs, beaten
4 cups flour
1 teaspoon cinnamon
1/4 teaspoon nutmeg
1/4 teaspoon ground cloves
1/4 teaspoon salt
1 tablespoon hot water
1 teaspoon baking soda
1 teaspoon vanilla
1 1/2 cups applesauce
1–2 pounds gumdrops and orange slices (cut in small pieces)
1 pound white raisins
2 cups chopped nuts

Cream margarine and sugar; add eggs. Sift together flour, cinnamon, nutmeg, cloves, and salt, reserving some flour mixture for raisins, nuts, and candy. Mix applesauce, hot water, baking soda, and vanilla; add to creamed mixture, alternating with flour mixture. Sift remaining flour mixture over candy, raisins, and nuts to keep them separated. Add to cake. Bake at 300° for 2 hours in tube pan. Cool; wrap in foil.

Down Memory Lane

Oatmeal Cake

COCONUT TOPPING:

½ cup brown sugar
1 stick margarine, melted
¼ cup evaporated milk
1 teaspoon vanilla
1 cup coconut
1 cup chopped nuts (optional)

Mix brown sugar, margarine, evaporated milk, vanilla, coconut, and nuts, if desired.

CAKE:

1 cup quick oats
1½ cups hot water
1 teaspoon baking soda
1 cup brown sugar
1 cup sugar
½ stick margarine, softened
½ teaspoon cinnamon
½ teaspoon salt
2 eggs
½ cup cooking oil
2 cups flour

Mix quick oats, hot water, and baking soda; let cool. Cream together sugars, margarine, cinnamon, salt, eggs, oil, and flour. Mix and add to oat mixture. Bake in a greased and floured 9x13-inch baking pan for 20 minutes in 375° oven. Remove from oven; spread Coconut Topping on hot cake and return to oven for 10–20 minutes longer.

Cakes...Cakes...and more Cakes

Molasses Stack Cake

1 cup butter or margarine, softened
1 cup sugar
1 cup molasses
3 eggs
5 cups all-purpose flour
1 teaspoon baking soda
1 teaspoon salt
1 cup buttermilk
Applesauce or apple butter

Cream together butter and sugar till light. Stir in molasses; add eggs, 1 at a time, beating after each. Stir together flour, baking soda, and salt; add to creamed mixture alternately with milk, beating after each addition. Cut wax paper rounds to fit 8-inch cake pans. Grease and flour. Pour 1⅓ cups batter into each pan. (Refrigerate remaining batter.) Bake at 350° until done, about 15 minutes. Remove from pans and cool on rack.

Wash pans, grease and flour. Repeat with remaining batter. I usually only get 5 layers unless I make them very thin. I find that you can put the batter in the pans, sprinkle with flour, and flour your hands and just pat it to the edges. Stack cakes with applesauce or apple butter.

Note: If using store-bought applesauce or apple butter, you might want to add a little cinnamon and nutmeg and a little sugar, and cook it down a little.

Keaton Mills Family Cookbook

Penuche Frosting

1 cup sugar
1 cup packed brown sugar
¼ cup milk
3 tablespoons butter
1 teaspoon vanilla
1½ cups powdered sugar

Combine sugars, milk, and butter, and cook in a double boiler 3 minutes. Cool to lukewarm and add vanilla. Beat in powdered sugar.

Cakes...Cakes...and more Cakes

Best Ever Carrot Cake

1½ cups oil
1¾ cups sugar
3 eggs
2 cups all-purpose flour
2 teaspoons baking soda
½ teaspoon salt
3 teaspoons cinnamon
1 teaspoon ground cloves
1 (8-ounce) can crushed pineapple
2 cups grated carrots
1 cup chopped nuts

Beat together oil, sugar, and eggs until well combined. Sift together flour, baking soda, salt, cinnamon, and cloves. Add to egg and sugar mixture, mixing well. Drain pineapple well; add carrots, nuts, and pineapple to mixture. Blend to mix well. Pour batter into a greased and floured 9- or 10-inch tube pan. Bake at 350° for 1 hour or until done. Let cool on rack. Cover with Frosting.

FROSTING:

2 (8-ounce) packages cream cheese, softened
1 cup powdered sugar
1 teaspoon vanilla
Coconut

Cream together cream cheese, powdered sugar, and vanilla, blending well. Spread over cake. Sprinkle with coconut.

Our Daily Bread

Cranberry Halloween Cake

1 package yellow or white cake mix
Grated rind of 1 orange

Prepare cake according to mix directions, adding the orange rind. While cake is baking in 2 (8-inch) greased and floured cake pans, prepare Cranberry Filling.

CRANBERRY FILLING:
2 cups fresh cranberries, rinsed and drained
⅓ cup orange juice
½ cup sugar
1 (14-ounce) package creamy white frosting mix (or canned prepared frosting)
Red and yellow food coloring

Combine cranberries, juice, and sugar, and boil for 10 minutes. Cool, then chill. Cool cake layers on a rack 10 minutes; remove from pans and finish cooling. Spread Cranberry Filling between layers. Prepare frosting mix according to directions, adding enough food coloring to make frosting a bright orange. Spread frosting on sides and top and decorate with Halloween candies.

Note: If cranberry seeds are a problem, cut cranberries in half and float in water; seeds will sink to the bottom of the bowl.

Cakes...Cakes...and more Cakes

The unique three-tiered Mannington Round Barn, originally built in 1912 and used as a dairy barn, is the only restored round barn in the state.

Strawberry Jelly Roll

4 eggs
1 tablespoon hot water
1 teaspoon vanilla, divided
1 cup sugar
3/4 cup flour
1 teaspoon baking powder
1/4 teaspoon salt
1/4 cup powdered sugar, divided
1 cup heavy cream
1 pint strawberries, sliced

Preheat oven to 375°. In a large bowl, beat eggs and water until thick and light colored. Add 1/2 teaspoon vanilla; gradually beat in sugar. In another bowl, sift flour, baking powder, and salt. Sift again onto egg mixture, then gently fold in. Grease 15 1/2 x 10 1/2 x 1-inch jellyroll pan. Line with wax paper; grease paper. Spread batter gently and evenly in pan. Bake 12–15 minutes or until golden brown.

Meanwhile, on a clean kitchen towel, sift 1–2 tablespoons powdered sugar to form a 15 1/2 x 10 1/2-inch rectangle; invert pan to turn cake onto sugared towel. Carefully peel off wax paper. Trim off any uneven edges of cake. Starting with narrow end, roll up cake and towel together. Place seam-side-down on a rack and let cool completely.

To prepare filling, whip cream with 2 tablespoons powdered sugar and 1/2 teaspoon vanilla until stiff. Unroll cake. Spread cream leaving 1/4-inch border around edges. Reserve 4 or 5 strawberry slices for garnish. Arrange remaining berries in a single layer on cream. Roll up cake, gently removing towel. Place seam-side-down on serving platter. Dust with powdered sugar. Garnish with rerserved strawberries. Slice and serve.

Dutch Pantry Cookin'

The New River Gorge Bridge near Fayetteville is the world's longest spanning, steel single-arch bridge.

Luscious Almond Amaretto Cheesecake

CRUST:

40 vanilla wafers
¾ cup toasted slivered almonds
⅓ cup sugar
¼ cup plus 2 tablespoons butter, melted

Combine first 3 ingredients in processor and process until crushed. Add butter and process until blended. If no processor, crush wafers by hand and mix all together. Press into bottom and 1¾ inches up side of 9-inch springform or regular cake pan; set aside.

FILLING:

3 (8-ounce) packages cream cheese, softened
1 cup plus 1 tablespoon sugar, divided
4 eggs
¼ cup plus 1 tablespoon amaretto, divided
⅓ cup heavy cream
2 teaspoons vanilla, divided
2 cups sour cream
Whipped cream, fresh raspberries, and toasted almonds for garnish

Beat cream cheese and 1 cup sugar. Add eggs 1 at a time. Beat in ¼ cup amaretto, cream, and 1 teaspoon vanilla; beat well. Pour into crust. Bake at 350° for 30 minutes, then reduce oven to 225° and bake 1 hour. Cool on rack 5 minutes.

Combine sour cream, 1 tablespoon sugar, 1 tablespoon amaretto, and 1 teaspoon vanilla. Spread evenly over cheesecake. Bake an additional 5 minutes. Remove from pan and cool 30 minutes. Cover and refrigerate overnight.

For garnish, at serving time, pipe rosette of whipped cream at intervals around edge. Place a raspberry on top of whipped cream. Sprinkle with almonds and serve. If you don't want to pipe the cream, just either spread it over the top or drop in dollops by spoon over cheesecake.

Enjoy at Your Own Risk! Cookbook

Chocolate Turtle Cheesecake

1 (7-ounce) package caramels, peeled
1/4 cup evaporated milk
3/4 cup chopped pecans, divided
1 (9-inch) chocolate-crumb pie crust
2 (3-ounce) packages cream cheese, softened
1/2 cup sour cream
1 1/4 cups milk
1 (3.9-ounce) package chocolate instant pudding mix
1/2 cup fudge topping

Place caramels and evaporated milk in a heavy saucepan. Heat over medium-low heat, stirring continually, until smooth, about 5 minutes. Stir in 1/2 cup chopped pecans. Pour into pie crust. Combine cream cheese, sour cream, and milk in blender. Process until smooth. Add pudding mix; process for about 30 seconds longer. Pour pudding mixture over caramel layer, covering evenly. Chill, loosely covered, until set, about 15 minutes. Drizzle fudge topping over pudding layer in a decorative pattern. Sprinkle top of cake with remaining pecans. Chill, loosely covered, until serving time.

Dutch Pantry Simply Sweets

COOKIES *and* CANDIES

PHOTO BY DAVID FATTALEH, COURTESY OF WEST VIRGINIA DIVISION OF TOURISM.

Sometimes known as the General Store or the Mercantile, the country store was the hub of day-to-day life in a West Virginia town. The Country Store at the Heritage Farm Museum and Village in Huntington was the first building completed there.

Mama's Raisin-Filled Cookies

1 cup shortening
2 cups sugar
1 cup sour milk*
5–5½ cups flour
1 teaspoon baking soda
1 teaspoon baking powder
1 teaspoon vanilla

Cream shortening and sugar. Combine 5 cups flour, baking soda, and baking powder; add creamed mixture and remaining ingredients. Add extra flour as needed to make a quite sticky dough. Refrigerate overnight.

Roll out half the dough on lightly floured board, thin. Cut with round cookie cutter and place on lightly greased cookie sheet. Place a teaspoonful of Mama's Raisin Filling on each. Roll remaining dough and cut with a doughnut cutter. Place on top of filled cookie. Bake at 350° for 10–15 minutes, or until lightly brown.

MAMA'S RAISIN FILLING:

1 (1-pound) box raisins
2 cups water
1 teaspoon vinegar

Grind raisins in food chopper (or in water in the blender). In a saucepan, add 2 cups water to raisins, bring to boil and add vinegar. Cook about 10 minutes and thicken with a thin paste of flour and water.

***Note:** To make sour milk, add 2 tablespoons lemon juice to sweet milk

Casseroles, Meats and Fish...Cookies

An abundance of trails, beautiful scenery and a variety of terrain make West Virginia a world class destination for mountain biking enthusiasts.

Raisin-Filled Cookies

COOKIES:
1 cup sugar
1 egg
½ cup milk
1 teaspoon vanilla
½ cup butter, softened
3½ cups flour
2 teaspoons cream of tartar
1 teaspoon baking soda

Cream sugar, egg, milk, vanilla, and butter. Add flour, cream of tartar, and baking soda. Mix well. Roll out thinly and cut out using a round cookie cutter.

FILLING:
1 cup raisins
1 cup sugar
1 cup water
2 tablespoons flour
¼ teaspoon salt

Grind raisins. Combine raisins, sugar, water, flour, and salt in a saucepan. Cook until very thick. Spoon 1 teaspoonful of Filling on ½ of the cut-out Cookies. Use remaining Cookies as tops and crimp edges to seal. Make small slits on the top cookie. Bake at 350° until lightly browned, 10–15 minutes.

Recipes for You & Your Best Friends

Best Bug Cookies

Shape this brown and white cookie dough into cute, crawly bugs. Decorate them, bake them and best of all, eat them.

½ cup margarine or butter
1¾ cups all-purpose flour, divided
½ cup sugar
½ cup brown sugar
¼ cup dairy sour cream
1 egg
1 teaspoon vanilla
½ teaspoon baking soda
¼ teaspoon salt
1 (1-ounce) square unsweetened chocolate, melted and cooled
Assorted nuts
Raisins

Beat margarine with an electric mixer on low to medium speed about 30 seconds or until softened. Add about ½ of the flour, all of the sugar, brown sugar, sour cream, egg, vanilla, baking soda, and salt. Beat on low to medium speed until thoroughly combined, scraping the sides of the bowl often. Then, beat or stir in remaining flour. Divide dough in half. Stir cooled chocolate into one half. (If dough is sticky, cover and chill about 2 hours.)

To form bugs, drop vanilla and chocolate dough by rounded teaspoonfuls onto ungreased cookie sheets so that mounds of dough just touch. Keep bugs 3 inches apart. Decorate as bugs with nuts, raisins or little blobs of dough. Bake in 375° oven for 8–10 minutes or until vanilla part of cookie is golden. Remove from cookie sheets. Cool on wire rack. Makes about 20.

For the Love of Kids

West Virginia's coal miners came from all over the world. African-Americans fleeing the deep South worked alongside European immigrants searching for a better life. More than 100,000 miners labored underground during the industry's glory years.

Lizzies

This is a particularly colorful cookie that has the essence of a fruitcake. The dough mixture simply holds the raisins, pecans, citron, and cherries together.

3 cups seedless raisins
½ cup bourbon
1½ cups all-purpose flour
1½ teaspoons baking soda
1½ teaspoons cinnamon
1½ teaspoons nutmeg
1½ teaspoons powdered cloves
¼ cup margarine, softened
½ cup lightly packed brown sugar
2 eggs
4 cups pecan halves
½ pound diced citron
1¼ cups whole candied cherries

Place raisins in a bowl; add bourbon. Mix well and let stand for 1 hour. Sift together flour, baking soda, cinnamon, nutmeg, and cloves. Place margarine in a mixing bowl; add brown sugar and eggs. Beat until fluffy. Add flour mixture and blend until smooth. Stir in raisins, pecans, citron, and cherries. Drop from teaspoon onto greased cookie sheets. Bake at 325° for 15 minutes or until firm. Makes 7–8 dozen cookies. Store in airtight container. Can be frozen.

West Virginia Librarians (bon) Appétit

Texas Lizzies

1/2 pound butter, softened
2 cups dark brown sugar
4 eggs, well beaten
1/2 cup thick peach juice
3 cups plain flour
1 teaspoon cinnamon
1 teaspoon nutmeg
3 teaspoons baking soda
1/2 pound candied cherries (red and green)
1/2 pound candied pineapple (1/4 white and 1/4 green)
1/4 pound white seedless raisins
3/4 pound dark seedless raisins
3/4 pound English walnuts or 1 1/2 pounds black walnuts
3/4 pound pecans

Cream butter and sugar. Add well-beaten eggs and peach juice; mix well. Add flour, spices, and baking soda; mix well. Add fruit (cut into small pieces) and nuts. Work with hands until well mixed. Chill overnight. Drop from spoon 2 inches apart. Bake in 350° oven for 20 minutes or until done. Will keep in refrigerator for a month. Bake as you need.

Home Cookin'

Pecan Crispies

Good. Easy to make.

1/2 cup butter, softened
6 tablespoons brown sugar
6 tablespoons sugar
1 egg
1/2 teaspoon vanilla
1 1/4 cups all-purpose flour
1 teaspoon baking powder
1/4 teaspoon baking soda
1/4 teaspoon salt
1 cup chopped pecans

Cream butter and sugars until light. Beat in egg and vanilla. Sift dry ingredients together. Blend into creamed mixture. Stir in pecans. Drop by teaspoon on ungreased cookie sheet. Bake at 350° for 10–12 minutes. Cool slightly before removing from pan. Makes 3 1/2 dozen.

Third Wednesday Homemakers Volume II

Almond Cookies

¾ pound butter, softened
2½ cups brown sugar
2½ cups sugar
4 or 5 eggs
3 tablespoons honey
1 tablespoon almond extract
6 cups flour
1 teaspoon baking powder
1 teaspoon baking soda
1 small bag coconut
1 pound slivered almonds

Cream butter, sugars, eggs, honey, and extract. Add dry ingredients, coconut, and almonds. Make into rolls and chill. Slice and bake at 350° for 12–15 minutes.

Treasures from Heaven

Aunt Ada's Oatmeal Cookies

1 cup butter
1 cup brown sugar
1 cup sugar
2 eggs
1 teaspoon vanilla
1 cup flour
1 teaspoon baking soda
1 teaspoon salt
½ cup chopped walnuts
3 cups oats (not quick)

Cream butter and sugars; add eggs, and vanilla. Add dry ingredients, then nuts and oats. Grease a cookie sheet and place small spoonfuls far apart, as these cookies need room to spread out. Bake at 350° for 10–15 minutes until browned. While warm (but not hot), remove cookies to cool on wire cookie racks. If they stick to pan, just warm them up a bit to remove them. You'll need to wash and regrease your cookie sheet after each batch (or use parchment paper) for best results. Keep in a tin or they will lose their crunch.

Take Two & Butter 'Em While They're Hot!

In West Virginia, 99% of the electricity comes from coal. More than 56% of the nation's electricity is generated from coal.

Yellow Cornmeal Cookies

¾ cup butter or margarine
¾ cup sugar
1 egg
1½ cups flour
½ cup cornmeal
1 teaspoon baking powder
¼ teaspoon salt
1 teaspoon vanilla
½ cup raisins (optional)

Mix butter or margarine and sugar in large bowl. Add egg and beat well. Add rest of ingredients and mix well. Drop by teaspoons onto a greased baking pan. Bake at 350° for about 15 minutes or until lightly brown. Makes 3 dozen cookies.

Tyrand Cooperative Ministries Cookbook

Foothill House Sweet Dreams

2 sticks unsalted butter
1½ cups firmly packed brown sugar
1 egg, room temperature
1 teaspoon vanilla
2 cups flour
1 teaspoon baking soda
1 teaspoon cinnamon
1 teaspoon ground ginger
½ teaspoon salt
1 (12-ounce) package semisweet chocolate chips
1 cup chopped walnuts
1 cup powdered sugar

Cream butter using an electric mixer. Beat in brown sugar, egg, and vanilla. Combine dry ingredients. Blend into butter mixture. Fold in chocolate chips and walnuts. Refrigerate until firm, or overnight. Preheat oven to 375°. Lightly grease cookie sheet. Break off small piece of dough and roll in palm until 1-inch round. Dredge in powdered sugar and arrange on cookie sheet approximately 2 inches apart. Bake 10 minutes. Let cool on pan for 5 minutes, then transfer to racks to finish cooling. Store in airtight containers.

Cookin' in a Coal Camp

Spell-Binders

1½ cups all-purpose flour
1½ teaspoons baking powder
1 teaspoon baking soda
1 cup firmly packed brown sugar
1 cup butter, softened
1 egg
1 cup quick-cooking oats
1 cup flaked coconut
1 cup salted Spanish peanuts
½ cup finely crushed cornflakes
Additional cornflake crumbs for dipping

Combine flour, baking powder, and baking soda. Gradually add sugar to butter; cream until light and fluffy. Add egg; beat well. Gradually add dry ingredients; blend well after each addition. Stir in oats, coconut, peanuts, and cornflakes. Flatten slightly with glass dipped in additional cornflake crumbs. Bake at 350° for 12–15 minutes. Drizzle with Glaze. Makes 4 dozen.

GLAZE:

2 tablespoons butter, melted
1 cup powdered sugar
1 tablespoon hot water
1 teaspoon vanilla

Combine all and beat well to consistency of Glaze.

Cookin' with the Stars

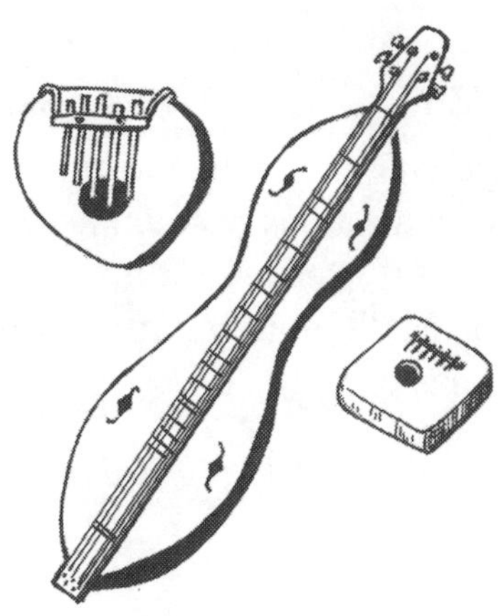

Mom-Mom's Sugar Cookie Cutouts with Glaze

At Mom-Mom's on Christmas Eve, there was homemade fudge, cakes, and cookies of all sorts, especially her frosted cut-out cookies—those were everybody's favorite. Everybody was happy. There was Christmas music playing; the tree was all decorated and the lights were on; everything was perfect.

COOKIES:

2 cups sifted flour
1 teaspoon cream of tartar
1/2 teaspoon baking soda
1/2 teaspoon salt
3/4 cup sugar
1/2 cup oil
2 eggs
1 teaspoon vanilla

Sift flour, cream of tartar, baking soda, and salt into a bowl. In another bowl, add sugar, oil, and eggs; beat until smooth. Add vanilla; mix thoroughly. Gradually add flour mixture to shortening mixture, beating after each addition. Chill dough until it can be easily handled.

Grease cookie sheets. Heat oven to 375°. Roll dough out, 1/2 at a time, on lightly floured table top to 1/8 inch thick. Use cutters to make cookies; dip cutters into flour to keep them from sticking. Place onto cookie sheets and bake at 375° for 10–12 minutes. Put on racks to cool. Frost with Glaze when cool. Makes 1 1/2–2 dozen cookies.

GLAZE:

3/4 cup powdered sugar
3–4 teaspoons milk

Mix powdered sugar and milk until smooth and of frosting consistency, adding a few more drops of milk, if needed. Glaze hardens as it stands.

You may want to add different colors of food coloring to each 3/4 cup Glaze that you make.

Mom-Mom's Cookbook

Old Fashioned Sugar Cookies

3 cups flour
1 teaspoon baking powder
1 teaspoon salt
1 teaspoon baking soda
1 cup sugar
1 cup shortening
2 eggs
4 tablespoons milk
2 teaspoons vanilla
12 ounces mini chocolate chips or 1 cup finely chopped nuts or 1 cup diced raisins (optional)
1 egg white, beaten
Sugar or colored sprinkles

Sift together flour, baking powder, salt, baking soda, and sugar. Cut shortening in with pastry blender until it resembles coarse meal. Blend in eggs, milk, and vanilla. Add any desired options. Chill. Roll out on floured board. Cut into desired shapes. Brush with beaten egg white and sprinkle with sugar or colored decorations.

Bake on ungreased cookie sheet at 400° for 6–8 minutes until lightly brown at edges.

West Virginia Country Cooking

Sour Cream Cookies

½ cup Crisco®
1½ cups packed brown sugar
2 eggs
2½ cups flour
½ teaspoon baking powder
1 teaspoon baking soda
1 cup sour cream
1 teaspoon vanilla

Combine Crisco, brown sugar, and eggs. In another bowl combine flour, baking powder, and baking soda. Add flour mixture alternately to brown sugar mixture with sour cream. Add vanilla. Drop by spoonfuls on greased cookie sheet. Bake at 375° for 12–15 minutes. Cool slightly, then top with Glaze. Makes approximately 5 dozen cookies.

GLAZE:
½ cup margarine
1½ cups powdered sugar
1 teaspoon vanilla
2 teaspoons water
Food coloring (optional)

Combine ingredients, adding food coloring, if desired, for holidays. Spread on slightly cooled cookies.

Cookin' with the Colts

Clothespin Cookies

COOKIES:
3 sticks butter
1 cup sour cream
3 cups flour
Powdered sugar

Cream butter and sour cream. Stir in flour. Chill. Roll dough out thinly. Cut into strips ½ inch wide and about 4–5 inches long. Wrap loosely around round wooden clothespins. Bake at 375° until lightly browned. Take cookies off the clothespins as soon as they are removed from oven; roll cookies in powdered sugar.

FILLING:
1 cup milk
2 tablespoons flour
Pinch salt
1 cup sugar
½ cup shortening
½ cup butter, softened
½ teaspoon vanilla extract
1 or 2 teaspoons almond extract
Food coloring (optional)

Mix milk, flour, and salt in a saucepan. Cook until thick over low heat. Remove from heat and cool. In a mixing bowl cream sugar, shortening, butter, vanilla, and almond extract until smooth. Add cooled mixture and beat for 15 minutes. Add color, if desired. Pipe into cookies, using a pastry bag.

Recipes for You & Your Best Friends

West Virginia Firsts: • The world's first and largest clothespin factory was located at Richwood. • In May 1860, the first well in the state for producing crude oil was drilled at Burning Springs. • The first spa open to the public was at Berkeley Springs, West Virginia, in 1756 (then, Bath, Virginia). • The first free school for African-Americans in the entire South opened in Parkersburg in 1862. • The first steamboat was launched by James Rumsey in the Potomac River at New Mecklensburg (Shepherdstown) on December 3, 1787. • The first iron furnace west of the Alleghenies was built by Peter Tarr on Kings Creek in 1794. • The first memorial building to honor World War I veterans was dedicated on May 30, 1923, in Welch. • The first federal prison exclusively for women in the United States was the Federal Industrial Institution for Women in Alderson, which received its first inmates in 1927. • On December 21, 1984, West Virginia University player Georgeann Wells became the first woman to dunk a basketball in a college game.

Chocolate Shortbreads

2 cups flour
½ cup cocoa
1 cup powdered sugar
¼ teaspoon salt
2 sticks unsalted butter (very cold and firm)
1 teaspoon vanilla

Sift all dry ingredients into a food processor fitted with a steel blade. Add cold butter, chopped into pieces, and vanilla. Process until mixture forms a ball. Roll out to ¼-inch thickness and cut with cookie cutters.

Bake on ungreased cookie sheets for 18–22 minutes at 300°. Cool on wire racks. Cookies should not become browned or crisp in oven. Remove them when still soft on top.

Carnegie Hall Cookbook

Cocoa Mint Wafers

1½ cups flour
¾ cup unsweetened cocoa
1¼ teaspoons baking powder
¼ teaspoon salt
¾ cup margarine or butter, softened
1¼ cups sugar
1 large egg
24 rectangular mint wafers (such as Andes)

Mix flour, cocoa, baking powder, and salt. In a large bowl, beat butter and sugar with electric mixer until fluffy. Beat in egg, and with mixer on low, gradually add flour mixture until blended. Divide dough in half. Shape each half into an 6-inch-long roll. Wrap and refrigerate about 4 hours until very firm. Heat oven to 375°. Lightly grease cookie sheets. Cut each roll into 32 slices. Place 1 inch apart on cookie sheets.

Bake 10–12 minutes until cookies look dry. Remove to a wire rack to cool completely. In a small saucepan, melt mints over low heat. Put in a zipper-type sandwich-size plastic bag. Snip off a small corner and drizzle chocolate over cooled cookies. Refrigerate 15 minutes for chocolate to harden.

Dutch Pantry Simply Sweets

Date Nut Balls

(No-Bake Cookies)

1/2 cup butter
3/4 cup sugar
1 1/2 cups chopped dates
1/3 cup maraschino cherries, chopped
3 cups Rice Krispies®
1 cup chopped nuts (or 1/2 cup nuts and 1/2 cup flaked coconut)

In saucepan, melt butter and sugar. Add dates and cherries and cook over medium heat until mixture becomes a smooth, soft paste. Stir constantly. Remove from heat and add Rice Krispies and nuts (or nuts and coconut). Mix thoroughly and form into balls. Place on waxed paper or parchment paper until cool. Store in a tight container when completely cold.

Treasured Recipes

Unbaked Chocolate Cookies

2 cups sugar
1/2 cup milk
6 tablespoons cocoa
2/3 cup peanut butter
1 teaspoon vanilla
2 cups uncooked oatmeal

Combine sugar, milk, and cocoa in a saucepan and boil 1 minute. Remove from heat and add peanut butter, vanilla, and oatmeal. Mix well, then drop by teaspoon onto waxed paper; cool.

Casseroles, Meats and Fish...Cookies

In 1921, West Virginia University played University of Pittsburgh in the first football game ever broadcast on the radio on station KDKA.

Mincemeat Cookies

1 cup shortening
$1\frac{1}{2}$ cups sugar
3 eggs, well beaten
1 package mincemeat, broken into small pieces
$3\frac{1}{4}$ cups sifted flour
$\frac{1}{2}$ teaspoon salt
1 teaspoon baking soda

Cream shortening and sugar; add eggs and beat until smooth. Add mincemeat. Sift dry ingredients and add to first mixture. Drop by teaspoonfuls onto greased baking sheet. Bake at 400° about 12 minutes.

Note: One cup honey may be substituted for the sugar.

Casseroles, Meats and Fish...Cookies

Lemon Ginger Cookies

1 package gingerbread mix
$\frac{1}{2}$ cup sour cream
1 tablespoon grated lemon peel
Lemon Frosting

Combine mix, sour cream, and peel and beat well on low speed. Shape dough into 1-inch balls and place about 3 inches apart on ungreased cookie sheet. Flatten to 2 inches with bottom of glass dipped in flour (or sugar). Bake until set, 9–11 minutes in 375° oven. Remove from cookie sheet, cool and frost.

LEMON FROSTING:
$1\frac{1}{4}$ cups powdered sugar
1 tablespoon margarine or butter, softened
2 tablespoons sour cream
1 teaspoon lemon juice

Mix until smooth and of spreading consistency.

Casseroles, Meats and Fish...Cookies

Lemon Bars

1 cup butter, softened
1/2 cup powdered sugar
2 cups flour
4 large eggs
2 cups sugar
1 tablespoon flour
1/2 teaspoon baking powder
1/3 cup fresh lemon juice
1 cup finely chopped pecans

Cream butter and powdered sugar. Gradually stir in 2 cups flour until blended. Pat over the bottom of an ungreased 9x13x2-inch baking pan. Bake in preheated 325° oven for 15 minutes. At once, beat the eggs slightly with fork; add sugar, 1 tablespoon flour, and baking powder. Add lemon juice, and pecans. Stir (do not beat) until well mixed. Pour over warm crust. Return to oven and bake 45 minutes or until lightly browned. Loosen edges and let cool. Then cut bars and remove. Freezes well.

A Taste of Fayette County

Easy Time Squares

1 1/2 cups sugar
1 cup margarine, softened
4 eggs
2 cups flour
1 tablespoon lemon juice
1 can pie filling
Powdered sugar

Gradually add sugar to margarine in a large mixing bowl, creaming at medium speed until light and fluffy. Add eggs, 1 at a time, beating well after each. At low speed, add flour and lemon juice. Pour into a well-greased 15x10-inch baking pan. Mark off the dough in 20 squares. Press down in the center of each square with the back of a spoon and place 1 tablespoon pie filling (tart cherry, blueberry, apple, or pineapple) in center of each square. Bake at 350° for 35–40 minutes. While still warm, sift powdered sugar over top of cake. Cool and cut into squares.

Casseroles, Meats and Fish...Cookies

Cherry Coconut Bars

1 cup flour
3 tablespoons powdered sugar
½ cup butter, softened

Heat oven to 350°. With hands, mix flour, powdered sugar, and butter until smooth. Spread thin in a greased 8-inch pan. Bake 15 minutes.

FILLING:
1 cup sugar
½ teaspoon baking powder
¼ teaspoon salt
½ cup coconut
¼ cup flour
½ cup quartered maraschino cherries
1 teaspoon vanilla
¾ cup chopped nuts
2 eggs, slightly beaten

Combine sugar, baking powder, salt, coconut, flour, cherries, vanilla, and nuts. Stir into beaten eggs and spread over top of baked pastry. Bake 25 minutes at 350°. Can be doubled and baked in a jellyroll pan.

Our Best Home Cooking

Caramel Dream Bars

BOTTOM LAYER:
1 package yellow cake mix
1/3 cup margarine
1 egg

Grease 9x13-inch pan. Combine dry cake mix, margarine, and egg. Mix until crumbly. Press into pan.

TOP LAYER:
1 can sweetened condensed milk
1 egg
1 teaspoon vanilla
1 cup chopped pecans
1/2 cup Heath® Bits 'O Brickle chips

In small bowl combine milk, egg, and vanilla; mix well. Stir in pecans and chips. Pour over cake base and spread to cover. Bake at 350° for 25–35 minutes or until browned. Center may appear loose, but will set up when cool.

Cookin' with the Stars

Rocky Road Fudge Bars

BARS:

½ cup butter or margarine
1 (1-ounce) square unsweetened chocolate or 1 envelope pre-melted unsweetened baking chocolate
1 cup sugar
1 cup flour, sifted
½ cup chopped pecans
1 teaspoon baking powder
1 teaspoon vanilla
2 eggs

Preheat oven to 350°. In saucepan over low heat, melt margarine and chocolate. In large mixing bowl, add remaining bar ingredients to margarine and chocolate; mix well. Spread in greased and floured 9x13-inch pan. Set aside.

FILLING:

1 (8-ounce) package cream cheese, softened (reserve 2 ounces for Frosting)
½ cup sugar
¼ cup butter or margarine, softened
2 tablespoons flour
1 egg
½ teaspoon vanilla
¼ cup chopped pecans
1 cup semisweet chocolate chips
2 cups miniature marshmallows

In small mixing bowl, combine 6 ounces cream cheese with sugar, butter, flour, egg, and vanilla. Beat 1 minute at medium speed until smooth and fluffy; stir in pecans. Spread in pan over chocolate mixture. Sprinkle with chocolate chips. Bake for 25–35 minutes. Check with toothpick inserted in center coming out clean. Remove from oven; sprinkle with marshmallows. Bake 2 minutes longer.

FROSTING:

¼ cup butter or margarine
1 (1-ounce) square unsweetened chocolate or 1 envelope pre-melted unsweetened baking chocolate
2 ounces reserved cream cheese
¼ cup milk
3 cups powdered sugar
1 teaspoon vanilla

In saucepan over low heat, melt margarine with chocolate. In small mixing bowl, combine this with cream cheese, milk, powdered sugar, and vanilla until smooth. Immediately pour over marshmallows and smooth with back of spoon. Cool. Cut into bars. Store in refrigerator. Yields 36 bars.

Almost Heaven

Philadelphia Cheesecake Brownies

1 (20½-ounce) package brownie mix (do not use mix that includes a syrup mix)
1 (8-ounce) package cream cheese, softened
⅓ cup sugar
½ teaspoon vanilla
1 egg

Prepare brownie mix as directed on package. Pour into greased 9x13-inch baking pan. Mix cream cheese, sugar, and vanilla with electric mixer on medium speed until well blended. Add egg; mix until blended. Pour over brownie mixture; cut through batter with knife several times for marble effect. Bake at 350° for 35–40 minutes or until cream cheese mixture is lightly browned. Cool; cut into squares. Makes 24 brownies.

Generations

Chocolate Caramel Brownies

1 (14-ounce) bag caramels
1 (5-ounce) can evaporated milk, divided
1 dark chocolate cake mix
½ cup margarine, melted
1 cup chopped nuts
1 (6-ounce) package chocolate chips

Melt caramels with ⅓ cup milk in double boiler. Combine remaining milk, cake mix, and margarine; mix well. Press half of the mixture in greased 9x13-inch pan. Bake at 350° for 6 minutes. Sprinkle nuts and chocolate chips over crust. Top with caramel mixture. Crumble remaining cake mixture over caramel mixture. Press gently. Bake at 350° for 20 minutes. Cool before cutting. Makes 2 dozen brownies.

Best Taste of Fairmont

Almond Fudge Brownies

Easy one-pan mixing—a White Grass favorite!

2/3 cup margarine (1 stick + 3 tablespoons)
3/4 cup cocoa powder
2 cups sugar
4 eggs
1/2 teaspoon almond extract
1/2 teaspoon vanilla
1 1/4 cups unbleached white or all-purpose flour
1 teaspoon baking powder
1 teaspoon salt
1 cup chopped nuts (optional)

Preheat oven to 350°. Grease and flour a 9x13x2-inch baking pan. In medium saucepan, melt margarine, then remove from heat. Add cocoa, sugar, eggs, and extracts, in that order, stirring after each addition. Then add remaining ingredients until just moistened. Spread into pan and bake 20–25 minutes.

Brownies are done if the center springs back when touched, and edges pull away from pan. It may be difficult to wait, but cool at least 20 minutes before cutting.

White Grass Cafe Cross Country Cooking

Best Ever Brownies

These are super!

2 cups sugar
1 cup salad oil
1 teaspoon vanilla
1 3/4 cups all-purpose flour
1/2 teaspoon salt
1/2 cup cocoa
5 eggs
1 cup chopped nuts (optional)
6 ounces semisweet chocolate chips

Put all ingredients except chips in large bowl. Mix well with spoon. Pour into greased 9x13x2-inch baking pan. Sprinkle chips on top and bake at 350° for 25–30 minutes or until toothpick inserted in center comes out clean. Yields 4–5 dozen squares.

Treat Yourself to the Best Cookbook

Golden Grahams S'Mores

¾ cup light corn syrup
3 tablespoons margarine or butter
1 (11.5-ounce) package milk chocolate chips
1 teaspoon vanilla
1 (12-ounce) box (9 cups) Golden Grahams® cereal
3 cups miniature marshmallows

Grease 9x13x2-inch pan. Heat syrup, margarine, and chocolate chips to boiling; stir constantly. Remove from heat; add vanilla. Pour over cereal in bowl; toss until coated. Fold in marshmallows, 1 cup at a time. Press in pan with buttered back of spoon. Let stand 1 hour. Cut into 2-inch squares. Store loosely at room temperature up to 2 days. Makes 24 squares.

Tyrand Cooperative Ministries Cookbook

Graham Cracker Goodies

44 graham crackers
¼ stick real butter
¼ stick margarine
½ cup sugar
1 cup chopped pecans
Powdered sugar

Lay graham crackers on a cookie sheet. Combine butter, margarine, and sugar in saucepan and boil 3 minutes. Pour over crackers and sprinkle chopped nuts over the crackers. Bake 8 minutes at 350°. Remove from oven and separate. Sprinkle with powdered sugar and serve.

Serving Our Best

The world's largest teapot, measuring 14 feet in diameter and approximately 14 feet high, is located in Chester.

Chocolate Cherry Bombs

1 cup margarine, softened
2 cups sugar
2 eggs
1 tablespoon vanilla extract
3 cups flour
½ teaspoon baking soda
½ teaspoon salt
½ teaspoon baking powder
1 cup baking cocoa
48 maraschino cherry halves (reserve juice)
1 (14-ounce) can sweetened condensed milk
2 cups chocolate chips
1 tablespoon maraschino cherry juice

Cream margarine, sugar, eggs, and vanilla in mixer bowl until light and fluffy. Add mixture of flour, baking soda, salt, baking powder, and cocoa; mix well. Shape into 1-inch balls. Place on ungreased cookie sheet. Bake at 350° for 12 minutes. Press cherry half into center of each cookie. Remove to wire rack.

Combine condensed milk, chocolate chips, and cherry juice in double boiler. Cook over hot water until smooth, stirring constantly. Frost warm cookies with chocolate mixture. Yields 48 cookies.

The Best of Wheeling

Peanut Butter Cups

3 boxes powdered sugar
1 quart peanut butter
1 pound margarine, softened to room temperature
1 (12-ounce) package chocolate chips
1 cake paraffin wax

Mix sugar, peanut butter, and margarine until well blended. Melt in double boiler the chocolate chips and paraffin wax. Make candy in rolls or patties; dip in hot chocolate/wax mixture. Place on wax paper until cool.

Tyrand Cooperative Ministries Cookbook

Cornflake Kisses

1 cup sugar
1 cup light Karo syrup
1 cup peanut butter
1 teaspoon vanilla
6 cups cornflakes

Bring sugar and light Karo syrup to a boil; remove from heat. Add peanut butter and vanilla. In large bowl, pour hot mixture over cornflakes; mix well. Put butter on hands and shape mixture into small balls.

Note: You could also use a small buttered funnel and make into the shape of Hershey's® Kisses.

Cooking for the New Era

Aunt Genevieve's Peanut Butter Fudge

2 cups sugar
⅔ cup milk
2 tablespoons Karo syrup
¼ cup peanut butter
1 teaspoon vanilla
2 tablespoons butter
Evaporated milk, if needed

Cook first 3 ingredients to the soft-ball stage (235°). Stir constantly. Add next 3 ingredients and mix. Cool mixture and beat until it loses its gloss and is smooth. If candy gets too hard, add enough evaporated milk to get the desired consistency. Put in an 8-inch buttered pan. Cool thoroughly and cut.

For the Love of Kids

Ooee Gooey Marshmallow Cream Fudge

1½ cups sugar
½ pound (32) marshmallows
1 cup evaporated milk
¼ cup margarine
⅛ teaspoon salt
1 (12-ounce) package semisweet chocolate morsels
1 teaspoon vanilla
½ cup chopped nuts

Combine sugar, marshmallows, evaporated milk, margarine, and salt in saucepan. Bring to a full boil, stirring constantly. Remove from heat. Stir in chocolate morsels until melted. Add vanilla and nuts. Pour into greased 8-inch-square pan. Chill until firm. Makes about 2¼ pounds candy.

A Taste of Fayette County

Mom-Mom's Southern-Style Pecan Fudge

1 pound powdered sugar
6 tablespoons butter
½ cup unsweetened cocoa
¼ cup milk
1 tablespoon vanilla
¼ teaspoon salt
1 cup chopped pecans

In a medium saucepan, heat sugar, butter, cocoa, milk, vanilla, and salt over low heat, stirring until smooth. Stir in nuts and spread mixture quickly into a buttered 8x4-inch pan. Cool and cut into squares. Makes 2 dozen.

Mom-Mom's Cookbook

Anna M. Jarvis is credited with originating our Mother's Day holiday. Anna led a small tribute to her mother at Andrews Methodist Church in Grafton on May 12, 1907, and dedicated her life to establishing a nationally recognized Mother's Day. The first official Mother's Day ceremonies were held on May 10, 1908, at Andrews Methodist Church and at the Wanamaker Store Auditorium in Philadelphia, Pennsylvania. Six years later, President Woodrow Wilson signed a Congressional Resolution setting aside Mother's Day as a national holiday to be celebrated on the second Sunday in May.

No-Fail Peanut Butter Candy

½ cup milk
Pinch of salt
2 cups sugar
1 teaspoon vanilla
1 cup peanut butter

Combine milk, salt, and sugar in saucepan. Stir until sugar dissolves. Bring to a boil; cook for 2 minutes exactly. Add vanilla and peanut butter. Stir well. Pour out on waxed paper or cookie sheet and cut in squares.

Cooking for the New Era

Peanut Butter Candy

3 cups sugar
1 cup milk
3 tablespoons Karo syrup
Dash of salt
1 teaspoon vanilla
¼ cup butter
1 or 2 heaping tablespoons peanut butter

Combine sugar, milk, Karo syrup, and salt. Cook over low heat. Boil till it forms a soft ball when dropped in cold water. Remove from heat and add vanilla, butter, and peanut butter. Beat until thick and creamy. Pour into buttered dish. Cool and cut into squares.

Gypsy, West Virginia 100th Anniversary Cookbook

Peanut Brittle

1 cup sugar
½ cup white Karo syrup
1 cup dry-roasted peanuts
1 tablespoon butter
1 teaspoon vanilla
1 teaspoon baking soda

Use a 4-cup Pyrex® dish. Combine sugar and Karo in dish. Microwave, uncovered, on HIGH 4 minutes. Mix with a spoon. Add peanuts. Microwave on HIGH 4 minutes. Add butter and vanilla. Microwave on HIGH 2 minutes. Take out of microwave. Add baking soda and whip quickly with spoon. Pour quickly onto a well-greased cookie sheet (metal). Let cool. Break into pieces.

For the Love of Kids

Honeyed Popcorn

This is usually kept on hand in the winter. It is not only a good snack but the price is right. I keep a special good-grade plastic bucket with lid to store this in. Popcorn balls can also be formed from this syrup. Pop 3/4 cup popcorn or whatever amount you need to get a gallon of popped corn.

Set the oven on 300°. Lightly butter a large bowl or pan and 2 large baking pans. Place 1/2 cup butter in cast-iron skillet; melt and add 1/2 cup honey. Heat to boiling while corn is popping. You can make more if you like, just use equal parts of real butter and honey.

As corn pops, empty into large bowl or pan. When all corn is popped, add the honey syrup. Mix well or make popcorn balls. Place loose popcorn on the large baking pans and place in oven to dry. Remove from oven and use or store in a tightly closed container.

Bootstraps and Biscuits

Popcorn Balls

2 cups sugar
1 cup white corn syrup
1 tablespoon butter
2 tablespoons vinegar
1/2 teaspoon baking soda
8 quarts popped corn

Boil sugar, syrup, butter, and vinegar to hard-ball stage; remove from heat and add baking soda. Stir well and pour over popcorn, stirring to coat. Form into balls.

Gypsy, West Virginia 100th Anniversary Cookbook

The first "trust" in the United States was the salt trust organized November 10, 1817, by the salt manufacturers of the city of Kanawha. It went into operation on January 1, 1818, at the Kanawha Salt Company and was formed in order to regulate the quality and price of salt and to discourage foreign competition.

Microwave Caramel Corn

16 cups air-popped popcorn
1 cup packed brown sugar
¼ cup corn syrup
½ cup margarine
½ teaspoon salt
½ teaspoon baking soda

Place popcorn in large oven baking bag. Combine brown sugar, corn syrup, margarine, and salt in large microwave-safe bowl. Microwave on HIGH for 1½ minutes or until mixture boils. Boil for 3 minutes. Remove from microwave. Add baking soda, stirring until foamy. Pour over popcorn.

Fasten bag loosely. Microwave on HIGH for 2 minutes, shaking bag after 1 minute. Microwave on HIGH for an additional 30 seconds; shake bag. Pour popcorn onto greased baking sheet. Cool. Yields 16 servings.

The Best of Wheeling

PIES *and* OTHER DESSERTS

PHOTO BY STEPHEN SHALUTA, COURTESY OF WEST VIRGINIA DIVISION OF TOURISM.

Tamarack, located near Beckley, is the nation's first and only statewide collection of hand-made crafts, arts and cuisine. Tamarack is a one-of-a-kind shopping and cultural experience with 59,000 square feet of retail area, and over 2,000 juried artists.

6 Easy Steps to the Perfect Pie

Follow these instructions for the perfect pie crust.

STEP 1

Gather these ingredients:

⅔ cup lard or shortening
2 cups flour
1 teaspoon salt
3–6 tablespoons cold water

STEP 2

Cut shortening into flour and salt mixture with a fork or pastry blender until crumbs are coarse and granular.

STEP 3

Add 3–6 tablespoons cold water, a little a time. Mix quickly and evenly through the flour until the dough just holds in a ball.

STEP 4

Roll ½ the dough to about ⅛-inch thickness. Lift edge of pastry cloth and roll crust onto rolling pin. Line pie pan allowing ½-inch crust to extend over edge.

STEP 5

Add filling of your choice. Roll out remaining ½ of dough (top crust), making several gashes to allow escape of steam. Place over filling. Allow top crust to overlap lower crust. Fold top crust under the lower crust and crimp edges.

STEP 6

And here will be your perfect pie, baked in a moderately hot oven (425°) for 35 minutes.

Generations

On February 14, 1824, at Harpers Ferry, John S. Gallaher published the *Ladies Garland,* one of the first papers in the nation devoted mainly to the interests of women.

Raisin Pie Filling

1 (15-ounce) box raisins
4 cups water
1 cup sugar
½ teaspoon nutmeg
¼ teaspoon salt
1 teaspoon vinegar
3 tablespoons brown sugar
4 tablespoons cornstarch
2 pie crusts

Preheat oven to 375°. Mix all ingredients, except cornstarch and pie crusts, in a 2-quart saucepan. Bring to a boil and cook about 5 minutes on medium heat. Mix cornstarch with a small amount of water and stir gradually into hot mixture until it thickens. Pour into bottom pie crust and cover with top crust. Bake at 375° for 45 minutes.

Treasured Recipes

Upside-Down Apple Pecan Pie

4 tablespoons butter
⅔ cup brown sugar
⅔ cup pecans
2 unbaked (9-inch) pastry circles
1 tablespoon flour
½ teaspoon nutmeg
½ teaspoon cinnamon
6 cups sliced apples
1 tablespoon lemon juice

Combine butter and brown sugar. Spread mixture evenly on the bottom of a 9-inch pie plate (be sure to butter rim of pie plate). Arrange pecan halves in design, pressing into sugar. Cover with plain pastry. Trim, leaving ½ inch hanging over all around.

Combine flour, nutmeg, and cinnamon with apples and lemon juice. Pile on pastry, leveling as much as possible. Cover with second crust. Fold edges and prick with a fork on top. Bake at 450° for 10 minutes. Reduce to 350° and bake for 30–45 minutes or longer. When syrup in pan stops bubbling (about 5 minutes), place serving plate over pie and invert. Remove pie plate. Serve with vanilla ice cream.

A Gracious Plenty

Shoofly Pie

1 cup brown sugar
1 cup dark molasses
1 egg, slightly beaten
1 teaspoon baking soda
1 teaspoon flour
2 cups boiling water
2 (9-inch) pie shells

Mix sugar, molasses, egg, baking soda, and flour. Add boiling water. Pour into 2 unbaked pie shells.

CRUMB TOPPING:
2 cups flour
1 cup brown sugar
½ cup shortening
1 teaspoon baking soda
Pinch salt

Mix all ingredients well and sprinkle over liquid in pie shells. Bake at 350° for 35–40 minutes.

Dutch Pantry Cookin' Volume II

Sour Cream Apple Pie

2 eggs
1 (8-ounce) carton sour cream
1 cup sugar
6 tablespoons all-purpose flour, divided
1 teaspoon vanilla extract
¼ teaspoon salt
3 cups chopped, peeled cooking apples
1 (9-inch) unbaked pie shell
¼ cup packed brown sugar
3 tablespoons cold butter

In a large bowl, beat eggs. Add sour cream. Stir in sugar, 2 tablespoons flour, vanilla, and salt; mix well. Stir in apples. Pour into pie shell. Bake at 375° for 15 minutes. Meanwhile, combine brown sugar and remaining flour; cut in butter until mixture is crumbly. Sprinkle over top of pie. Return to oven for 20–25 minutes or until filling is set. Cool completely on wire rack. Serve, or cover and refrigerate. Yields 8 servings.

Best Taste of Fairmont

Rhubarb Creme Pie

- Double crust pastry, 8 or 9 inches
- 3 cups rhubarb, cleaned and sliced ½ inch
- 3 tablespoons flour
- ½ teaspoon nutmeg
- 1½ cups sugar
- 2 eggs, well beaten
- 1–2 tablespoons butter

Line pie plate with pastry. Arrange rhubarb slices evenly in pastry lined plate. Combine flour, nutmeg, and sugar, then add well beaten eggs to dry ingredients. Pour over rhubarb slices. Dot with butter before laying top crust on. Bake at 350° until golden brown (about 30 minutes). Yields 6–8 servings.

The Way Pocahontas County Cooks

Lemon Meringue Pies

- 2¼ cups sugar, divided
- 2 tablespoons butter, softened
- 6 eggs, separated
- ½ cup fresh lemon juice and grated rind of 2 lemons
- 3 cups boiling water
- 1 cup cold water
- 3 heaping tablespoons cornstarch
- 2 (9-inch) pie shells, baked
- ⅛ teaspoon cream of tartar

In a 3-quart saucepan, mix 2 cups sugar with the butter. Stir in 6 egg yolks alternately with lemon juice and rind. Stir, and when blended, add boiling water. Have ready cold water with cornstarch added. When lemon mixture boils almost to the top of the saucepan, pour cornstarch mixture in and keep stirring. When the first bubble comes to the top, remove from heat. Pour into baked shells.

Beat egg whites and cream of tartar. When it starts to peak, add ¼ cup sugar and continue beating until peaks are stiff. Spread on pie and bake about 7 minutes at 350° or until golden.

Serving Our Best

Yogurt Pie

CRUST:

24 Ritz® Crackers
1/4 teaspoon baking powder
1/2 cup chopped pecans
1 teaspoon vanilla
3 egg whites
1 cup sugar

Crush Ritz Crackers until fine. Add baking powder, pecans, and vanilla. Beat egg whites until stiff. Add sugar. Fold cracker mixture into egg whites. Pour into a buttered 9-inch pie pan. Bake at 325° for 30 minutes. Cool.

FILLING:

1 (10-ounce) package frozen strawberries, thawed
1 carton strawberry yogurt
1 (8-ounce) container whipped topping

Crush and drain strawberries. Fold yogurt into whipped topping and add strawberries. Pour into cooled pie crust. Chill.

Stout Memorial Culinary Treasures

Praline Pie

1/3 cup butter
1/3 cup firmly packed brown sugar
1/2 cup chopped pecans
1 small box butterscotch pudding and pie filling
1 (8-inch) pie crust, lightly baked (do not brown)
Whipped topping
Nuts for garnish

Cook and stir butter and sugar until sugar melts and it boils vigorously. Remove from heat. Add nuts. Pour into crust and bake for 5 minutes at 425° (it will be bubbly). Meanwhile, prepare pudding as directed; cool, stirring twice. Spoon into crust. Chill. Serve with whipped topping. Garnish with nuts.

Homemade with Love

Coconut Caramel Pie

¼ cup butter
1 (7-ounce) package flaked coconut
½ cup chopped pecans
1 (8-ounce) package cream cheese, softened
1 (14-ounce) can condensed milk
1 (16-ounce) carton Cool Whip®, thawed
2 (9-inch) pie shells, baked
1 (12-ounce) jar caramel ice cream topping, divided

Melt butter in large skillet. Add coconut and chopped pecans; cook until golden brown. Stir frequently. Set mixture aside. Combine cream cheese and condensed milk; beat until smooth. Fold in Cool Whip. Lay ¼ cream cheese mixture in each pie shell. Drizzle ¼ caramel topping over cream cheese mixture. Sprinkle ¼ coconut mixture evenly over each pie. Repeat layers with remaining ingredients. Cover and freeze until firm. Let frozen pie stand at room temperature for 5 minutes before slicing.

Dutch Pantry Simply Sweets

Coconut Macaroon Pie

1 cup sugar
2 eggs
½ teaspoon salt
½ cup butter, softened
¼ cup flour
½ cup milk
1½ cups shredded coconut, divided
1 (9-inch) pie shell

Beat sugar, eggs, and salt until mixture is lemon colored. Add butter and flour. Blend well. Add milk. Fold in 1 cup coconut. Pour into pie shell. Top with remaining coconut. Bake at 325° for about 60 minutes. Remove from oven; cool. Makes 6–7 servings.

Our Daily Bread

Peanut Butter Pie

1 cup powdered sugar
½ cup chunky peanut butter
1 (9-inch) pastry shell, baked

Blend sugar and peanut butter with fork until mixture is crumbly. Spread ½ mixture in bottom of baked pastry shell; reserve remainder.

FILLING:
¼ cup cornstarch
⅔ cup sugar
3 egg yolks (reserve whites)
½ teaspoon vanilla
1 tablespoon peanut butter
¼ teaspoon salt
2 cups milk

Combine cornstarch, sugar, egg yolks, vanilla, peanut butter, salt, and milk and cook in double boiler until thickened, stirring constantly. Spoon Filling over peanut butter mixture.

MERINGUE:
3 egg whites
3 tablespoons sugar
½ teaspoon salt

Beat egg whites, sugar, and salt until stiff and spread over pie. Sprinkle remaining peanut butter mixture on top. Bake at 325° for 20 minutes or until Meringue is firm and brown.

More...Home Town Recipes

Real Butterscotch Pie

Brown that butter!!!

6 tablespoons butter
1 cup dark brown sugar
1 cup boiling water
3 tablespoons cornstarch
2 tablespoons flour
½ teaspoon salt
1⅔ cups milk
3 egg yolks
1 teaspoon vanilla
1 (9-inch) pie shell, baked

Melt butter in heavy skillet over low heat. When butter is golden brown, add brown sugar. Boil until foamy, 2–3 minutes, stirring constantly. Stir in boiling water; remove from heat.

In saucepan, mix cornstarch, flour, and salt. Stir in milk gradually until smooth. Stir in brown sugar mixture. Cook over low heat, stirring constantly. Boil 1 minute. Remove from heat. Stir a little of hot mixture into slightly beaten egg yolks. Then blend it all back into hot mixture in saucepan. Boil 1 minute longer. Remove from heat. Blend in vanilla. Cool, stirring occasionally. Pour into pie shell. Chill.

MERINGUE:
3 egg whites
3 tablespoons sugar

Make meringue with egg whites and sugar beaten until stiff peaks form. Top pie with Meringue; brown lightly in oven.

Keaton Mills Family Cookbook

Three's Company Chocolate Mousse Pie

CRUST:

1¼ cups Oreo® cookie crumbs

¼ cup butter, melted

Combine crust ingredients and press into bottom of 10-inch pie plate, quiche dish, or shallow casserole; set aside.

FILLING:

2 (1-ounce) squares unsweetened chocolate

1 (7-ounce) jar marshmallow cream

1 teaspoon vanilla

2 tablespoons cream or milk

2 cups heavy cream for whipping, divided

½ ounce semisweet chocolate for garnish

In small bowl, melt chocolate in microwave; or melt in small saucepan on low heat. Remove from heat. In mixing bowl, combine marshmallow cream, vanilla, and melted chocolate. Mix until well blended. Gradually add milk, blending until smooth. Beat 1 cup of cream just till stiff peaks form; fold into chocolate mixture. Spread in crust.

Whip remaining cream, sweetening slightly with sugar. Gently spread over mousse layer. Grate chocolate evenly over whipped cream topping. Cover and refrigerate at least 2 hours. Refrigerate leftovers. Makes 1 (10-inch) pie.

Enjoy at Your Own Risk! Cookbook

Blueberry Crumble

FILLING:

1/3 cup packed brown sugar
2 tablespoons flour
1/2 teaspoon cinnamon
2 1/2 pints blueberries
2 tablespoons lemon juice

Combine brown sugar, flour, and cinnamon in a bowl. Gently stir in the blueberries and lemon juice. Spoon into a greased 2-quart baking dish.

TOPPING:

1/2 cup packed brown sugar
1/2 cup flour
1/4 cup butter or margarine
3/4 cup rolled oats
Whipped cream or vanilla ice cream (optional)

Combine brown sugar and flour in a bowl. Cut in butter until the mixture resembles coarse crumbs. Stir in oats. Sprinkle evenly over blueberry mixture. Bake at 375° for 40 minutes or until Topping is browned and the Filling is bubbly. Serve with whipped cream or vanilla ice cream, if desired. Yields 8 servings.

Note: May substitute any of the following fruits for the blueberries: 2 1/2 pints raspberries or blackberries, 3 cups apples or peaches, or 4 cups cherries.

Everything but the Entrée

Judy's Peach Crisp

5–6 cups sliced peaches
1/2 cup sugar
1 tablespoon flour

Mix fruit, sugar, and flour; pour in greased 1 1/2-quart baking dish.

TOPPING:
1/3 cup margarine
1/2 cup flour
1/2 cup rolled oats
3/4 cup brown sugar
1/2–1 teaspoon cinnamon

Mix margarine, flour, rolled oats, brown sugar, and cinnamon and put on top of fruit mixture. Bake at 350° for 30–35 minutes.

Tyrand Cooperative Ministries Cookbook

Summer Harvest Cobbler

1/2 cup margarine
1 cup flour
1 cup sugar
1 cup milk
2 teaspoons baking powder
1 (21-ounce) can fruit or pie filling (any flavor)
Whipped cream (optional)

Place margarine in a 2-quart shallow baking dish. Place in a cold oven. Set oven temperature to 325°. Remove from oven when margarine is melted.

Combine flour, sugar, milk, and baking powder in a bowl, mixing until smooth. Pour into center of melted margarine. Do not stir. Pour fruit or pie filling into center of batter. Do not stir. Bake for 1 hour or until top is browned. Serve with whipped cream, if desired. Yields 8 servings.

Everything but the Entrée

Cherry Cobbler

2 (16-ounce) cans pitted sour cherries (see note)
1 cup sugar, divided
2 tablespoons cornstarch
1¼ teaspoons almond extract
1 cup quick or old-fashioned oats, uncooked
1 cup flour
2 teaspoons baking powder
¼ teaspoon salt (optional)
⅓ cup margarine or butter, chilled
½ cup milk
Whipped cream or ice cream (optional)

Drain cherries, reserving 1 cup liquid. In medium saucepan, combine ¾ cup sugar and cornstarch; stir in reserved liquid. Bring to a boil over medium heat. Stir constantly until thickened and clear. Reduce heat. Boil 1 minute. Stir in cherries and extract. Pour mixture into a greased 8-inch-square glass baking dish. Heat oven to 400°. Combine oats, flour, ¼ cup sugar, baking powder, and salt; mix well. Cut in margarine until mixture resembles coarse crumbs. Add milk and mix with fork just until dry ingredients are moistened. Drop by rounded tablespoons over hot filling. Bake 25–30 minutes or until topping is light golden brown. Serve warm with whipped cream or ice cream, if desired.

Note: May substitute 2 (20-ounce) cans cherry pie filling and omit ¾ cup sugar and 2 tablespoons cornstarch.

Christ Reformed Church Historical Cookbook

Cherry Surprise

1 (6-ounce) package vanilla instant pudding
2 cups cold milk
1 cup thawed Cool Whip®
14 graham crackers
1 can cherry pie filling

Combine pudding mix and milk; beat well. Allow to stand 5 minutes. Fold in Cool Whip. Line square baking dish with graham crackers. Pour 1/2 of pudding over crackers. Add another layer of crackers and top with remaining pudding. Add another layer of crackers. Spoon cherry pie filling on top. Refrigerate at least 3 hours before serving.

Christ Reformed Church Historical Cookbook

Peaches and Cream

3/4 cup flour
1 teaspoon baking powder
1/2 teaspoon salt
1 (3 3/4-ounce) package vanilla pudding (not instant)
1 egg
1/2 cup milk
1 (15-ounce) can sliced peaches, drain and reserve juice
1/2 cup sugar
1 (8-ounce) package cream cheese, softened
3 tablespoons reserved juice
Cinnamon/sugar mixture

Combine flour, baking powder, salt, pudding mix, egg, and milk in bowl. Mix for 2 minutes on medium speed. Pour into greased oblong pan or dish. Spread peaches over mixture. Blend sugar, cream cheese, and peach juice for 2 minutes on medium speed. Spoon over peaches and sprinkle with cinnamon/sugar. Bake 30–35 minutes at 350°. Serve warm or cold.

Stout Memorial Culinary Treasures

Cranberry Casserole

3 cups chopped unpeeled apples
2 cups cranberries
1 cup sugar
½ stick butter
½ cup brown sugar
½ cup quick cooking oats
½ cup chopped nuts

Place apples and cranberries in 2-quart baking dish and sprinkle with sugar. Melt butter and brown sugar; add oats and nuts. Sprinkle this mixture over apples and cranberries. Bake, uncovered, 45 minutes at 325°.

United Methodist Ministers' Wives Cook Book

Cranberry Dessert

2 cups cranberries
1⅔ cups sugar, divided
½ cup chopped walnuts or pecans
2 eggs
1 cup flour
½ cup butter, melted
¼ cup shortening, melted

Spread bottom of 2 (10-inch) pie pans with cranberries, ⅔ cup sugar, and nuts. Beat eggs. Gradually add 1 cup sugar, beating continually. Add flour, melted butter, and melted shortening. Continue beating. Pour over cranberries and bake at 300° about 1 hour. Serve with ice cream. Serves 8–9.

Recipes for You & Your Best Friends

The first electric railroad in the world, built as a commercial enterprise, was constructed between Huntington and Guyandotte.

Boiled Apple Dumplings

2 cups milk
1 tablespoon vinegar
½ teaspoon baking soda
1 teaspoon salt
½ cup butter, melted
3–4 cups flour
6–8 apples
Brown sugar
Cinnamon

Combine milk, vinegar, baking soda, and salt. Mix in melted butter. Add enough flour to make dough a little stiffer than a biscuit dough.

Divide dough into 6–8 portions. Peel and core apples, leaving them whole. Roll out each portion of dough. Set an apple in the center of each portion of dough and fill apple with brown sugar and a sprinkle of cinnamon. Wrap dough around apple and pinch edges together tightly.

Take a white cotton cloth the size of a man's handkerchief and set the dumpling in the center of it. Bring up the four corners of the cloth and tie them together or tie with string. Have water boiling in a big kettle. Add ½ teaspoon salt to the water. Put dumplings into boiling water and keep them covered with water throughout cooking. Boil 40 minutes. Remove cloth and serve warm with rich milk poured over, or with ice cream.

Keaton Mills Family Cookbook

Baked Curried Fruit

1 (1-pound, 14-ounce) can cling peach halves, drained
1 (1-pound, 14-ounce) can pear halves, drained
1 (1-pound, 13½-ounce) can sliced pineapple, drained
½ cup maraschino cherries, drained
1 (1-pound, 14-ounce) can apricot halves, undrained
½ cup syrup from apricots
⅓ cup butter or margarine
3 teaspoons curry powder
¾ cup light brown sugar

Drain all fruits, except apricots. Reserve ½ cup apricot syrup, then drain. Pat fruits lightly with paper towels. Arrange fruits in large shallow pan or 3-quart casserole. In small skillet combine apricot syrup, butter, curry powder, and brown sugar. Heat to boiling, stirring until butter melts and sugar dissolves. Drizzle syrup mixture over fruit. Bake in 350° oven for 45 minutes.

Cookin' in a Coal Camp

Caramel Apple Pizza

1 package sugar cookie dough
1 cup peanut butter
1 large Granny Smith apple
1 bottle caramel syrup
¼ cup chopped peanuts

Let cookie dough come to room temperature and spread evenly onto pizza pan. Bake at 350° for 15 minutes or until lightly browned. Cool. Spread with a thin layer of peanut butter. Layer on thinly sliced apple and caramel syrup. Sprinkle with chopped nuts.

Feeding the Flock—MOPs of Westminister

Every October, the Salem Apple Butter Festival is held at Depot Park in downtown Salem, where festival goers get the unique opportunity to watch apple butter being made in copper kettles suspended over slow-burning wood fires.

Pumpkin Yummies

2 cups graham cracker crumbs
½ cup unsalted butter, melted
¼ cup sugar
2 cups solid-pack canned pumpkin
½ cup packed light brown sugar
1 teaspoon cinnamon
½ teaspoon salt
¼ teaspoon ginger
¼ teaspoon ground cloves
1 quart vanilla ice cream, softened
Brown sugar, cinnamon, and sugar for sprinkling

Combine graham cracker crumbs, butter, and ¼ cup sugar in a 9x13-inch baking pan. Spread evenly over bottom of pan. Combine pumpkin, ½ cup brown sugar, 1 teaspoon cinnamon, salt, ginger, and cloves in a large bowl, mixing well. Fold in ice cream. Spoon over graham cracker crust, smoothing with a spatula. Combine additional brown sugar, cinnamon, and sugar in a bowl. Sprinkle over the top. Cover with plastic wrap. Freeze until firm. Yields 15 servings.

Everything but the Entrée

Mountain Momma Mudslide

1 stick butter, softened
1 cup flour
1 cup chopped nuts
1 (8-ounce) package cream cheese, softened
1 cup powdered sugar
1 (13-ounce) carton Cool Whip®, thawed, divided
1 (4-ounce) package chocolate instant pudding
1 (4-ounce) package butterscotch instant pudding
2 cups milk

Combine butter, flour, and nuts. Press into 9x13-inch pan. Bake 20 minutes at 350°; cool about 30 minutes. Combine cream cheese and powdered sugar, and beat till fluffy. Fold in ½ of Cool Whip; spread over crust. Combine puddings and milk; beat until stiff. Pour over cheese mixture; spread evenly. Spread remaining Cool Whip on top. Chill about 30 minutes. Serve.

Dutch Pantry Cookin'

Cream Puffs or Eclairs

1 stick butter
1 cup water
1 cup flour
4 eggs

Bring butter and water to a boil in medium saucepan. Add flour all at once. Stir vigorously until ball forms in center of pan. Remove from heat. Add eggs 1 at a time, beating after each egg. Shape on a slightly greased cookie sheet with spoon or pastry bag, forming an oval for eclairs or round for cream puffs. Bake at 375° for 1 hour or until bubbles of moisture disappear. Cut off tops when cool. Spoon out soft center, if present. Fill with Vanilla Filling and ice with Glossy Chocolate Icing, or fill with vanilla ice cream and top with chocolate syrup and garnish with nuts.

VANILLA FILLING:

2 cups milk, divided
1/3 cup flour
2/3 cup sugar
1/4 teaspoon salt
3 egg yolks
2 tablespoons butter
1/2 teaspoon vanilla

Scald 1 1/2 cups milk. Mix together flour, sugar, salt, and remaining 1/2 cup milk. Gradually add mixture to scalded milk. Stir constantly in top of double boiler or directly over low heat. Add well-beaten egg yolks and butter. Cook until thick. Add vanilla. Cool.

GLOSSY CHOCOLATE ICING:

3 tablespoons butter or margarine
9 tablespoons cocoa
2 cups powdered sugar
5 tablespoons milk
3 teaspoons vanilla

Melt butter and cocoa together. Mix powdered sugar and milk together and add to cocoa mixture. Add vanilla.

Somebody's Cookbook

The citizens of a community in Ritchie County, deciding a name change was in order, exercised a once-in-a-lifetime opportunity, changing the town's name from Mole Hill to Mountain, settling the argument once and for all that you *can* make a mountain out of a mole hill.

Bread Pudding with Lemon Sauce

3 eggs
3 (12-ounce) cans evaporated milk
1¼ cups sugar
¼ cup butter or margarine
1 teaspoon ground cinnamon
½–1 cup golden raisins (optional)
2 teaspoons vanilla
½ teaspoon salt
1 (1-pound) loaf bread, cut in cubes

In a large bowl, beat eggs. Add milk, sugar, butter, cinnamon, raisins, vanilla, and salt; mix well. Add bread cubes; stir gently. Pour into greased 9x13x2-inch baking dish. Bake at 325° for 50–60 minutes until knife in center comes out clean.

SAUCE:
¼ cup sugar
2 tablespoons cornstarch
1 cup water
4 tablespoons lemon juice
2 teaspoons grated lemon peel
1 tablespoon butter or margarine

Combine sugar and cornstarch in saucepan. Stir in water until smooth; bring to boil over medium heat. Boil for 1–2 minutes, stirring constantly. Remove from heat; stir in lemon juice, peel, and butter until butter melts. Serve over warm or cold pudding. Store leftovers in refrigerator.

Just Plain Country

Apple Cinnamon Pudding

2 tablespoons butter
½ cup brown sugar
½ cup raisins, divided
½ cup red cinnamon candies, divided
1 can apple pie filling
2 cans refrigerated cinnamon rolls
½ cup chopped nuts

Melt butter in 9x13-inch baking dish; sprinkle with brown sugar, ¼ cup raisins, and ¼ cup cinnamon candy. Add pie filling and remaining candy. Place rolls, cinnamon side up, on top of filling. Sprinkle with remaining raisins and nuts. Cover. Bake at 275° for 30 minutes. Serves 10.

Cookin' with the Stars

Cracker Pudding

4 cups milk
2 eggs, separated
½ cup + 3 tablespoons sugar, divided
2 cups coarse cracker crumbs
1 cup shredded coconut
1 teaspoon vanilla

Scald milk in top of double boiler. Beat egg yolks and add ½ cup sugar. Add this mixture gradually to scalded milk. Stir constantly. Allow to cook for 1 minute and then add cracker crumbs and coconut. Stir until cracker crumbs are soft and mixture is thick. Remove from heat and add vanilla. Pour into a buttered baking dish. Spread with meringue made by beating 3 tablespoons sugar into stiffly beaten egg whites. Bake at 350° until meringue is golden brown. Makes 6–8 servings.

Elkins Manor Cookbook

Poor Pudding

(Berisford Christmas Pudding)

SAUCE:

1 cup brown sugar
2 tablespoons butter
2 cups water
1 teaspoon vanilla
½ cup chopped walnuts (optional)

Boil ingredients until dissolved, then place in a 9-inch-square baking pan.

PUDDING:

1 heaping cup flour
2 teaspoons baking powder
Pinch of salt
½ cup brown sugar
3 tablespoons butter, melted
½ cup milk
¾ cup cut or chopped dates and/or raisins (optional)

Sift flour, baking powder, and salt into medium-size bowl. Add sugar, butter, milk, and fruit. Drop by spoonfuls into Sauce and bake in 350° oven about 25 minutes. Serve warm or cold with the Sauce for topping. Also good topped with ice cream or whipped topping.

United Methodist Ministers' Wives Cook Book

Pawpaw Pudding

Pawpaw is known as the West Virginia banana.

2 cups mashed pawpaws
2 teaspoons powdered ginger
1 teaspoon cinnamon
½ teaspoon nutmeg
½ cup milk
½ cup honey
¾ cup sugar

Mix in order given. Beat well. Pour into a prepared pan and bake 1 hour at 350°.

Bootstraps and Biscuits

Chocolate Mousse for Two

¾ cup light cream
⅔ cup chocolate pieces
1 egg yolk
1 tablespoon orange liqueur
2 tablespoons whipped topping

Combine cream and chocolate pieces in the top of double boiler. Heat and stir just to boiling. Remove from heat. Beat together egg yolk and liqueur. Gradually add about ½ of hot mixture and return to saucepan with remaining hot mixture. Cook and stir 1 minute longer. Pour mixture into 2 dessert dishes and chill at least 3 hours, covered. Top with 1 tablespoon whipped topping to serve.

Dutch Pantry Simply Sweets

Berry Mousse

1½ cups fresh strawberries or 8 ounces frozen berries
1 (8-ounce) package cream cheese, cut in cubes
½ cup sifted powdered sugar
1 (4-ounce) container frozen whipped topping, thawed
Sliced almonds, toasted

In a blender, combine strawberries, cream cheese, and powdered sugar. Cover and blend until mixture is smooth. Pour into mixing bowl and fold in whipped topping. Spoon mousse mixture into 6 dessert dishes. Chill 3–4 hours or overnight. To serve, sprinkle with toasted sliced almonds.

Carnegie Hall Cookbook

"Paws-Paws," a tropical fruit nicknamed the "West Virginia banana," originated in the state and took their name from the little town of Paw Paw, located in Morgan County.

Lemon Cool

PART 1:

2 cups all-purpose flour
2 sticks margarine, melted
½ cup finely chopped nuts

Mix together; press in 9x13-inch baking dish and 1 inch up the sides. Bake at 350° for 25 minutes.

PART 2:

1 (8-ounce) container Cool Whip®
2 cups powdered sugar
1 (8-ounce) package cream cheese, softened

Mix together and spread over cooled crust.

PART 3:

2 boxes lemon instant pudding
3 cups milk

Mix until thick; let stand a few minutes. Put on cheese layer.

PART 4:

1 (8-ounce) carton Cool Whip
½ (8-ounce) package cream cheese, softened
½ cup powdered sugar
½ cup chopped pecans

Mix together. Spoon over pudding. Refrigerate.

Third Wednesday Homemakers Volume II

Orange "Pushup" Gelatin Dessert

This dessert is equally as wonderful made with all sugar-free ingredients.

1 angel food cake
2 cans mandarin oranges, drained
2 small packages orange gelatin
2 cups boiling water
1 pint orange sherbet
1 (12-ounce) carton Cool Whip®

Tear cake in pieces, put in a 9x13-inch glass dish. Place mandarin oranges over cake pieces. Set aside. In small bowl, mix gelatin with boiling water. Add sherbet and mix. Put in refrigerator until syrupy (about 7 minutes); whip until frothy; add Cool Whip and blend well. Pour over cake and oranges. Use a knife to separate cake so gelatin reaches bottom of dish. Make sure all cake has been covered or coated. Cover with plastic wrap and refrigerate several hours or overnight.

Our Favorite Recipes

Orange Fluff

1 (6-ounce) package orange gelatin
2½ cups boiling water
2 (11-ounce) cans mandarin oranges, drained
1 (8-ounce) can crushed pineapple, undrained
1 (6-ounce) can frozen orange juice concentrate, thawed
1 (8-ounce) package cream cheese, softened
1 cup cold milk
1 (3.4-ounce) package vanilla instant pudding mix

In a bowl, dissolve gelatin in boiling water. Stir in oranges, crushed pineapple, and orange juice concentrate. Coat a 9x13x2-inch dish with nonstick cooking spray; add gelatin mixture. Refrigerate until firm. In a mixing bowl, beat cream cheese until light. Gradually add milk and pudding mix; beat until smooth. Spread over orange layer. Chill until firm.

Feeding the Flock—HCCLA

Ice Cream Lover's Dream

12 ice cream sandwiches
1 carton caramel-flavored ice cream topping
1 (8-ounce) carton whipped topping, divided
3 candy bars (any kind), crushed

Unwrap the ice cream sandwiches and line the bottom of a pan; cover with caramel topping. Add a layer of whipped topping, then a layer of crushed candy. Cover with a layer of whipped topping. Cover and place in freezer for 1 hour.

Feeding the Flock—HCCLA

Double Chocolate Peanut Butter Ice Cream

6 (1-ounce) squares semisweet chocolate
2 cups milk
1 cup sugar
½ cup smooth peanut butter
2 cups whipping cream
2 teaspoons vanilla extract
⅔ cup peanut butter cups, chopped

Combine chocolate, milk, and sugar in 2-quart heavy saucepan. Cook over medium heat, stirring frequently, until chocolate melts. Stir in peanut butter. Cool to lukewarm. Stir in whipping cream and vanilla. Chill 1 hour. Churn-freeze. After freezing, transfer ice cream to a plastic freezer container. Stir in chopped peanut butter cups. Ripen in freezer at least 3 hours before serving. Yields 2 quarts.

For the Love of Kids

The first patent for a soda fountain was granted in 1833 to George Dulty in Wheeling.

Cheesecake Dessert

CRUST:
3 tablespoons sugar
2½ cups graham cracker crumbs
⅔ cup margarine or butter, melted

Mix sugar and graham cracker crumbs, then stir in melted butter. Press in bottom of 9x13-inch cake pan.

CHEESECAKE:
2 (8-ounce) packages cream cheese, softened
⅔ cup sugar
2 (8-ounce) tubs Cool Whip®
Fruit pie filling of choice

Beat cream cheese and sugar until well mixed. Add Cool Whip, beating just until blended. Pour on Crust. Chill about 1 hour. Top with your choice of fruit pie filling and serve. Store covered with plastic wrap in refrigerator.

More...Home Town Recipes

Strawberry Wonderful

¼ cup brown sugar
1 cup flour
½ cup butter
½ cup ground pecans
1 can condensed milk
2 tablespoons lemon juice
2 (10-ounce) cartons frozen strawberries, thawed
1 (8-ounce) carton Cool Whip®

Mix as a pie crust the sugar, flour, butter, and pecans. Press on a baking sheet and bake 20–25 minutes at 350°. Cool and break into pieces. Place in the bottom of a pan or freezer-safe container. Save some pieces to sprinkle on top.

Mix condensed milk, lemon juice, and strawberries with mixer. Beat well. Fold in Cool Whip. Place on top of pieces and then cover with reserved pieces. Freeze. Serve frozen.

Generations

Oreo Cake

1 large can evaporated milk
1 stick margarine, divided
1 cup sugar
2 (1-ounce) squares chocolate
1 pound Oreo® cookies, divided
½ gallon vanilla ice cream, divided
1 small carton Cool Whip®

Bring milk, ½ stick margarine, sugar, and chocolate to a boil in saucepan. Cook until thick. Cool. Crush cookies in a blender or put in plastic bag and crush with rolling pin. Save ¾ cup crumbs to sprinkle on top. Mix remaining cookie crumbs with ½ stick melted margarine. Press in a 9x13-inch pan. Slice the ice cream in half; lay 1 slice on top of cookie mixture. Pat down well. Spoon ½ of the chocolate sauce over ice cream. Lay remaining slice of ice cream over sauce. Spread rest of chocolate sauce on top of ice cream. Cover with Cool Whip. Sprinkle reserved crumbs on top. Freeze.

Cookin' in a Coal Camp

CATALOG *of* CONTRIBUTING COOKBOOKS

PHOTO BY DAVID FATTALEH, COURTESY OF WEST VIRGINIA DIVISION OF TOURISM.

Nestled in the mountains of West Virginia, Cass Scenic Railroad State Park transports you back in time to relive an era when steam-driven locomotives were an essential part of everyday life. The Cass Scenic Railroad is the same line built in 1901 to haul lumber to the mill in Cass.

CATALOG *of* CONTRIBUTING COOKBOOKS

All recipes in this book have been selected from the cookbooks shown on the following pages. Individuals who wish to obtain a copy of any particular book may do so by sending a check or money order to the address listed by each cookbook. Please note the postage and handling charges that are required. State residents add tax only when requested. Prices and addresses are subject to change, and the books may sell out and become unavailable. Retailers are invited to call or write to same address for discount information.

THE ALL OR NOTHING COOKBOOK

by Judy Grigoraci
1971 Parkwood Road
Charleston, WV 25314
Phone 304-342-5491
jagrigoraci@citynet.net

A 60-recipe, 28-page short collection of delicious, quick, simple but unique family recipes in which you use all of the ingredients that are called for with nothing (bags, boxes, jars) to store. You may have leftovers of finished dish, but not products it took to put recipe together.

$8.95 Retail price
$.54 Tax for West Virginia residents
$3.00 Postage and handling

Make check payable to Judy Grigoraci

ALMOST HEAVEN

Junior League of Huntington
617 Ninth Avenue
Huntington, WV 25701
Phone 304-523-4165

Discover West Virginia, from its luxury and culture of historic areas and cities, to the wild, natural beauty of its hills and streams. West Virginia is, indeed, *Almost Heaven.* Heavenly, too, are the recipes we've collected, tested and presented in this collection that is as rich and varied as our heritage.

$11.95 Retail price
$.72 Tax for West Virginia residents
$2.00 Postage and handling

Make check payable to Junior League of Huntington ISBN 0-9612712-0-5

THE BEST OF WHEELING

Junior League of Wheeling
907 1/2 National Road
Wheeling, WV 26003
Phone 304-232-3164
Fax 304-232-3109

The Best of Wheeling takes the reader on a walking tour through our Victorian past, containing vintage photographs, amusing anecdotes and a diverse collection of recipes. Proclaimed "Official Cookbook of Wheeling" by the mayor, *The Best of Wheeling's* 222 pages will appeal to cooks of all levels.

$15.95 Retail price
$.96 Tax for West Virginia residents
$3.50 Postage and handling

Make check payable to Junior League of Wheeling - Cookbook
ISBN 0-87197-404-5

BEST TASTE OF FAIRMONT

The Woman's Club of Fairmont
1511 Farrell Street
Fairmont, WV 26554
Phone 304-366-2127

A beautiful 112-page cookbook with a variety of wonderful recipes. The Woman's Club of Fairmont is housed in the Thomas Parks Fleming Home, built in the early 1900s. It is the center of cultural, civic and social life of this community and listed on the National Register of Historic Places.

$8.00 Retail price
$1.50 Postage and handling

Make check payable to The Woman's Club of Fairmont

BOOTSTRAPS AND BISCUITS

by Anna Lee Robe-Terrya
Pictorial Histories Distribution
1416 Quarrier Street
Charleston, WV 25301
Phone 888-982-7472
Fax 304-343-0594
wvbooks@intelos.net

Learn how to explore or forage for wild food stuffs and turn them into tasty down-home cooking. From Dandelion Wine to Squirrel Pot Pie—perfect for anyone wanting to cook and eat in an adventurous fashion. You will appreciate the meal more by getting fresh air while gathering the ingredients.

$12.95 Retail price
$.78 Tax for West Virginia residents
$3.50 Postage and handling

Make check payable to Pictorial Histories

ISBN 1-891852-14-0

CAKES...CAKES...AND MORE CAKES

by Mariwyn McClain Smith
P. O. Box 401
Parsons, WV 26287
Phone 800-654-7179
Fax 304-478-4658
gsmith@neumedia.net

The first of two cookbooks using recipes from the weekly column, Merry Wind, which has appeared since 1971 in *The Parsons Advocate*. Nearly 200 recipes—from very simple to very complicated—are included along with dozens of frosting recipes.

$10.00 Retail price
$.96 Tax for West Virginia residents
$6.00 Postage and handling (UPS)

Make check payable to McClain Printing Co.

ISBN 0-87012-491-9

CARNEGIE HALL COOKBOOK

Carnegie Hall, West Virginia
105 Church Street
Lewisburg, WV 24901
Phone 304-645-7917
Fax 304-645-5228
webmaster@carnegiehallwv.com

Lewisburg is home not only to Carnegie Hall, West Virginia—recognized as a leader in rural arts and education—but also a lot of honest country cooking. From Aunt Cleta's Rhubarb Bread to Sweet Potato Casserole and Christmas Oysters to Berry Mousse, *Carnegie Hall Cookbook* includes over 200 delightful recipes.

$8.00 Retail price
$2.00 Postage and handling

Make check payable to Carnegie Hall

CASSEROLES, MEATS AND FISH...COOKIES

by Mariwyn McClain Smith
P. O. Box 401
Parsons, WV 26287
Phone 800-654-7179
Fax 304-478-4658
gsmith@neumedia.net

The second volume of two cookbooks using recipes from the column, Merry Wind, which has appeared since 1971 in *The Parsons Advocate*. A portion of the profits is donated to the local library.

$15.00 Retail price
$1.26 Tax for West Virginia residents
$6.00 Postage and handling (UPS)

Make check payable to McClain Printing Co.

ISBN 0-87012-574-5

CHRIST REFORMED CHURCH HISTORICAL COOKBOOK

Christ Reformed Church
101 Jefferson Street
Martinsburg, WV 25401
Phone 304-263-0290
snoopy5@wv.adelphia.net

This 190-page cookbook is a collection of tried-and-true recipes, many of which go far back in time, some even to the Civil War. Many historical notes are included. A great addition to any collection. This book features 286 recipes along with historical articles and photos of the Martinsburg area.

$10.00 Retail price
$3.50 Postage and handling

Make check payable to Christ Reformed Church

COOKIN' IN A COAL CAMP

by Glenna R. Pack
1821 Devondale Circle
Charleston, WV 25314
Phone 304-345-1634

Reveals lifelong recipes from the times I lived in numerous coal camps. Features vintage black-and-white pictures of coal camps and coal people. There are 183 treasured favorites in the 81-page spiral-bound cookbook that contains a variety of categories. A great resource for the novice or experienced cook.

$12.00 Retail price
$3.00 Postage and handling

Make check payable to Glenna R. Pack

ISBN 0-615-11719-8

COOKIN' WITH THE COLTS

Philip Barbour High School Marching Band
Lilah Phillips
301 Shenandoah Lane
Philippi, WV 26416
Phone 304-457-3638

This book features 387 recipes which were collected from boosters and band members and their families from the Philip High School Marching Band, "The Pride of Barbour County," for the purpose of purchasing new uniforms and percussion for the band. This is an ongoing fund raiser.

$10.00 Retail price
$3.00 Postage and handling

Make check payable to P.B.H.S. Band

COOKIN' WITH THE STARS

Buffalo #150 Order of Eastern Star
300 Plantation Road
Fraziers Bottom, WV 25082 Phone 304-937-2865

This cookbook is filled with the best of recipes. It contains 500 recipes which have been tested by our families and friends. There is quite a variety because our group is made up of all walks of life.

$8.00 Retail price
$2.00 Postage and handling

Make check payable to Buffalo #150 OES

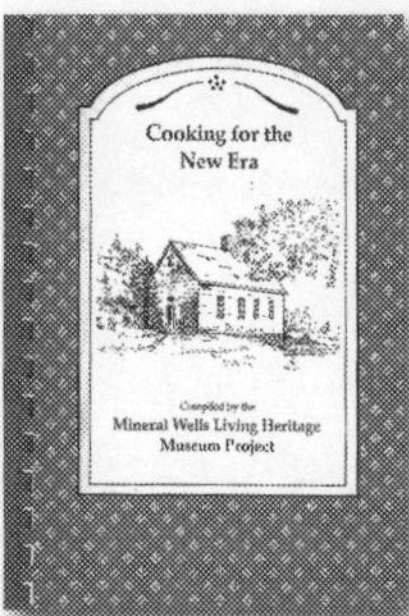

COOKING FOR THE NEW ERA

Living Heritage Museum Phone 304-489-1670
P. O. Box 340 Fax 304-489-2637
Mineral Wells, WV 26150 lcarroll@access.k12.wv.us

"New Era" is a little one-room school built in 1884 that is used as a demonstration classroom. The cookbook is a community project with over 900 recipes. These are mostly traditional favorites. Contributors indicated which West Virginia school they attended. Delightful reading and tasty treats.

$16.00 Retail price
$.96 Tax for West Virginia residents
$2.00 Postage and handling

Make check payable to Living Heritage Museum

A DOORYARD HERB COOKBOOK

by Linda O. Rago
Pictorial Histories Distribution Phone 888-982-7472
1416 Quarrier Street Fax 304-343-0594
Charleston, WV 25301 wvbooks@intelos.net

A West Virginia herbalist, Rago has grown and cooked with herbs for decades. Armed with her grandmother's herbal folk tales and years of research, Rago travels through twelve months of recipes, giving guidelines to cooking in a seasonal fashion.

$9.95 Retail price
$.60 Tax for West Virginia residents
$3.50 Postage and handling

Make check payable to Pictorial Histories ISBN 1-891852-15-9

DOWN MEMORY LANE

Straight Fork CEOS Club
Route 1 Box 26
Crawford, WV 26343 Phone 304-924-5385

Down Memory Lane contains treasured recipes that are true examples of our heritage and can be made with common ingredients. Throughout the book there are helpful cooking hints and words of wisdom. Included are 416 household hints that are indexed. Ringbound, Laminated Cover, Index, 500 recipes, 202 pages.

$8.00 Retail price
$.48 Tax for West Virginia residents
$1.52 Postage and handling

Make check payable to Straight Fork CEOS

DUTCH PANTRY COOKIN'

Dutch Pantry Family Restaurant
Route 31 & I-77 — Phone 304-375-7757
Williamstown, WV 26187 — Fax 304-375-7789

Our employees have put together this collection of their favorite recipes. We hope that you will enjoy these recipes in your own home. *Dutch Pantry Cookin'* contains 86 pages full of wonderful recipes, helpful hints, and home remedies. Enjoy!

$3.99 Retail price
$.24 Tax for West Virginia residents
$1.33 Postage and handling

Make check payable to Dutch Pantry

DUTCH PANTRY COOKIN' VOLUME II

Dutch Pantry Family Restaurant
Route 31 & I-77 — Phone 304-375-7757
Williamstown, WV 26187 — Fax 304-375-7789

Our employees have put together this collection of their favorite recipes. We hope that you will enjoy these recipes in your own home. *Dutch Pantry Cookin' Volume II* contains 107 pages of our families' favorites. Our new book, *Down-Home Cooking: Main Dishes and Casseroles* is also available for $3.99. Enjoy!

$3.99 Retail price
$.24 Tax for West Virginia residents
$1.33 Postage and handling

Make check payable to Dutch Pantry

DUTCH PANTRY SIMPLY SWEETS

Dutch Pantry Family Restaurant
Route 31 & I-77 — Phone 304-375-7757
Williamstown, WV 26187 — Fax 304-375-7789

Our employees have put together this collection of their favorite recipes. We hope that you will enjoy these recipes in your own home. *Dutch Pantry Simply Sweets* contains recipes to satisfy anyone's sweet tooth. Enjoy!

$4.99 Retail price
$.30 Tax for West Virginia residents
$1.33 Postage and handling

Make check payable to Dutch Pantry

ELKINS MANOR COOKBOOK: SECRETS OF THE SENIOR COOKS

Elkins Manor
JoAnn Frederick
100 Tallman Avenue
Elkins, WV 26241 — Phone 304-637-4800

Elkins Manor Cookbook was created with a goal in mind. The proceeds will be used to build raised vegetable garden beds for handicap residents. It has 350 recipes on 140 pages from the manor residents, their families, and friends.

$8.00 Retail price
$2.00 Postage and handling

Make check payable to Elkins Manor

ENJOY AT YOUR OWN RISK! COOKBOOK

by Judy Grigoraci
1971 Parkwood Road — Phone 304-342-5491
Charleston, WV 25314 — jagrigoraci@citynet.net

A 200-recipe, 90-page cookbook of good tasting recipes we are supposed to feel "guilty" about eating. This cookbook follows two others that I wrote which were "healthy"—modified in fat, sugar, cholesterol, and sodium. Family favorites from various sources in which no one has dared count calories.

$9.95 Retail price
$.60 Tax for West Virginia residents
$3.00 Postage and handling

Make check payable to Judy Grigoraci

EVERYTHING BUT THE ENTRÉE

Junior League of Parkersburg
1301 Murdoch Avenue — Phone 304-422-6961
Parkersburg, WV 26101 — tiaknopp@wirefire.com

Everything but the Entrée is just what you need to complement main dishes. From accompaniments, soups and breads, to desserts, breakfast and brunch, this cookbook is the long-overdue addition to your collection. Along with a variety of recipes and food tips, there's historical tidbits about the Parkersburg area. 190 pages, 200+ recipes.

$19.95 Retail price
$1.20 Tax for West Virginia residents
$3.00 Postage and handling

Make check payable to Junior League of Parkersburg ISBN 0-9669807-0-0

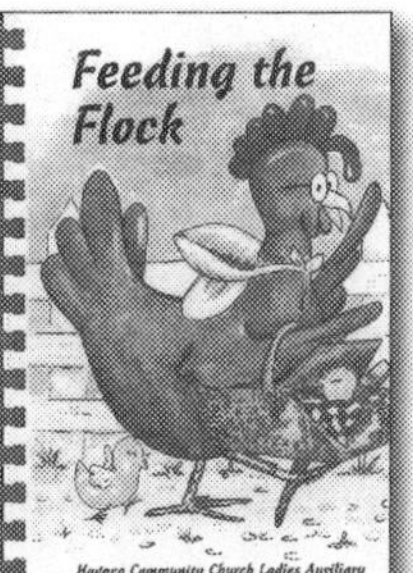

FEEDING THE FLOCK

Havaco Community Church Ladies Auxiliary
178 Havaco Drive — Phone 304-436-3765
Welch, WV 24801 — adonithan@citlink.net

Feeding the Flock is a collection of recipes compiled by the Havaco Community Church ladies. All of the recipes are treasured by us and we would like to share them with you. From appetizers to desserts, you are certain to find something destined to become one of your favorites.

$10.00 Retail price
$3.00 Postage and handling

Make check payable to Havaco Community Church

FEEDING THE FLOCK

MOPS of Westminister (Mothers of Preschoolers)
Route 4 Box 451-A
Bluefield, WV 24701 — Phone 304-589-5934

Our cookbook is 114 pages of recipes that are "tried and true"—easy-to-do for the busy mom or anyone who is looking for quick and easy cooking. Many of our recipes are suitable for a brunch-type meal. This cookbook makes a wonderful gift for anyone.

$12.00 Retail price
$4.00 Postage and handling

Make check payable to MOPS of Westminister

FOR THE LOVE OF KIDS

Marshall County Day Care Friends
R D 4 Box 435
Cameron, WV 26033

A collection of recipes from friends and West Virginia University Extension Service classes. One section is devoted to kids. The dividers feature art work by second graders of Cameron Elementary School. Proceeds from the book will purchase music, books, and equipment for the Marshall County Day Care. 500 recipes on 186 pages.

$10.00 Retail price
$4.00 Postage and handling

Make check payable to Marshall County Day Care

GENERATIONS

Smithville Elementary PTO
P. O. Box 30
Smithville, WV 26178
Phone 304-477-3273
Fax 304-477-3118

Generations is a 170-page cookbook put together by the students, staff, and parents of Smithville Elementary. It contains recipes for appetizers, soups, salads, sauces, main dishes, meats, vegetables, breads, pies, pastries, cookies, cakes, and low-calorie dishes.

$10.00 Retail price
$3.50 Postage and handling

Make check payable to Smithville Elementary PTO

GOOD MORNING WEST VIRGINIA!

Mountain State Association of Bed & Breakfasts
P. O. Box 501
Greensburg, IN 47240
Phone 812-663-4948
tmwinters@juno.com

A spectacular, 160-page cookbook featuring tried-and-true favorites from Mountain State Inns. These recipes are a sampling of the special treatment waiting for you. Find a wonderful getaway and wake up to stunning scenery, warm hospitality and palate-tempting breakfasts. Inns are arranged by regions—discover all the treasures of West Virginia.

$12.95 Retail price
$2.00 Postage and handling

Make check payable to Winters Publishing

ISBN 1-883651-05-0

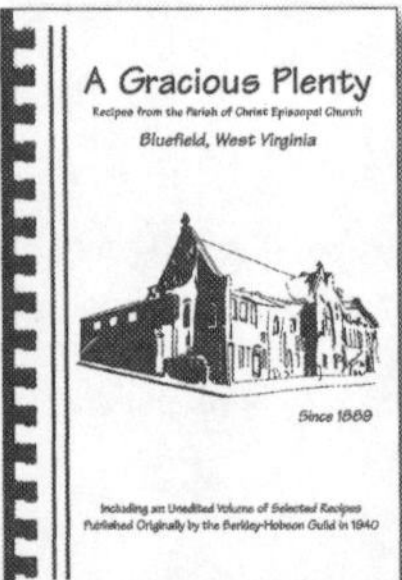

A GRACIOUS PLENTY

Christ Episcopal Church
200 Duhring Street
Bluefield, WV 29701
Phone 309-327-6861
christchurch@bluefield.org

This cookbook takes us on a historical journey through the kitchens of Christ Episcopal Church churchwomen who have fed husbands, children, and grandchildren, and nurtured the spirits of those whom they loved. This book is the first one printed in 60 years and includes the 1940 cookbook, *Selected Recipes.*

$15.00 Retail price
$3.75 Postage and handling

Make check payable to Christ Episcopal Church

GYPSY, WEST VIRGINIA 100TH ANNIVERSARY COOKBOOK

Gypsy Comm.-Gypsy Youth Fellowship
P. O. Box 45 Phone 304-592-2480
Gypsy, WV 26361 Fax 304-592-2401

The history of a model coal-mining community and other historical information. Recipes from 1900 to 2000 and pictures and history of the community.

$15.00 Retail price
$3.00 Postage and handling

Make check payable to Gypsy Church Ladies Aid

HEAVENLY HELPINGS

Fort Gay United Methodist Church Women

Heavenly Helpings is a collection of recipes submitted by the Fort Gay United Methodist Church Women. Included are down-home favorites passed down through the generations. From appetizers to desserts, it's a treasure chest full of goodies sure to please the taste buds. This book is currently out of print.

HOME COOKIN'

Fellowship Baptist Ladies Auxiliary
Barbara Sturgill
HC 70 Box 140
Lenore, WV 25676 Phone 304-475-3751

We had so much fun (and heartburn) putting together *Home Cookin'*. So many ladies in our church submitted delicious and easy-to-follow recipes. Most ingredients are usually on hand. 122-pages. Currently out of print.

HOMEMADE WITH LOVE

Attn: Linda Mullenax
Beverly Elementary Phone 304-636-9162
P. O. Box 209 Fax 304-636-9163
Beverly, WV 26253 wvgrammy152@hotmail.com

This cookbook was written by the family, friends, and alumni of what was once Beverly High School (closed in 1966) and is now Beverly Elementary School. A second edition will be available Spring 2003.

$12.00 Retail price
$3.00 Postage and handling

Make check payable to Beverly Elementary

JUST PLAIN COUNTRY

by Alice Lantz
P. O. Box 102 — Phone 304-636-4543
Glady, WV 26268 — southpaw@neumedia.net

This cookbook is from the "Hills" of West Virginia and is dedicated to my mom who will be 95-years-young. Family and friends have also contributed to the 300 recipes in the book. Recipes for all, from bread and jams to delectable desserts.

$12.00 Retail price
$2.50 Postage and handling

Make check payable to Alice Lantz

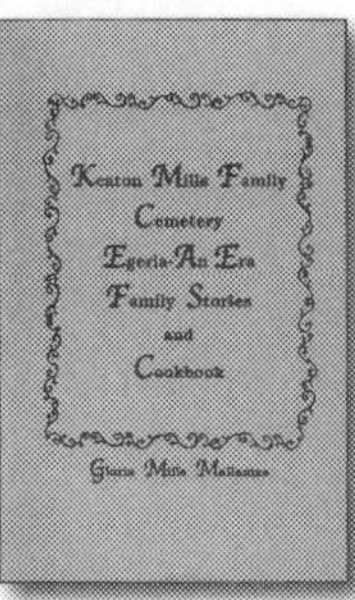

KEATON MILLS FAMILY COOKBOOK

by Gloria Mills Mallamas
138 Sunrise Avenue — Phone 304-252-5050 (Summer)
Beckley, WV 25801 — 407-889-9450 (Winter)

The book has 348 pages. The cookbook section consists of 57 pages. The book is mostly about our family history, the Cherokee Indian connection, family stories, and the way my generation lived.

$20.00 Retail price
$3.00 Postage and handling

Make check payable to Gloria Mallamas

ISBN 0-87012-585-0

MOM-MOM'S COOKBOOK

by Marilyn Hudson — Phone 304-339-6629
HC 86 Box 111 — ma6629@hotmail.com
Monterville, WV 26282 — www.cookbooksandmore.net

This is a heritage cookbook—I wrote it as a memorial to my mother and both of my grandmothers. It is filled with wonderful family recipes and short stories—some funny and some serious—all interesting. My grandfather was a fisherman and there is a very interesting recipe in this book for eel.

$12.50 Retail price
$.75 Tax for West Virginia residents
$1.75 Postage and handling

Make check payable to Cookbooks and More

MORE...HOME TOWN RECIPES

South Fork Volunteer Fire Department, Inc., Auxiliary
Box 297 — Phone 304-249-5422
Brandywine, WV 26802 — dnbland@mountain.net

A collection of 350 recipes by outstanding cooks that will test your taste buds with cooking tips and helpful hints.

$8.00 Retail price
$3.00 Postage and handling

Make check payable to South Fork Volunteer Fire Department, Inc. Auxiliary

MORE THAN BEANS AND CORNBREAD

by Barbara McCallum
Pictorial Histories Distribution
1416 Quarrier Street
Charleston, WV 25301
Phone 888-982-7472
Fax 304-343-0594
wvbooks@intelos.net

Old West Virginia recipes to keep you eating well, using common, simple ingredients. Celebrate a time when cooking and eating were ends in themselves...not just the joyless science it is becoming. 190 pages, 7¼ x 10, indexed.

$12.95 Retail price
$.78 Tax for West Virginia residents
$3.50 Postage and handling

Make check payable to Pictorial Histories

ISBN 1-891852-10-8

OUR BEST HOME COOKING

by Vienna Baptist Church

This cookbook was an idea of the crafters in the Vienna Baptist Church. Favorite recipes were solicited from members of the church and compiled in our cookbook, *Our Best Home Cooking*. There are 126 pages and 327 recipes in the book. This book is currently out of print.

OUR DAILY BREAD

Fellowship Memorial Baptist Ladies Aid Society
131 Shirley Donnelly Road
Oak Hill, WV 25901
Phone 304-469-6714

This book was put together with love by our Ladies Aid Society. We compiled recipes from church members and their families or friends. It has some of the best recipes I've ever tried in it. There are 460 recipes in this book.

$8.00 Retail price
$3.00 Postage and handling

Make check payable to Fellowship Memorial Ladies Aid

OUR FAVORITE RECIPES

West Virginia Public Health Association
210 Maple Street, Suite 10
Ronceverte, WV 24970
Phone 304-647-7430
Fax 304-647-7431
sperry57@hotmail.com

The Professional Clerical Section of the West Virginia Public Health Association has gathered 450 recipes from throughout West Virginia. Some of these recipes have been handed down from generation to generation, and some are original creations.

$10.00 Retail price
$2.50 Postage and handling

Make check payable to Professional Clerical Section

POCAHONTAS COUNTY HUNTER'S COOKBOOK

Pocahontas Communications Cooperative — Phone 304-799-6004
Route 1 Box 139 — Fax 304-799-7444
Dunmore, WV 24934 — amr@neumedia.com

This 170-page book represents a wide range of wild game recipes from Pocahontas County, the hunting capital of West Virginia. Meats discussed range from the familiar (venison, rabbit, squirrel) to the unusual (groundhog, possum). The book also features hunters' tall tales and photos of great hunts in years past.

$15.00 Retail price
$.90 Tax for West Virginia residents
$1.00 Postage and handling

Make check payable to Pocahontas Communications

RECIPES FOR YOU & YOUR BEST FRIENDS

Putnam County Humane Society, Inc.
P. O. Box 461
Scott Depot, WV 25560 — putnamcountyhumanesocietyinc@msn.com

Our cookbook consists of 300 meat-free recipes, and includes a section for animal treats. Proceeds from the cookbook benefit our spay/neuter and emergency medical assistance programs.

$10.00 Retail price
$4.00 Postage and handling

Make check payable to PCHS

SERVING OUR BEST

Elkins Regional Convalescent Center Auxiliary
1175 Beverly Pike
Elkins, WV 26241 — Phone 304-636-1391

Auxiliary members, staff and friends submitted favorite recipes for the cookbook. It contains 106 pages of recipes and a section on "Household Hints." From appetizers to desserts, this book has it all!

$6.50 Retail price
$.39 Tax for West Virginia residents
$2.50 Postage and handling

Make check payable to Elkins Regional Convalescent Center Auxiliary

SOMEBODY'S COOKBOOK

Wood's Pharmacy Employees and Friends

"I wondered why somebody didn't do something, then I realized . . . I was somebody." Woods Pharmacy published our cookbook to help the Fayette Plateau Ministerial Association Food Pantry. Over the years, we have donated $1,928.00 to help ensure that everyone has enough food to eat. This book is currently out of print.

STOUT MEMORIAL CULINARY TREASURES

Stout Memorial United Methodist Women
3329 Broad Street
Parkersburg, WV 26104 Phone 304-428-1179

A 130-page collection of favorite recipes from members of our church congregation. Some recipes will bring back memories while others suggest new and interesting ideas. Enjoy!

$5.00 Retail price
$2.00 Postage and handling

Make check payable to Stout Memorial UMW

TAKE TWO & BUTTER 'EM WHILE THEY'RE HOT

by Barbara Swell
Native Ground Music
109 Bell Road
Asheville, NC 28805
Phone 800-752-2656 or 828-299-7031
Fax 828-298-5607
banjo@nativeground.com
www.nativeground.com

Cook your heart out with generations of hand-me-down recipes and food lore. The book also includes folklore, food insults, old-timey remedies, vintage photos, romance superstitions, hearth crafts, and 19th century chores. 72 pages, 60 recipes

$5.95 Retail price
$3.50 Postage and handling ($1.00 each additional book)

Make check payable to Native Ground Music ISBN 1-883206-32-4

A TASTE OF FAYETTE COUNTY

New River Convention & Visitors Bureau
310 Oyler Avenue
Oak Hill, WV 25901
Phone 800-927-0263
Fax 304-465-5618
sharon@newrivercvb.com

A Taste of Fayette County features many recipes from our area restaurants, lodging properties, mayors, several delegates and, of course, the staff from the visitors center and chamber. It offers everything from appetizers to desserts. Enjoy our Southern hospitality!

$10.00 Retail price
$.60 Tax for West Virginia residents
$3.00 Postage and handling

Make check payable to New River Convention & Visitors Bureau

THIRD WEDNESDAY HOMEMAKERS

Fraziers Bottom Pliny Extension Homemakers
300 Plantation Road
Fraziers Bottom, WV 25082 Phone 304-937-2865

Third Wednesday Homemakers is a collection of wonderful recipes put together by a group of ladies who really know how to cook! This treasured keepsake is full of family recipes used again and again. This book is no longer in print, however, the second edition (pictured next page) is available.

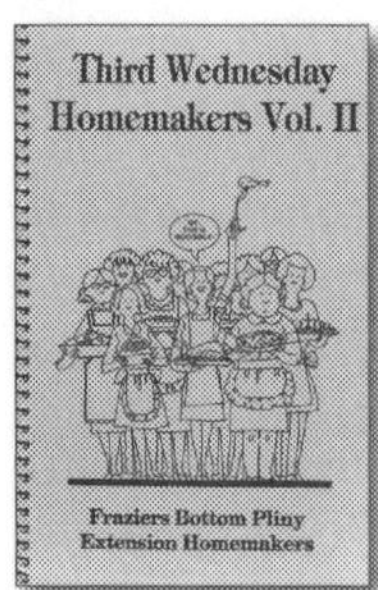

THIRD WEDNESDAY HOMEMAKERS VOLUME II

Fraziers Bottom Pliny Extension Homemakers
300 Plantation Road
Fraziers Bottom, WV 25082 Phone 304-937-2865

A wonderful cookbook with tried-and-true favorites. Most of the recipes use ingredients in your kitchen. Some old recipes—some new, but all are down-home cooking. Cookbook contains 500 recipes from members and friends.

$8.00 Retail price
$2.00 Postage and handling

Make check payable to Fraziers Bottom Pliny Homemakers

TREASURED RECIPES

Cross Restoration Committee
1319 41st Street
Parkersburg, WV 26104 Phone 304-485-6785

Our cookbook is a collection of recipes from new and seasoned cooks. Some recipes are old family and church dinner favorites and some have won prizes in cooking contests.

$8.00 Retail price
$3.50 Postage and handling

Make check payable to Christ United Methodist Church

TREASURES FROM HEAVEN

Vincent Memorial United Methodist Women
205 Bagwell Avenue Phone 304-622-3274
Nutter Fort, WV 26301 Kbetler@aol.com

Treasures from Heaven contains 435 recipes (185 pages) contributed by members, friends, and families of Vincent Memorial United Methodist Women. Sections include appetizers, relishes and pickles; soups, salads and sauces; main dishes; meats, poultry and seafood; vegetables; breads, rolls, pies and pastries; cakes, cookies and confections; desserts; beverages, sandwiches and misc.

$10.00 Retail price
$3.00 Postage and handling

Make check payable to Vincent Memorial UMW

TREAT YOURSELF TO THE BEST COOKBOOK

Junior League of Wheeling
907 1/2 National Road Phone 304-232-3164
Wheeling, WV 26003 Fax 304-232-3109

Treat Yourself to the Best was recognized as a finalist in the R.T. Toastmaster Cookbook Competition and is currently in its 4th edition. With over 425 recipes from family, friends, chefs at the Greenbrier, and many prominent West Virginians, it will offer a "taste" for everyone.

$14.95 Retail price
$.89 Tax for West Virginia residents
$3.50 Postage and handling

Make check payable to Junior League of Wheeling - Cookbook
ISBN 0-9613428-0-3

TYRAND COOPERATIVE MINISTRIES COOKBOOK

Tyrand Cooperative Ministries, Inc.
P. O. Box 365
Mill Creek, WV 26280
Phone 304-335-2788
Fax 304-335-2788
tcm@meer.net

Tyrand Cooperative Ministries, Inc. is a ecumenical mission. The cookbook was compiled by the volunteers and staff. These are some of our favorite recipes.

$8.00 Retail price
$.48 Tax for West Virginia residents
$3.00 Postage and handling

Make check payable to Tyrand Cooperative Ministries, Inc.

UNITED METHODIST MINISTERS' WIVES COOK BOOK

West Virginia Conference United Methodist Ministers' Wives Association
98 Elm Street
Buckhannon, WV 26201
Phone 304-599-1436
mccauley98@mountain.net

This is the sixth anniversary cook book our ministers' wives have published. They are recipes that have been used many times and favorite recipes of many parishioners. There are approximately 500 recipes.

$7.00 Retail price
$2.50 Postage and handling

Make check payable to WV Conference UM Ministers' Wives Assoc.

THE WAY POCAHONTAS COUNTY COOKS

Pocahontas Communications Cooperative
Route 1, Box 139
Dunmore, WV 24934
Phone 304-799-6004
Fax 304-799-7444
amr@neumedia.net

The Way Pocahontas County Cooks has over 500 recipes and a number of household hints sent in by listeners to the program "Cook's Corner" on radio station WVMR in Frost, West Virginia. The book is especially strong on breads, pies, cakes, and cookies. Over 200 country cooks contributed to this volume.

$15.00 Retail price
$.90 Tax for West Virginia residents
$1.00 Postage and handling

Make check payable to Pocahontas Communications

WEST VIRGINIA COUNTRY COOKING: YESTERDAY AND TODAY

by Janese Tennant
P. O. Box 4701
Parkersburg, WV 26104-4701
Phone 304-422-8564
janese@janese.com

Gathered from my grandmother's and great-grandmother's files are 175 of my ancestors' best recipes. Some were written on envelopes and on margins of cookbooks. I have translated the archaic measurements to modern terminology for excellent results every time.

$9.99 Retail price
$.60 Tax for West Virginia residents
$3.50 Postage and handling

Make check payable to Janese Can Cook

WEST VIRGINIA LIBRARIANS (BON) APPÉTIT

West Virginia Library Association
Patsy Stephenson/Marketing Chair
1 John Marshall Drive
Huntington, WV 25755-2060
Phone 304-696-6573
Fax 304-696-5228
stephens@marshall.edu

This cookbook was compiled by the Cookbook Committee of the West Virginia Library Association. Consisting of everything from mouth-watering meals to time-saving tips—this cookbook is sure to please! Enjoy dishes like Bourbon Dogs, Wyatt Divan, Peanut Butter Bread, Tomato Jelly and more. Bon Appétit!

$4.00 Retail price
$2.00 Postage and handling

Make check payable to WVLA

WHITE GRASS CAFE CROSS COUNTRY COOKING

by Laurie Little and Mary Beth Gwyer
HC 70 Box 299
Davis, WV 26260
Phone 304-866-4114
Fax 304-866-4706
chip@whitegrass.com

Simple, wholesome, and delicious! This cookbook contains easy recipes for even a beginner cook, while gourmet taste buds can still be thrilled! 140 of our favorite recipes from 20 years in the kitchen at White Grass Cafe and Cross Country Ski Center in Canaan Valley, West Virginia.

$12.95 Retail price
$.73 Tax for West Virginia residents
$2.50 Postage and handling

Make check payable to White Grass Cafe

ISBN 0-87012-570-2

INDEX

PHOTO BY MIKE BAILEY FOR NRAO/AUI.

The Green Bank Telescope, located at the National Radio Astronomy Observatory in Green Bank, Pocahontas County, is the world's largest fully steerable radio telescope.

A

B

C

D

Q

R

S

Best of the Best State Cookbook Series

Best of the Best from
ALABAMA
288 pages, $16.95

Best of the Best from
ALASKA
288 pages, $16.95

Best of the Best from
ARIZONA
288 pages, $16.95

Best of the Best from
ARKANSAS
288 pages, $16.95

Best of the Best from
BIG SKY
288 pages, $16.95

Best of the Best from
CALIFORNIA
384 pages, $16.95

Best of the Best from
COLORADO
288 pages, $16.95

Best of the Best from
FLORIDA
288 pages, $16.95

Best of the Best from
GEORGIA
336 pages, $16.95

Best of the Best from the
GREAT PLAINS
288 pages, $16.95

Best of the Best from
IDAHO
288 pages, $16.95

Best of the Best from
ILLINOIS
288 pages, $16.95

Best of the Best from
INDIANA
288 pages, $16.95

Best of the Best from
IOWA
288 pages, $16.95

Best of the Best from
KENTUCKY
288 pages, $16.95

Best of the Best from
LOUISIANA
288 pages, $16.95

Best of the Best from
LOUISIANA II
288 pages, $16.95

Best of the Best from
MICHIGAN
288 pages, $16.95

Best of the Best from the
MID-ATLANTIC
288 pages, $16.95

Best of the Best from
MINNESOTA
288 pages, $16.95

Best of the Best from
MISSISSIPPI
288 pages, $16.95

Best of the Best from
MISSOURI
304 pages, $16.95

Best of the Best from
NEW ENGLAND
368 pages, $16.95

Best of the Best from
NEW MEXICO
288 pages, $16.95

Best of the Best from
NEW YORK
288 pages, $16.95

Best of the Best from
NO. CAROLINA
288 pages, $16.95

Best of the Best from
OHIO
352 pages, $16.95

Best of the Best from
OKLAHOMA
288 pages, $16.95

Best of the Best from
OREGON
288 pages, $16.95

Best of the Best from
PENNSYLVANIA
320 pages, $16.95

Best of the Best from
SO. CAROLINA
288 pages, $16.95

Best of the Best from
TENNESSEE
288 pages, $16.95

Best of the Best from
TEXAS
352 pages, $16.95

Best of the Best from
TEXAS II
352 pages, $16.95

Best of the Best from
VIRGINIA
320 pages, $16.95

Best of the Best from
WASHINGTON
288 pages, $16.95

Best of the Best from
WEST VIRGINIA
288 pages, $16.95

Best of the Best from
WISCONSIN
288 pages, $16.95

Cookbooks listed above have been completed as of December 31, 2003. All cookbooks are ring-bound except California, which is paperbound.

Note: Big Sky includes Montana and Wyoming; Great Plains includes North Dakota, South Dakota, Nebraska, and Kansas; Mid-Atlantic includes Maryland, Delaware, New Jersey, and Washington, D.C.; New England includes Rhode Island, Connecticut, Massachusetts, Vermont, New Hampshire, and Maine.

Special discount offers available! *(See previous page for details.)*

To order by credit card, call toll-free **1-800-343-1583** or visit our website at **www.quailridge.com.**
Use the form below to send check or money order.

Call 1-800-343-1583 or email info@quailridge.com to request a free catalog of all of our publications.

Order form

Use this form for sending check or money order to:
QUAIL RIDGE PRESS • P. O. Box 123 • Brandon, MS 39043

❑ Check enclosed

Charge to: ❑ Visa ❑ MC ❑ AmEx ❑ Disc

Card # ____________________

Expiration Date ____________________

Signature ____________________

Name ____________________

Address ____________________

City/State/Zip ____________________

Phone # ____________________

Email Address ____________________

Qty.	Title of Book (State) or Set	Total

Subtotal ________

7% Tax for MS residents ________

Postage ($4.00 any number of books) + 4.00

Total ________